SELF-INTEREST

An Anthology of Philosophical Perspectives

SELF-INTEREST

An Anthology of Philosophical Perspectives

Edited by Kelly Rogers

Routledge
New York and London

Published in 1997 by
Routledge
29 West 35th Street
New York, NY 10001

Published in Great Britain by
Routledge
11 New Fetter Lane
London EC4P 4EE

The text was set in Centaur.
Book design: Jeff Hoffman
Printed in the United States of America on acid-free paper.

Library of Congress Cataloging-in-Publication Data

Self-interest: an anthology of philosophical perspectives / edited by
Kelly Rogers
p.   cm.
Includes bibliographical references.
ISBN 0-415-91251-2. — ISBN 0-415-91252-0 (pbk.)
I. Self-interest. I. Rogers, Kelly, 1966—   .
BJ1474.S394   1996   96-48798
171'.9—DC21   CIP

For Mom and Dad

CONTENTS

INTRODUCTION

That human beings naturally care a great deal for themselves is plain. We could not survive otherwise. The drive for self-preservation is, as the Stoics observed, a human being's first impulse. In the imperative of self-love, however, philosophers have also perceived a tacit threat: "the excessive love of self is in reality the source to each man of all offenses" (Plato, *Laws* V, 731b). What has seemed required is a sort of balancing act, whereby the inevitability of self-concern is reconciled with its manifest potential for harm.

But how is such a reconciliation possible? Philosophers are as vexed today as ever by this problem. Some ethicists have tried to show that virtue is at least partly constitutive of our well-being, and thus that there is no inherent opposition between pursuing one's best interest and being a good person.[1] Others argue for the rationality of altruistic concern or point to a sympathetic principle in human nature which tempers self-interest with other-regard.[2] Still others deny conflicts of interest by rejecting metaphysical individualism.[3] Political philosophers grapple with the tension between "self" and "society," and the interpersonal issues to which it gives rise.[4] Decision theorists scrutinize the nature of rationality and its ends—whether they are wholly self-centered, and if not, how the good of others gets taken into rational account.[5]

These issues are not confined to philosophy. Religionists examine the concept of salvation, which involves survival of the self in another realm. Economists study the nature of rational choice and its relation to self-concern, and view market activity as the archetype of self-interested behavior.[6] Psychologists study egoism as a factor in motivation and self-esteem.[7] Biologists address its role in evolution, from the standpoint of genes which perpetuate themselves even at the cost of the parent's life.[8] Political scientists have developed so-called "public choice theory," modeling political activity on personal self-interest.[9] Throughout the humanities and sciences, the idea of self-regard plays a central role—even if in our personal lives, as Voltaire quipped, "we need it, we cherish it, it gives us pleasure, and we must hide it."[10]

By "it" philosophers have traditionally meant something with two basic aspects. They distinguish being *motivated* by self-interest from self-interest understood as the *interests of the self.* The terms "self-love," "self-concern," and "self-regard" tend to be connected with the former, though they are often used simply to denote the attitude of caring about one's own good. "Selfish" and "egoistic" function similarly, though they frequently carry a more pejorative sense. A number of our authors attach special meanings to some of these terms, but for the purpose of this discussion and unless noted otherwise, I will use them more or less interchangeably. I am less interested here in terminological differences than in the substantive distinction mentioned initially, between *having* interests and being *motivated* by them.

On the subject of motivation, the central question concerns the extent to which human action is driven by concern for the self. Some philosophers embrace the theory known as "psychological egoism," which views human pursuits as motivated exclusively by self-regard. On this view, apparent cases of disinterest—the giving of charity, for instance—are really just disguised self-seeking: we do not assist others for *their* sake, but only to bring satisfaction for ourselves. Yet, opponents of psychological egoism insist that individuals may well be motivated by matters other than their own welfare—take, for example, the concern shown to children by their parents—though these philosophers disagree over the strength and scope of motivational disinterest, some claiming that we can extend our concern impartially to all human beings (possibly even to members of the wider animal kingdom), others that our concern is limited to those with whom we stand in special relationships.

These questions bear heavily upon our understanding of socio-political interaction. If it is held that individuals are naturally other-regarding and that society is an expression of this fact, the state's primary objective is seen not to be the masking of restraining of deep anti-social impulses, but rather the establishment of the best conditions for people to cooperate in effecting their common good. For those thinkers who, in contrast, view social relationships as at root narrowly self-interested, political association tends to be viewed in contractual terms, as a covenant guaranteeing mutual self-restraint: each individual will limit the pursuit of his or her self-interest if others agree to do the same. Whether we should adhere to the social contract even when we can violate it without detection then becomes a central questions. Certain ancient Sophists defended the rationality of injustice, but most philosophers since antiquity have argued that it is never beneficial to breech the social contract—either because of the detrimental effects of wrong-doing upon one's character, or because one can never be sure one won't get caught.

The views taken on the role of self-interest in human motivation depend in part upon how the interests of the self are conceived, so let us briefly consider that subject. Is self-interest determined subjectively, on the basis of whatever desires and preferences a person happens to have? Or, is the good of the self objective, consisting in such things as wealth and honor, or perhaps in spiritual goods, such as rationality and virtue? If the latter, and assuming that virtue is concerned with others' good, motivation by self-interest may, paradoxically, not be exclusively self-regarding. But we say that an individual's good encompasses the welfare of certain others—for instance, that of his friends—or are the interests of different people utterly distinct? If there is a link between friends' interests, it seems that we are automatically motivated by our friends' good when motivated by our own. Of course, this does not mean that concern for the self and concern for others is equivalent, or that we will be motivated by others' good at all if it bears no connection to our own, but it does suggest that a certain form of other-regard may be inherent in self-interested motivation.

Most philosophers would agree that, whatever the nature and motivational strength of self-interest, it plays an important role in human life. But the question remains what role it *should* play, and disagreements at the descriptive level carry over to the normative realm. Some philosophers have denied entirely the moral relevance of self-concern, on the grounds either that it is automatic and therefore not the proper object of moral obligation, or that morality is strictly other-regarding. Proponents of the latter view say that self-regard is the concern not of morality, but of prudence. On the other side, there are philosophers who identify self-interest as the ultimate aim and proper motive of morality.

In political philosophy, the central normative concern is how the self-interest of different individuals should be related to the collective good. If the state's good is not identifiable with the individual's, is he always obligated to bow to the greater social welfare, or is his private good at least sometimes sovereign? What principles are available for adjudicating conflicts of interests? Some philosophers simply deny any ultimate incompatibility of individual interests, but still they face questions about issues such as the assignment of rights and duties in the state, as well as the larger matter of how the citizens must be cooperate if they are to realize their shared good.

These issues represent only a small sample of the kinds of questions to which the concept of self-interest has given rise; I have outlined just a few of the standard replies. By bringing together the major philosophical sources on the subject, this collection invites further reflection upon self-interest and the wide variety of interpretations it has received throughout the centuries, affording a broad perspective from which to approach afresh the question of what it is to care for and pursue the interests of a self.

The writings are organized chronologically, and divided into five historical periods: Classical, Medieval, Early Modern, Nineteenth Century, and Twentieth Century. Each period is prefaced with an overview of its unique features and concerns, and historical continuity is noted, where it seems to exist.

In a collection of this sort, it is not possible to include every thinker and text, so I should briefly mention what I have chosen to exclude.

The early modern era produced so much on the topic of self-regard that, even having included more writings from this period than any other, I had to omit here more than I would have liked. Despite his interesting distinction between *amour d'soi* and *amour propre*, Rousseau was not included because his work lacked extended discussions of self-interest. I excluded as well Pierre Nicole, who discusses the similarities between self-love and charity; Lord Shaftesbury, who defends something similar to the Stoic view of a universal harmony of interests; Samuel Clarke, who claims that divine law dictates the appropriate duties to both self and others (personal upkeep in the first case, equity and love in the second); Samuel Pufendorf, who defends against Hobbes the natural sociability of men, while admitting that by nature all are principally recommended to their own care; John Gay, who sees all motivation as self-interested, but believes that over time, we can come to take pleasure in benefiting others without explicitly consulting our own interests; and Claude Helvétius, who combines Hobbesian egoism with a version of Stoic universalism.

The Industrial Revolution and rise of socialism in the nineteenth century prompted a host of new writings on the problem of self-regard, many of which, again, I was forced to leave out. I exclude Marx, who does not engage in any extended philosophical analysis of self-interest. Emerson's essay, "Self-Reliance," is a poetic tribute to proper self-regard, but lacks the philosophical rigor that characterizes the other selections. Kierkegaard's *Works of Love*, a theological philippic against self-love, is reminiscent of Augustine. Other writers of this era with original ideas about self-interest for whom space was lacking: Max Stirner (*The Ego and Its Own*), Auguste Comte (*System of Positive Polity*), Francis H. Bradley (*Ethical Studies*), and Herbert Spencer (*The Principles of Ethics*).

The twentieth century proved most difficult of all, and due to space limitations and the historical orientation of the collection, I was forced to omit a good deal of important material. I have tried partially to compensate for this by including a lengthier bibliography for this era.

These decisions were difficult to make, and I entreat the reader to delve into the full range of historical materials on self-interest, as well as the more recent treatments by the philosophers of this century. In a subject of such enduring importance and continuing perplexity, what we require, far from provincialism, is exposure to all of the available resources. By gathering many of the best writings on self-regard in a single collection, this anthology aims to be an initial step in that direction.

I | CLASSICAL ERA

𝒯houghts of self-love and self-interest were never far from the minds of the classical philosophers. Theirs was a tradition in which self-concern was not only considered acceptable, but the foundation of the moral life. The dominant ethical paradigm at the time held that the moral purpose of each individual is to promote his own personal happiness (*eudaimonia*). The philosophical debate concerned not whether we are justified in pursuing our self-interest, but what are the best means for doing so.

The two most influential views on this were developed by the sophists and Socrates (469–399 B.C.), respectively. The Sophists were a group of educators who sought to prepare young men for civic life. Though some were politically conservative, a number of Sophists challenged traditional Greek morality by emphasizing its tension with self-interest. For instance, Callicles and Thrasymachus (*fl.* late fifth century B.C.)—whose views are presented by Plato in our first selection—argue that self-interest consists in having the power to do what one desires, whatever the consequences for others. The weak have devised a conventional conception of justice that enables them artificially to restrain the strong and so promote their own interests, but in reality justice is "nothing but the advantage of the stronger."

Socrates, the Sophists' greatest critic, left no writings, but his views have been preserved in the works of Xenophon (c. 428–c. 354 B.C.) and Plato (427–347 B.C.), which depict him firmly rejecting the Sophists' equation of injustice and happiness. Virtue and law are not "bonds on nature"—as Antiphon (c. 480–411 B.C.) had asserted—but expressions of man's natural condition. Indeed, rationality and virtue are definitive of human nature. Since a being who lives in violation of its nature cannot flourish, it is only people who exercise reason and virtue that are capable of discovering true happiness. "The wrongdoer is more unfortunate than the person wronged": the latter may suffer incidental harm, but the former's vice undermines the very foundation of his well-being.

Plato, the first philosopher from whom we read, presents both the Sophistic and Socratic views in his writings, but sides firmly with Socrates in the debate over self-interest. For Plato, happiness must be understood in terms of the proper functioning of the soul, and the soul operates correctly to the extent that reason regulates the appetites and emotions. A well-ordered soul exhibits balance and virtue, and fosters psychological health in just the same way that bodily harmony fosters physical health. Inasmuch as inner harmony carries over to one's interpersonal relations, leading one to treat others justly, it fosters social well-being, too.

Despite his concern with personal well-being, some commentators suggest that Plato ultimately subordinates self-interest to the interests of society. For instance, in the *Republic* Plato claims to be less interested in the happiness of any one group in the state than with that of state as a whole, and in the *Laws* he asserts that, "the purpose of all that happens is . . . to win bliss for the life of the whole; it is not made for you, but you for it." Yet, though there are undoubtedly collectivist elements to Plato's thought, we should not lose sight of his enduring concern with the personal benefits to be had from practicing virtue within the framework of a righteous state.

Although the topic of self-interest is broached in a number of the Platonic dialogues, it is only in his late work, the *Laws*, that Plato offers his explicit thoughts on self-love. His earlier works seem to imply that true self-love consists in obedience to reason; for if the self's good consists in being properly ordered, and if proper order is achieved only through rational control, one who loves one's self and wants its good will obey reason. It would follow from this that true self-love could never be excessive, since, for Plato, a person can never be too rational.

In the *Laws*, however, Plato puts the matter differently, indicating that he does think an excess of self-love possible. Human beings naturally love themselves most of all, he observes, and this partiality may lead them to subvert "real fact" or "justice" in the pursuit of their own ends—holding others to standards of righteousness to which they will not submit themselves. The good man, recognizing this human tendency, refuses to focus on himself at all; rather, his concern lies with justice. This does not mean the good man abandons his own fulfillment, however. On the contrary, since the just person considers the facts, as opposed to the distorted state of affairs projected through biased self-preference, he is actually best able to secure his interests, as well as those of everyone else.

Is self-love a good or an evil, then, in Plato's view? He never explicitly addresses this question, although he seems to think something like the following. If by "self-love" we mean love of psychic harmony and rational control, self-love can never be but a force for good. Self-love in the ordinary sense of self-preference, however, inevitably must lead to "all manner of misdeeds in every one of us." Plato's illustrious pupil, Aristotle, would later offer an explicit account of this distinction, which, in Plato, remains only tacit.

The conception of psychic and social harmony defined by Plato is embraced by Aristotle (384–322 B.C.), who agrees that rationality and virtue are the keys to personal happiness. But Aristotle gives the non-rational elements of the soul a more explicit role in well-being. It is not sufficient to have reason control appetite and emotion, our non-rational side must be trained to take pleasure in virtue, too.

Although Aristotle conceives internal harmony—summed up in his doctrine of the mean—as the essence of happiness, he denies that an individual's interests can be specified entirely in terms of the soul. A healthy soul is crucial, but material prosperity, as well good friends, are preconditions of total flourishing.

However, Aristotle does not always appear consistent on this point. In particular, the tenth book of the *Nicomachean Ethics* seems to offer a purely spiritual conception of well-being. Aristotle declares that human beings possess theoretical understanding (*nous*), a godlike trait, and that *eudaimonia* actually consists of withdrawal into a life of uninterrupted contemplation. Insofar as human life possesses a physical dimension, people cannot live by contemplation alone, but they are happiest to the extent they spend their time in purely theoretical pursuits. Was *Ethics* X intended to supplant the more "earthly" conception of the good developed in *Ethics* I–IX? Or does *Ethics* X assume that human nature is more complex, and that its fulfillment requires the flourishing of both its divine and mortal aspects? Scholars are deeply divided on this question, to which we may never arrive at a satisfactory answer.

The meaning of Aristotle's remaining remarks about self-interest are, fortunately, far less opaque. First, Aristotle explains the importance of friendship to our well-being, and how it functions both as a model for and an outgrowth of self-love. True friends love each other for their own sakes, he observes, and since this kind of loving occurs above all in a person's relationship toward himself, the ultimate paradigm of friendship is love of self. Though we naturally love ourselves most of all, however, there may be people in our lives—particularly, our equals in virtue—to whom we can extend this love, and come to regard as "second selves."

Next, Aristotle employs the Greek ideal of nobility (*to kalon*) to explain how self-interest and the interests of others coincide through virtue. Behaving nobly involves acting in a way that is wholly appropriate—at the right time, in the right amount, towards the right people, and so forth. Since appropriate action is a manifestation of virtue—the cornerstone of happiness—nobility is among the greatest goods one can possess. What counts as appropriate action is dictated in large part by appeal to human nature, and man is by nature a "political animal"—that is, he naturally forms social bonds and wishes to share his life with others. Thus, nobility involves a substantial social component and a host of interpersonal virtues, including justice. Practicing these virtues becomes as essential an ingredient of our nobility and well-being as practicing the more self-confined virtues, such as temperance. And so Aristotle remarks that "when everyone competes to achieve what is noble and strains to do the noblest actions, everything that is right will be done for the common good, and each person individually will receive the greatest of goods, since that is the character of virtue." (*Nichmachean Ethics* IX.8 1169A9–12).

Finally, Aristotle rejects Plato's political analysis of self-interest, denying the danger of such institutions as private property. For Plato, private ownership engenders personal interests that interfere with civic loyalty. Aristotle takes the opposite view: the state fares best when each citizen is allowed to attend to his own affairs. It is not private interests that create civil strife but, rather, wicked characters. Furthermore, if private property is abolished, so too is the possibility of genuine liberality: one cannot give others that which does not belong to one.

In his *Politics*, Aristotle expresses agreement with Plato that self-love can run to excess, but makes it clear in the *Nicomachean Ethics* that this is true only of "bad" self-love; of "good" self-love, there can never be too much. The difference between the two is a question of the sort of *self* that is loved. Vicious self-lovers are those who favor the non-rational elements of their soul, identifying with their appetites. Heedless of reason, they end up doing harm to everyone, themselves included. Paradoxically, says Aristotle, although such people are commonly derided as "self-lovers" and, indeed, give self-love a bad name, they are not actually *capable* of self-love, for their selves are not good, and what is bad is not lovable. Good self-lovers, by contrast, are those who identify with their rational element. Since reason consults the good of all, this type of person, far from deserving condemnation, is a great social asset.

In Aristotle's account of self-love, as that of private property, we notice a common theme: It is not human nature or institutions that corrupt people, but corrupt people that put these things to their improper use. What we must do is help people understand their true interests and so become lovers of nobility and goodness. That done, self-love, far from the source of the vice, is transformed into a manifestation, as well as a reward, of virtue.

Epicurus (c.341–c. 270 B.C.) and his followers defended what was perhaps the narrowest conception of self-interest in antiquity, identifying it strictly with pleasure. They were careful to distinguish their brand of hedonism from the advocacy of intemperate living, however. Although pleasure is intrinsically good, they said, one does not always attain the most pleasure by pursuing it directly; sometimes a pleasant end can be had only by painful means. Further, the desire for pleasure can itself often be painful, and certain desires, when fulfilled, may actually result in pain. The best way to pursue pleasure, therefore, is to seek freedom from urgent and painful desires. The Epicureans called this condition "tranquillity" (*ataxaria*), and deemed it the essence of happiness.

Tranquillity was thought to be a condition partly of the body, but the Epicureans identified the individual's true interests more with the soul. The greatest happiness, in their view, consists less in satisfying the needs of the body—which can be trained to require very little—than in cultivating peace of mind. This can be accomplished largely by two means. First, one must exercise "prudence," so that one does not get ensnared by harmful or unnecessary desires. Second, one must cultivate scientific knowledge, in order to dispel one's fears about death and the gods.

Insofar as the pleasure which the Epicureans advocate is that of the individual, Epicureanism has traditionally been regarded as an egoistic doctrine. This has been thought to create a tension with the Epicurean defense of both virtue and friendship. Let us consider this criticism.

Epicureanism takes as its starting-point the idea that pleasure is the ultimate good, and this would seem to imply that virtue is requisite for self-interest only in cases where it is accompanied by pleasure, or at least an absence of pain; since virtue can at times be very demanding, however, and in that sense painful, the Epicurean appears committed to rejecting the view that vice is never in one's interests. Nonetheless, Epicurus insists that "it is impossible to live pleasantly without living prudently, honorably, and justly." In the case of justice, for instance, the practice of this virtue brings social advantages and peace of mind. In general, he thinks, only the virtuous possess the knowledge, self-control, and self-sufficiency required to lead a truly pleasant life.

Friendship poses a problem for Epicureanism insofar as friends are thought to care for each other non-instrumentally, that is, for the sake of themselves, whereas the Epicurean seems committed to saying that, as with virtue, concern for friends is limited by its prospects for securing personal pleasure. Accordingly, Epicurus frequently stresses the pleasures of friendship, going so far as to consider it the single greatest means to happiness. At the same time, though, he feels it is important to benefit one's friends, and even to die for them in certain cases. Torquatus attempts to resolve this problem by arguing that although friendship begins with personal pleasure, eventually there evolves intrinsic concern for the friend. In his view, it is only one who loves his friends for their own sakes who can attain the true joys and benefits of friendship.

Despite their explicit ideas about self-interest, the Epicureans devoted no special attention to the matter of self-love. Yet, insofar as they understood the purpose of life as a certain sort of personal fulfillment, theirs was clearly in some fundamental sense a self-loving creed.

For Zeno of Citium (c.336–c.265 B.C.) and his fellow Stoics, the last classical philosophers we shall consider, self-love and self-interest can ultimately be understood only from the standpoint of the Universe. This is because human beings form part of the larger natural order, and their nature and interests cannot be conceived in isolation from it.

The key to self-interest, in the Stoic sense, is understanding the difference between what in the universe is up to us and what is not. The universe is a coherent and orderly Whole in which all occurrences are determined by preceding events. Most of what happens, therefore, is beyond our control—everything, in fact, other than the operation of our souls. Since we are powerless to alter the course of events, we must identify our interests with whatever in fact happens to us—a feat we accomplish simply by regarding all external events and entities with equal acceptance. The alternative is to resist Nature, making ourselves frustrated and ill-content, and further, impeding our true good, since everything that happens by Nature does so for the best.

As for that aspect of life over which we do exercise control—namely, the operation of our souls—we determine our interests here again by consulting Nature, but in a slightly different manner. Rather than adopting an attitude of resignation, we must come to grasp the end toward which Nature propels us, since Nature directs all of its elements toward their true interests. In the case of human beings, we are directed toward virtue, hence our self-interest consists entirely in virtuous living.

Their conception of the natural order leads the Stoics to deny the possibility of antagonism between the interests of the self and those of other people. Since we are all part of a thoroughly ordered Whole, we exist in a harmonious relation to one another. This is suggested by man's natural sociability, and also by the fact that we discern in nature principles of justice that promote the common good. This does not imply that we ought not to pursue our own personal interests, and instead focus only upon the collective. Rather, nature has created us in such a way that we cannot attain our self-interest in a way that does not at the same time contribute to the commonweal.

The Stoic view of self-love complements their conception of self-interest. As noted, the Stoics view Nature as directing all entities toward their proper ends. Self-love, which they regard as one of the two primary impulses to action—the second being love-of-others—is the mechanism by which Nature accomplishes this. By endearing each thing to itself, it is brought about that every being repels injury and is drawn to that which furthers its natural purpose.

Although we are purely self-loving at birth, according to Stoicism, as we begin to mature we develop concern for other people that is independent of our concern for ourselves. At first, we start to care about our family-members. Later, friends and fellow countrymen are loved, too. Eventually our concern extends to the "remotest Mysian"—the Stoic metaphor for humanity. The process by which this occurs is called "familiarization" (*oikeiosis*), and eventually it leads us to a universal standpoint from which we exhibit impartial concern for all. One way of understanding the relation of this to the Stoic conception of self-interest is as follows: once we take the universal and impartial standpoint, we become able to transcend our narrow concerns, thus ideally situating ourselves for virtuous resignation to the course of nature.

Though they were divided in their conceptions of self-interest, and though we find some variation in their appraisals of self-love, classical philosophers were marked by a generally positive attitude toward self-concern, frequently associating it with virtue and social harmony. The medieval thinkers who follow embrace a different vision. Though they find a certain measure of self-love natural and necessary, they emphasize the negative features of self-interested behavior, particularly its connection with sin.

PLATO

$(427-347 \text{ B.C.})$

The Sophists on how injustice promotes self-interest[11]

CALLICLES: [B]y nature everything that is worse is more shameful, suffering wrong for instance, but by convention it is more shameful to do it. For to suffer wrong is not even fit for a man but only for a slave, for whom it is better to be dead than alive, since when wronged and outraged he is unable to help himself or any other for whom he cares. But in my opinion those who framed the laws are the weaker folk, the majority. And accordingly they frame the laws for themselves and their own advantage, and so too with their approval and censure, and to prevent the stronger who are able to overreach them from gaining the advantage over them, they frighten them by saying that to overreach others is shameful and evil, and injustice consists in seeking the advantage over others. For they are satisfied, I suppose, if being inferior they enjoy equality of status. That is the reason why seeking an advantage over the many is by convention said to be wrong and shameful, and they call it injustice. But in my view nature herself makes it plain that it is right for the better to have the advantage over the worse, the more able over the less. And both among all animals and in entire states and races of mankind it is plain that this is the case—that right is recognized to be the sovereignty and advantage of the stronger over the weaker. For what justification had Xerxes in invading Greece or his father in invading Scythia? And there are countless other similar instances one might mention. But I imagine that these men act in accordance with the true nature of right, yes and, by heaven, according to nature's own law, though not perhaps by the law we frame. We mold the best and strongest among ourselves, catching them young like lion cubs, and by spells and incantations we make slaves of them, saying that they must be content with equality and that this is what is right and fair. But if a man arises endowed with a nature sufficiently strong, he will, I believe, shake off all these controls, burst his fetters, and break loose. And trampling upon our scraps of paper, our spells and incantations, and all our unnatural conventions, he rises up and reveals himself our master who was once our slave, and there shines forth nature's true justice. . . .

[T]he naturally noble and just is what I now describe to you with all frankness — namely that anyone who is to live aright should suffer his appetites to grow to the greatest extent and not check them, and through courage and intelligence should be competent to minister to them at their greatest and to satisfy every appetite with what it craves. But this, I imagine, is impossible for the many; hence they blame such men through a sense of shame to conceal their own impotence, and, as I remarked before, they claim that intemperance is shameful and they make slaves of those who are naturally better. And because they themselves are unable to procure satisfaction for their pleasures, they are led by their own cowardice to praise temperance and justice. For to those whose lot it has been from the beginning to be the sons of kings or whose natural gifts enable them to acquire some office or tyranny or supreme power, what in truth could be worse and more shameful than temperance and justice? For though at liberty without any hindrance to enjoy their blessings, they would themselves invite the laws, the talk, and the censure of the many to be masters over them. And surely this noble justice and temperance of theirs would make miserable wretches of them, if they could bestow no more upon their friends than on their enemies, and that too when they were rulers in their own states. But the truth, Socrates, which you profess to follow, is this. Luxury and intemperance and license, when they have sufficient backing, are virtue and happiness, and all the rest is tinsel, the unnatural catchwords of mankind, mere nonsense and of no account.

• • •

THRASYMACHUS: I affirm that the just is nothing else than the advantage of the stronger. . . . [J]ustice and the just are literally the other fellow's good — the advantage of the stronger and the ruler, but a detriment that is all his own of the subject who obeys and serves — while injustice is the contrary and rules those who are simple in every sense of the word and just, and they being thus ruled do what is for his advantage who is the stronger and make him happy by serving him, but themselves by no manner of means. And you must look at the matter, my simple-minded Socrates, in this way, that the just man always comes out at a disadvantage in his relation with the unjust. To begin with, in their business dealings in any joint undertaking of the two you will never find that the just man has the advantage over the unjust at the dissolution of the partnership but that he always has the worst of it. Then again, in their relations with the state, if there are direct taxes or contributions to be paid, the just man contributes more from an equal estate and the other less, and when there is a distribution the one gains much and the other nothing. And so when each holds office, apart from any other loss the just man must count on his own affairs' falling into disorder through neglect while because of his justice he makes no profit from the state, and thereto he will displease his friends and his acquaintances by his unwillingness to serve them unjustly. But to the unjust man all the opposite advantages accrue. I mean, of course, the one I was just speaking of, the man who has the ability to overreach on a large scale. Consider this type of man, then, if you wish to judge how much more profitable it is to him personally to be unjust than to be just. And the easiest way of all to understand this matter will be to turn to the most consummate form of injustice which makes the man who has done the wrong most happy and those who are wronged and who would not themselves willingly do wrong most miserable. And this is tyranny, which both by stealth and by force takes away what belongs to others, both sacred and profane, both private and public, not little by little but at one swoop. For each several part of such wrongdoing the malefactor who fails to escape detection is fined and incurs the extreme of contumely, for temple robbers, kidnappers, burglars, swindlers, and thieves are the appellations of those who commit these several forms of injustice. But when in addition to the property of the citizens men kidnap and enslave the citizens themselves, instead of these opprobrious names they are pronounced happy and blessed not only by their fellow citizens but by all who hear the story of the man who has committed complete and entire injustice. For it is not the fear of doing but of suffering wrong that calls forth the reproaches of those who revile injustice.

Thus, Socrates, injustice on a sufficiently large scale is a stronger, freer, and more masterful thing than justice, and, as I said in the beginning, it is the advantage of the stronger that is the just, while the unjust is what profits a man's self and is for his advantage.

Wrong-doing is always contrary to self-interest [12]

SOCRATES: But surely the goodness of anything, whether implement or body or soul or any living thing, does not best come to it merely by haphazard, but through a certain rightness and order and through the art that is assigned to each of them. Is this so?

CALLICLES: I certainly agree.

SOCRATES: Then the goodness of anything is due to order and arrangement?

CALLICLES: I should agree.

SOCRATES: It is then the presence in each thing of the order appropriate to it that makes everything good?

CALLICLES: So it appears to me.

SOCRATES: The soul then that has its own appropriate order is better than that which has none?

CALLICLES: Necessarily.

SOCRATES: But further, the soul possessed of order is orderly?

CALLICLES: Of course.

SOCRATES: And the orderly is the temperate?

CALLICLES: Most necessarily.

SOCRATES: Then the temperate soul is the good. I myself can offer no objection to this, my dear Callicles, but if you can, please instruct me.

CALLICLES: Go on, my good sir.

SOCRATES: I assert then that, if the temperate soul is good, then the soul in the opposite condition to the temperate is evil, and this, we saw, was the foolish and undisciplined.

CALLICLES: Certainly.

SOCRATES: Moreover the sound-minded man would do his duty by gods and men, for he would not be sound of mind if he did what was unfitting.

CALLICLES: That must necessarily be so.

SOCRATES: And doing his duty by men, he would be acting justly, and doing it by the gods, piously, and the doer of just and pious deeds must be just and pious.

CALLICLES: That is so.

SOCRATES: And further, he must be brave, for it is not the part of a man of sound mind to pursue or avoid what he should not, but to pursue or avoid what he should, whether it things, or people, or pleasures, or pains, and to stand his ground, where duty bids, and remain steadfast. So there is every necessity, Callicles, that the sound-minded and temperate man, being, as we have demonstrated, just and brave and pious, must be completely good, and the good man must do well and finely whatever he does, and he who does well must be happy and blessed, while the evil man who does ill must be wretched, and he would be the opposite of the temperate man, the undisciplined creature of whom you approve. This then is the position I take, and I affirm it to be true, and if it is true, then the man who wishes to be happy must, it seems, pursue and practice temperance, and each of us must flee from indiscipline with all the speed in his power and contrive, preferably to have no need of being disciplined, but if he or any of his friends, whether individual or city, has need of it, then he must suffer punishment and be disciplined, if he is to be happy. This I consider to be the mark to which a man should look throughout his life, and all his own endeavors and those of his city he should devote to the single purpose of so acting that justice and temperance shall dwell in him who is to be truly blessed. He should not suffer his appetites to be undisciplined and endeavor to satisfy them by leading the life of a brigand—a mischief without end. For such a man could be dear neither to any other man nor to God, since he is incapable of fellowship, and where there is no fellowship, friendship cannot be. Wise men, Callicles, say that the heavens and the earth, gods and men, are bound together by fellowship and friendship, and order and temperance and justice, and for this reason they call the sum of things the "ordered" universe, my friend, not the world of disorder or riot. But it seems to me that you pay no attention to these things in spite of your wisdom, but you are unaware that geometric equality is of great importance among gods and men alike, and you think we should practice overreaching others, for you neglect geometry. Well, either we must refute this argument and prove that happiness does not come to the happy through the possession of justice and temperance, nor does misery come through the possession of wickedness, or, if my argument is true, we must consider the consequences. And the consequences are all those previously mentioned, about which you asked me, Callicles, if I was speaking seriously when I said that a man should accuse himself and his son and his friend, if guilty of any wrong deed, and should employ rhetoric for this purpose, and what you thought Polus admitted through a sense of shame is true after all— that it is as much more evil as it is more shameful to do than to suffer wrong, and he who is to become a rhetorician in the right way must after all be a just man with a knowledge of what is just—an admission which Gorgias in turn made, according to Polus, through a sense of shame.

This being so, let us consider whether or not you spoke aright in your reproaches to me, when you said that I am not able to help myself or any of my friends and relations, or to save them from the gravest perils, but like outlawed men am at the mercy of anyone, whether he wishes to box my ears, as you so forcefully expressed it, or rob me of my money, or drive me out of the city, or, worst of all, put me to death, and, according to your view, to be in this plight is of all things the most shameful. But as to my own view, though it has often been expressed already, there is no harm in my expressing it once more. I maintain, Callicles, that it is not the most shameful of things to be wrongfully boxed on the ears, nor again to have either my purse or my person cut, but it is both more disgraceful and more wicked to strike or to cut me or what is mine wrongfully, and, further, theft and kidnapping and burglary and in a word any wrong done to me and mine is at once more shameful and worse for the wrongdoer than for me the sufferer. These facts, which were shown to be as I state them some time earlier in our previous discussion, are buckled fast and clamped together—to put it somewhat crudely—by arguments of steel and adamant—at least so it would appear as matters stand. And unless you or one still more enterprising than yourself can undo them, it is impossible to speak aright except as I am now speaking. For what I say is always the same—that I know not the truth in these affairs, but I do know that of all whom I have ever met either before or now no one who put forward another view has failed to appear ridiculous. And so once more I hold these things to be so, and if they are, and if injustice is the greatest of evils to the wrongdoer and, greatest though it be, it is an even greater evil, if that be possible, to escape punishment when one does wrong, what is that help the failure to avail himself of which makes a man in very truth ridiculous? Is it not that which will avert from us the greatest harm? This must surely be the help which it is most shameful to be unable to render to oneself and one's friends and relations, and next to this the second most shameful, and after that the third and so with the rest; as is the magnitude of the evil in each case, so too will be the beauty of being able to help oneself to meet such evil and the shame of being unable. Am I right or wrong, Callicles?

CALLICLES: You are right.

SOCRATES: Of these two then, inflicting and suffering wrong, we say it is a greater evil to inflict it, a lesser to suffer it.

Our true well-being lies in harmony of soul [13]

[SOCRATES:] Does it not belong to the rational part [of the soul] to rule, being wise and exercising forethought in behalf of the entire soul, and to the principle of high spirit to be subject to this and its ally?

[CALLICLES:] Assuredly.

Then is it not, as we said, the blending of music and gymnastics that will render them concordant, intensifying and fostering the one with fair words and teachings and relaxing and soothing and making gentle the other by harmony and rhythm?

Quite so, said he.

And these two, thus reared and having learned and been educated to do their own work in the true sense of the phrase, will preside over the appetitive part which is the mass of the soul in each of us and the most insatiate by nature of wealth. They will keep watch upon it, lest, by being filled and infected with the so-called pleasures associated with the body and so waxing big and strong, it may not keep to its own work but may undertake to enslave and rule over the classes which it is not fitting that it should, and so overturn the entire life of all.

By all means, he said.

Would not these two, then, best keep guard against enemies from without also in behalf of the entire soul and body, the one taking counsel, the other giving battle, attending upon the ruler, and by its courage executing the ruler's designs?

That is so.

Brave, too, then, I take it, we call each individual by virtue of this part in him, when, namely, his high spirit preserves in the midst of pains and pleasures the rule handed down by the reason as to what is or is not to be feared.

Right, he said.

But wise by that small part that ruled in him and handed down these commands, by its possession in turn within it of the knowledge of what is beneficial for each and for the whole, the community composed of the three.

By all means.

And again, was he not sober by reason of the friendship and concord of these same parts, when, namely, the ruling principle and its two subjects are at one in the belief that the reason ought to rule, and do not raise faction against it?

The virtue of soberness certainly, said he, is nothing else than this, whether in a city or an individual.

But surely, now, a man is just by that which and in the way we have so often described.

That is altogether necessary.

Justice . . . means that a man must not suffer the principles in his soul to do each the work of some other and interfere and meddle with one another, but that he should dispose well of what in the true sense of the word is properly his own, and having first attained to self-mastery and beautiful order within himself, and having harmonized these three principles, the notes or intervals of three terms quite literally the lowest, the highest, and the mean, and all others there may be between them, and having linked and bound all three together and made of himself a unit, one man instead of many, self-controlled and in unison, he should then and then only turn to practice if he find aught to do either in the getting of wealth or the tendance of the body or it may be in political action or private business—in all such doings believing and naming the just and honorable action to be that which preserves and helps to produce this condition of soul, and wisdom the science that presides over such conduct, and believing and naming the unjust action to be that which ever tends to overthrow this spiritual constitution, and brutish ignorance to be the opinion that in turn presides over this. . . . Next after this, I take it, we must consider injustice.

Obviously.

Must not this be a kind of civil war of these three principles, their meddlesomeness and interference with one another's functions, and the revolt of one part against the whole of the soul that it may hold therein a rule which does not belong to it, since its nature is such that it befits it to serve as a slave to the ruling principle? Something of this sort, I fancy, is what we shall say, and that the confusion of these principles and their straying from their proper course is injustice and licentiousness and cowardice and brutish ignorance and, in general, all turpitude.

Precisely this, he replied.

Then, said I, to act unjustly and be unjust and in turn to act justly —the meaning of all these terms becomes at once plain and clear, since injustice and justice are so.

How so?

Because, said I, these are in the soul what the healthful and the diseaseful are in the body; there is no difference.

In what respect? he said.

Healthful things surely engender health and diseaseful disease.

Yes.

Then does not doing just acts engender justice and unjust injustice?

Of necessity.

But to produce health is to establish the elements in a body in the natural relation of dominating and being dominated by one another, while to cause disease is to bring it about that one rules or is ruled by the other contrary to nature.

Yes, that is so.

And is it not likewise the production of justice in the soul to establish its principles in the natural relation of controlling and being controlled by one another, while injustice is to cause the one to rule or be ruled by the other contrary to nature?

Exactly so, he said.

Virtue, then, as it seems, would be a kind of health and beauty and good condition of the soul, and vice would be disease, ugliness, and weakness.

It is so.

Then is it not also true that beautiful and honorable pursuits tend to the winning of virtue and the ugly to vice.

Of necessity.

And now at last, it seems, it remains for us to consider whether it is profitable to do justice and practice honorable pursuits and be just, whether one is known to be such or not, or whether injustice profits, and to be unjust, if only a man escape punishment and is not bettered by chastisement.

Nay, Socrates, he said, I think that from this point on our inquiry becomes an absurdity—if, while life is admittedly intolerable with a ruined constitution of body even though accompanied by all the food and drink and wealth and power in the world, we are yet to be asked to suppose that, when the very nature and constitution of that whereby we live is disordered and corrupted, life is going to be worth living, if a man can only do as he pleases, and pleases to do anything save that which will rid him of evil and injustice and make him possessed of justice and virtue—now that the two have been shown to be as we have described them.

In forming the state, we must focus not on individual, but on collective, interests [14]

[SOCRATES:] In the first place, none [of the guardians of the state] must possess any private property save the indispensable. Secondly, none must have any habitation or treasure house which is not open for all to enter at will. Their food, in such quantities as are needful for athletes of war sober and brave, they must receive as an agreed stipend from the other citizens as the wages of their guardianship, so measured that there shall be neither superfluity at the end of the year nor any lack. And resorting to a common mess like soldiers on campaign they will live together. Gold and silver, we will tell them, they have of the divine quality from the gods always in their souls, and they have no need of the metal of men nor does holiness suffer them to mingle and contaminate that heavenly possession with the acquisition of mortal gold, since many impious deeds have been done about the coin of the multitude, while that which dwells within them is unsullied. . . .

And Adimantus broke in and said, What will be your defense, Socrates, if anyone objects that you are not making these men very happy, and that through their own fault? For the city really belongs to them and yet they get no enjoyment out of it as ordinary men do by owning lands and building fine big houses and providing them with suitable furniture and winning the favor of the gods by private sacrifices and entertaining guests and enjoying too those possessions which you just now spoke of, gold and silver and all that is customary for those who are expecting to be happy. But they seem, one might say, to be established in idleness in the city, exactly like hired mercenaries, with nothing to do but keep guard. . . .

By following the same path I think we shall find what to reply. For we shall say that while it would not surprise us if these men thus living prove to be the most happy, yet the object on which we fixed our eyes in the establishment of our state was not the exceptional happiness of any one class but the greatest possible happiness of the city as a whole. . . . If then we are forming true guardians and keepers of our liberties, men least likely to harm the commonwealth, but the proponent of the other ideal is thinking of farmers and "happy" feasters as it were in a festival and not in a civic community, he would have something else in mind than a state. Consider, then, whether our aim in establishing the guardians is the greatest possible happiness among them or whether that is something we must look to see develop in the city as a whole, but these helpers and guardians are to be constrained and persuaded to do what will make them the best craftsmen in their own work, and similarly all the rest. And so, as the entire city develops and is ordered well, each class is to be left to the share of happiness that its nature comports.

• • •

Why, our discourse must persuade the young man that he who provides for the world has disposed all things with a view to the preservation and perfection of the whole, wherefore each several thing also, so far as may be, does and has done to it what is proper. And for each and all there are, in every case, governors appointed of all doing and being-done-to, down to the least detail, who have achieved perfection even to the minute particulars. Your own being also, fond man, is one such fragment, and so, for all its littleness, all its striving is ever directed toward the whole, but you have forgotten in the business that the purpose of all that happens is what we have said, to win bliss for the life of the whole; it is not made for you, but you for it. For any physician or craftsman in any profession does all his work for the sake of some whole, but the part he fashions for the sake of the whole, to contribute to the general good, not the whole for the part's sake. And yet you murmur because you see not how in your own case what is best for the whole proves best also for yourself in virtue of our common origin. And seeing that a soul, in its successive conjunction first with one body and then with another, runs the whole gamut of change through its own action or that of some other soul, no labor is left for the mover of the pieces but this — to shift the character that is becoming better to a better place, and that which is growing worse to a worser, each according to its due, that each may meet with its proper doom.

The danger of self-love[15]

ATHENIAN: But every man's most precious possession, as we said, is his soul; no man, then, we may be sure, will of set purpose receive the supreme evil into this most precious thing and live with it there all his life through. And yet, though a wrongdoer or a man in evil case is always a pitiable creature, it is with him whose disease is curable that there is scope for pity. With him one may curb and tame one's passion, and not scold like a vixen, but against the unqualified and incorrigible offender, the utterly corrupt, we must give the rein to wrath. This is why we say it is meet for a good man to be high-spirited and gentle, as occasion requires. But of all faults of soul the gravest is one which is inborn in most men, one which all excuse in themselves and none therefore attempts to avoid — that conveyed in the maxim that "everyone is naturally his own friend," and that it is only right and proper that he should be so whereas, in truth, this same violent attachment to self is the constant source of all manner of misdeeds in every one of us. The eye of love is blind where the beloved is concerned, and so a man proves a bad judge of right, good, honor, in the conceit that more regard is due to his personality than to the real fact, whereas a man who means to be great must care neither for self nor for its belongings, but for justice, whether exhibited in his own conduct, or rather in that of another. From this same fault springs also that universal conviction that one's own folly is wisdom, with its consequences that we fancy we know everything when we know as good as nothing, refuse to allow others to manage business we do not understand, and fall into inevitable errors in transacting it for ourselves. Every man, then, must shun extreme self-love and follow ever in the steps of his better, undeterred by any shame for his case.

After studying in Athens under Plato for nearly twenty years, Aristotle went on to develop his own distinctive philosophy. Readers will find Plato's influence throughout his writings on self-interest, but they will also find him critical of Plato on certain points—for instance, on the political implications of self-concern.

ARISTOTLE
(384–322 B.C.)

Our true well-being lies in rational activity [16]

Presumably, however, to say that happiness is the chief good seems a platitude, and a clearer account of what it is still desired. This might perhaps be given, if we could first ascertain the function of man. For just as for a flute-player, a sculptor, or any artist, and, in general, for all things that have a function or activity, the good and the "well" is thought to reside in the function, so would it seem to be for man, if he has a function. Have the carpenter, then, and the tanner certain functions or activities, and has man none? Is he naturally functionless? Or as eye, hand, foot, and in general each of the parts evidently has a function, may one lay it down that man similarly has a function apart from all these? What then can this be? Life seems to be common even to plants, but we are seeking what is peculiar to man. Let us exclude, therefore, the life of nutrition and growth. Next there would be a life of perception, but it also seems to be common even to the horse, the ox, and every animal. There remains, then, an active life of the element that has a rational principle (of this, one part has such a principle in the sense of being obedient to one, the other in the sense of possessing one and exercising thought); and as this too can be taken in two ways, we must state that life in the sense of activity is what we mean; for this seems to be the more proper sense of the term. Now if the function of man is an activity of soul in accordance with, or not without, rational principle, and if we say a so-and-so and a good so-and-so have a function which is the same in kind, e.g. a lyre-player and a good lyre-player, and so without qualification in all cases, eminence in respect of excellence being added to the function (for the function of a lyre-player is to play the lyre, and that of a good lyre-player is to do so well): if this is the case, . . . human good turns out to be activity of soul in conformity with excellence, and if there are more than one excellence, in conformity with the best and most complete.

But we must add "in a complete life." For one swallow does not make a summer, nor does one day; and so too one day, or a short time, does not make a man blessed and happy. . . .

Yet evidently, as we said, it needs the external goods as well; for it is impossible, or not easy, to do noble acts without the proper equipment. In many actions we use friends and riches and political power as instruments; and there are some things the lack of which takes the luster from blessedness, as good birth, satisfactory children, beauty; for the man who is very ugly in appearance or ill-born or solitary and childless is hardly happy, and perhaps a man would be still less so if he had thoroughly bad children or friends or had lost good children or friends by death. As we said, then, happiness seems to need this sort of prosperity in addition. . . .

The highest good is contemplation [17]

If happiness is activity in accordance with excellence, it is reasonable that it should be in accordance with the highest excellence; and this will be that of the best thing in us. Whether it be intellect or something else that is this element which is thought to be our natural ruler and guide and to take thought of things noble and divine, whether it be itself also divine or only the most divine element in us, the activity of this in accordance with its proper excellence will be complete happiness. That this activity is contemplative we have already said.

Now this would seem to be in agreement both with what we said before and with the truth. For this activity is the best (since not only is intellect the best thing in us, but the objects of intellect are the best of knowable objects); and, secondly, it is the most continuous, since we can contemplate truth more continuously than we can do anything. And we think happiness has pleasure mingled with it, but the activity of wisdom is admittedly the pleasantest of excellent activities; at all events philosophy is thought to offer pleasures marvelous for their purity and their enduringness, and it is to be expected that those who know will pass their time more pleasantly than those who inquire. . . .

The activity of intellect, which is contemplative, seems both to be superior in worth and to aim at no end beyond itself, and to have its pleasure proper to itself (and this augments the activity), and the self-sufficiency, leisureliness, unweariedness (so far as this is possible for man), and all the other attributes ascribed to the blessed man are evidently those connected with this activity, it follows that this will be the complete happiness of man, if it be allowed a complete term of life (for none of the attributes of happiness is incomplete).

But such a life would be too high for man; for it is not in so far as he is man that he will live so, but in so far as something divine is present in him; and by so much as this is superior to our composite nature is its activity superior to that which is the exercise of the other kind of excellence. If intellect is divine, then, in comparison with man, the life according to it is divine in comparison with human life. But we must not follow those who advise us, being men, to think of human things, and, being mortal, of mortal things, but must, so far as we can, make ourselves immortal, and strain every nerve to live in accordance with the best thing in us; for even if it be small in bulk, much more does it in power and worth surpass everything. This would seem, too, to be each man himself, since it is the authoritative and better part of him. It would be strange, then, if he were to choose not the life of himself but that of something else. And what we said before will apply now; that which is proper to each thing is by nature best and most pleasant for each thing; for man, therefore, the life according to intellect is best and pleasantest, since intellect more than anything else is man. This life therefore is also the happiest. . . .

But, being a man, one will also need external prosperity; for our nature is not self-sufficient for the purpose of contemplation, but our body also must be healthy and must have food and other attention. Still we must not think that the man who is to be happy will need many things or great things, merely because he cannot be blessed without external goods; for self-sufficiency and action do not depend on excess, and we can do noble acts without ruling earth and sea; for even with moderate advantages one can act excellently (this is manifest enough; for private persons are thought to do worthy acts no less than despots—indeed even more); and it is enough that we should have so much as that; for the life of the man who is active in accordance with excellence will be happy.

Self-Friendship[18]

Friendly relations with one's neighbors, and the marks by which friendships are defined, seem to have proceeded from a man's relations to himself. For men think a friend is one who wishes and does what is good, or seems so, for the sake of his friend, or one who wishes his friend to exist and live, for his sake; which mothers do to their children, and friends do who have come into conflict. And others think a friend is one who lives with and has the same tastes as another, or one who grieves and rejoices with his friend; and this too is found in mothers most of all. It is by some one of these characteristics that friendship too is defined.

Now each of these is true of the good man's relation to himself (and of all other men in so far as they think themselves good; excellence and the good man seem, as has been said, to be the measure of every class of things). For his opinions are harmonious, and he desires the same things with all his soul; and therefore he wishes for himself what is good and what seems so, and does it (for it is characteristic of the good man to exert himself for the good), and does so for his own sake (for he does it for the sake of the intellectual element in him, which is thought to be the man himself); and he wishes himself to live and be preserved, and especially the element by virtue of which he thinks. For existence is good to the good man, and each man wishes himself what is good, while no one chooses to possess the whole world if he has first to become some one else (for that matter, even now God possesses the good); he wishes for this only on condition of being whatever he is; and the element that thinks would seem to be the individual man, or to be so more than any other element in him. And such a man wishes to live with himself; for he does so with pleasure, since the memories of his past acts are delightful and his hopes for the future are good, and therefore pleasant. His mind is well stored too with subjects of contemplation. And he grieves and rejoices, more than any other, with himself; for the same thing is always painful, and the same thing always pleasant, and not one thing at one time and another at another; he has, so to speak, nothing to regret.

Therefore, since each of these characteristics belongs to the good man in relation to himself, and he is related to his friend as to himself (for his friend is another self), friendship too is thought to be one of these attributes, and those who have these attributes to be friends. Whether there is or is not friendship between a man and himself is a question we may dismiss for the present; there would seem to be friendship in so far as he is two or more, to judge from what has been said, and from the fact that the extreme of friendship is likened to one's love for oneself.

But the attributes named seem to belong even to the majority of men, poor creatures though they may be. Are we to say then that in so far as they are satisfied with themselves and think they are good, they share in these attributes? Certainly no one who is thoroughly bad and impious has these attributes, or even seems to do so. They hardly belong even to inferior people; for they are at variance with themselves, and have appetites for some things and wishes for others. This is true, for instance, of incontinent people; for they choose, instead of the things they themselves think good, things that are pleasant but hurtful; while others again, through cowardice and laziness, shrink from doing what they think best for themselves. And those who have done many terrible deeds and are hated for their wickedness even shrink from life and destroy themselves. And wicked men seek for people with whom to spend their days, and shun themselves; for they remember many a grievous deed, and anticipate others like them, when they are by themselves, but when they are with others they forget. And having nothing lovable in them they have no feeling of love to themselves. Therefore also such men do not rejoice or grieve with themselves; for their soul is rent by faction, and one element in it by reason of its wickedness grieves when it abstains from certain acts, while the other part is pleased, and one draws them this way and the other that, as if they were pulling them in pieces. If a man cannot at the same time be pained and pleased, at all events after a short time he is pained because he was pleased, and he could have wished that these things had not been pleasant to him; for bad men are laden with regrets. Therefore the bad man does not seem to be amicably disposed even to himself because there is nothing in him to love; so that if to be thus is the height of wretchedness, we should strain every nerve to avoid wickedness and should endeavor to be good; for so one may be both friendly to oneself and a friend to another.

And since what is natural is pleasant, and things akin to each other seem natural to each other, therefore all kindred and similar things are for the most part pleasant to each other; for instance, one man, horse, or young person is pleasant to another man, horse, or young person. Hence the proverbs "mate delights mate," "like to like," "beast knows beast," "jackdaw to jackdaw," and the rest of them. But since everything like and akin to oneself is pleasant, and since every man is himself more like and akin to himself than anyone else is, it follows that all of us must be more or less fond of ourselves. For all this resemblance and kinship is present particularly in the relation of an individual to himself. And because we are all fond of ourselves, it follows that what is our own is pleasant to all of us, as for instance our own deeds and words. That is why we are for the most part fond of our flatterers, our lovers, and honor; also of our children, for our children are our own work.

Good versus bad self-love [19]

The question is also debated, whether a man should love himself most, or someone else. People criticize those who love themselves most, and call them self-lovers, using this as an epithet of disgrace, and a bad man seems to do everything for his own sake, and the more so the more wicked he is—and so men reproach him, for instance, with doing nothing of his own accord—while the good man acts for honor's sake, and the more so the better he is, and acts for his friend's sake, and sacrifices his own interest.

But the facts clash with these arguments, and this is not surprising. For men say that one ought to love best one's best friend, and a man's best friend is one who wishes well to the object of his wish for his sake, even if no one is to know of it; and these attributes are found most of all in a man's attitude towards himself, and so are all the other attributes by which a friend is defined; for, as we have said, it is from this relation that all the characteristics of friendship have extended to others. All the proverbs, too, agree with this, e.g., "a single soul," and "what friends have is common property," and "friendship is equality," and "charity begins at home"; for all these marks will be found most in a man's relation to himself; he is his own best friend and therefore ought to love himself best. It is therefore a reasonable question, which of the two views we should follow; for both are plausible.

Perhaps we ought to mark off such arguments from each other and determine how far and in what respects each view is right. Now if we grasp the sense in which each party uses the phrase "lover of self," the truth may become evident. Those who use the term as one of reproach ascribe self-love to people who assign to themselves the greater share of wealth, honors, and bodily pleasures; for these are what most people desire, and busy themselves about as though they were the best of all things, which is the reason, too, why they become objects of competition. So those who are grasping with regard to these things gratify their appetites and in general their feelings and the irrational element of the soul; and most men are of this nature thus the epithet has taken its meaning from the prevailing type of self-love, which is a bad one; it is just, therefore, that men who are lovers of self in this way are reproached for being so. That it is those who give themselves the preference in regard to objects of this sort that most people usually call lovers of self is plain; for if a man were always anxious that he himself, above all things, should act justly, temperately, or in accordance with any other of the excellences, and in general were always to try to secure for himself the honorable course, no one will call such a man a lover of self or blame him.

But such a man would seem more than the other a lover of self; at all events he assigns to himself the things that are noblest and best, and gratifies the most authoritative element in himself and in all things obeys this; and just as a city or any other systematic whole is most properly identified with the most authoritative element in it, so is a man; and therefore the man who loves this and gratifies it is most of all a lover of self. Besides, a man is said to have or not to have self-control according as his intellect has or has not the control, on the assumption that this is the man himself; and the things men have done from reason are thought most properly their own acts and voluntary acts. That this is the man himself, then, or is so more than anything else, is plain, and also that the good man loves most this part of him. Whence it follows that he is most truly a lover of self, of another type than that which is a matter of reproach, and as different from that as living according to reason is from living as passion dictates, and desiring what is noble from desiring what seems advantageous. Those, then, who busy themselves in an exceptional degree with noble actions all men approve and praise; and if all were to strive towards what is noble and strain every nerve to do the noblest deeds, everything would be as it should be for the common good, and every one would secure for himself the goods that are greatest, since excellence is the greatest of goods.

Therefore the good man should be a lover of self (for he will both himself profit by doing noble acts, and will benefit his fellows), but the wicked man should not; for he will hurt both himself and his neighbors, following as he does evil passions. For the wicked man, what he does clashes with what he ought to do, but what the good man ought to do he does; for the intellect always chooses what is best for itself, and the good man obeys his intellect. It is true of the good man too that he does many acts for the sake of his friends and his country, and if necessary dies for them; for he will throw away both wealth and honors and in general the goods that are objects of competition, gaining for himself nobility; since he would prefer a short period of intense pleasure to a long one of mild enjoyment, a twelvemonth of noble life to many years of humdrum existence, and one great and noble action to many trivial ones. Now those who die for others doubtless attain this result; it is therefore a great prize that they choose for themselves. They will throw away wealth too on condition that their friends will gain more; for while a man's friend gains wealth he himself achieves nobility; he is therefore assigning the greater good to himself. The same too is true of honor and office; all these things he will sacrifice to his friend; for this is noble and laudable for himself. Rightly then is he thought to be good, since he chooses nobility before all else. But he may even give up actions to his friend; it may be nobler to become the cause of his friend's acting than to act himself. In all the actions, there-fore, that men are praised for, the good man is seen to assign to himself the greater share in what is noble. In this sense, then, as has been said, a man should be a lover of self; but in the sense in which most men are so, he ought not.

Private property does not divide the interests of self and society [20]

Property should be in a certain sense common, but, as a general rule, private; for, when everyone has a distinct interest, men will not complain of one another, and they will make more progress, because everyone will be attending to his own business. And yet by reason of goodness, and in respect of use, "Friends," as the proverb says, "will have all things common." Even now there are traces of such a principle, showing that it is not impracticable, but, in well-ordered states, exists already to a certain extent and may be carried further. For, although every man has his own property, some things he will place at the disposal of his friends, while of others he shares the use with them. The Lacedaemonians, for example, use one another's slaves, and horses, and dogs, as if they were their own; and when they lack provisions on a journey, they appropriate what they find in the fields throughout the country. It is clearly better that property should be private, but the use of it common; and the special business of the legislator is to create in men this benevolent disposition. Again, how immeasurably greater is the pleasure, when a man feels a thing to be his own; for surely the love of self is a feeling implanted by nature and not given in vain, although selfishness is rightly censured;

this, however, is not the mere love of self, but the love of self in excess, like the miser's love of money; for all, or almost all, men love money and other such objects in a measure. And further, there is the greatest pleasure in doing a kindness or service to friends or guests or companions, which can only be rendered when a man has private property. These advantages are lost by excessive unification of the state. The exhibition of two excellences, besides, is visibly annihilated in such a state: first, temperance towards women (for it is an honorable action to abstain from another's wife for temperance sake); secondly, liberality in the matter of property. No one, when men have all things in common, will any longer set an example of liberality or do any liberal action; for liberality consists in the use which is made of property.

Such legislation may have a specious appearance of beneficence; men readily listen to it, and are easily induced to believe that in some wonderful manner everybody will become everybody's friend—especially when someone is heard denouncing the evils now existing in states, suits about contracts, convictions for perjury, flatteries of rich men and the like, which are said to arise out of the possession of private property. These evils, however, are due not to the absence of communism, but to wickedness. Indeed, we see that there is much more quarreling among those who have all things in common, though there are not many of them when compared with the vast numbers who have private property.

The shared interests of the virtuous [21]

Unanimity also seems to be a friendly relation. For this reason it is not identity of opinion; for that might occur even with people who do not know each other; nor do we say that people who have the same views on any and every subject are unanimous, e.g., those who agree about the heavenly bodies (for unanimity about these is not a friendly relation), but we do say that a city is unanimous when men have the same opinion about what is to their interest, and choose the same actions, and do what they have resolved in common. It is about things to be done, therefore, that people are said to be unanimous, and, among these, about matters of consequence and in which it is possible for both or all parties to get what they want; e.g., a city is unanimous when all its citizens think that the offices in it should be elective, or that they should form an alliance with Sparta, or that Pittacus should be their ruler—at a time when he himself was also willing to rule. But when each of two people wishes himself to have the thing in question, like the captains in the Phoenissai, they are in a state of faction; for it is not unanimity when each of two parties thinks of the same thing, whatever that may be, but only when they think of the same thing in relation to the same person, e.g., when both the common people and those of the better class wish the best men to rule; for thus do all get what they aim at. Unanimity seems, then, to be political friendship, as indeed it is commonly said to be; for it is concerned with things that are to our interest and have an influence on our life.

Now such unanimity is found among good men; for they are unanimous both in themselves and with one another, being, so to say, of one mind (for the wishes of such men are constant and not at the mercy of opposing currents like a strait of the sea), and they wish for what is just and what is advantageous, and these are the objects of their common endeavor as well. But bad men cannot be unanimous except to a small extent, any more than they can be friends, since they aim at getting more than their share of advantages, while in labor and public service they fall short of their share; and each man wishing for advantage to himself criticizes his neighbor and stands in his way; for if people do not watch it carefully the common interest is soon destroyed. The result is that they are in a state of faction, putting compulsion on each other but unwilling themselves to do what is just.

*Epicurus (c.341–c.270 B.C.)
came to Athens in his thirties and
founded a community of learning
and friendship called the Garden.
It is the central principle of his
philosophy that pleasure is the
ultimate good and so constitutes
the essence of happiness. What
follows are excerpts from some of
Epicurus' own writings, as well
as from other Epicureans, including Lucretius (?94–55 B.C.).*

EPICUREANISM

Tranquil pleasure constitutes human beings' supreme good [22]

We must reckon that some desires are natural and others empty, and of the natural some are necessary, others natural only; and of the necessary some are necessary for happiness, others for the body's freedom from stress, and others for life itself. For the steady observation of these things makes it possible to refer every choice and avoidance to the health of the body and the soul's freedom from disturbance, since this is the end belonging to the blessed life. For this is what we aim at in all our actions to be free from pain and anxiety.

Once we have got this, all the soul's tumult is released, since the creature cannot go as if in pursuit of something it needs and search for any second thing as the means of maximizing the good of the soul and the body. For the time when we need pleasure is when we are in pain from the absence of pleasure. <But when we are not in pain> we no longer need pleasure. This is why we say that pleasure is the beginning and end of the blessed life. For we recognize pleasure as the good which is primary and congenital; from it we begin every choice and avoidance, and we come back to it, using the feeling as the yardstick for judging every good thing.

Since pleasure is the good which is primary and congenital, for this reason we do not choose every pleasure either, but we sometimes pass over many pleasures in cases when their outcome for us is a greater quantity of discomfort; and we regard many pains as better than pleasures in cases when our endurance of pains is followed by a greater and long-lasting pleasure. Every pleasure, then, because of its natural affinity, is something good, yet not every pleasure is choiceworthy. Correspondingly, every pain is something bad, but not every pain is by nature to be avoided. However, we have to make our judgement on all these points by a calculation and survey of advantages and disadvantages. For at certain times we treat the good as bad and conversely the bad as good.

We also regard self-sufficiency as a great good, not with the aim of always living off little, but to enable us to live off little if we do not have much, in the genuine conviction that they derive the greatest pleasure from luxury who need it least, and that everything natural is easy to procure, but what is empty is hard to procure. Plain flavors produce pleasure equal to an expensive diet whenever all the pain of need has been removed; and bread and water generate the highest pleasure whenever they are taken by one who needs them. Therefore the habit of simple and inexpensive diet maximizes health and makes a man energetic in facing the necessary business of daily life; it also strengthens our character when we encounter luxuries from time to time, and emboldens us in the face of fortune.

So when we say that pleasure is the end, we do not mean the pleasures of the dissipated and those that consist in having a good time, as some out of ignorance and disagreement or refusal to understand suppose we do, but freedom from pain in the body and from disturbance in the soul. For what produces the pleasant life is not continuous drinking and parties or pederasty or womanizing or the enjoyment of fish and the other dishes of an expensive table, but sober reasoning which tracks down the causes of every choice and avoidance, and which banishes the opinions that beset souls with the greatest confusion.

Of all this the beginning and the greatest good is prudence. Therefore prudence is even more precious than philosophy, and it is the natural source of all the remaining virtues: it teaches the impossibility of living pleasurably without living prudently, honorably and justly, <and the impossibility of living prudently, honorably and justly without living pleasurably>. For the virtues are naturally linked with living pleasurably, and living pleasurably is inseparable from them.

• • •

When winds are troubling the waters on a great sea, it is a pleasure to view from the land another man's great struggles; not because it is a joy or delight that anyone should be storm-tossed, but because it is a pleasure to observe from what troubles you yourself are free. It is a pleasure too to gaze on great contests of war deployed over the plains when you yourself have no part in the danger. But pleasantest of all is to be master of those tranquil regions well fortified on high by the teaching of the wise. From there you can look down on others and see them wandering this way and that and straying in their quest for a way of life—competing in talent, fighting over social class, striving night and day with utmost effort to rise to the heights of wealth and become owners of substance. O miserable minds of men, O unseeing hearts! How great the darkness of life, how great the dangers too in which this portion of time, whatsoever it be, is spent. Do you not see that nature screams out for nothing but the removal of pain from the body and the mind's enjoyment of the joyous sensation when anxiety and fear have been taken away? So we see that our bodily nature needs only the few things which remove pain, in such a way that they can also furnish many delights rather pleasurably from time to time. Nor does nature itself require it, if there are no golden statues of youths in the entrance halls grasping fiery torches in their right hands to provide evening banquets with light, or if the house does not gleam with silver and shine with gold and a carved and gilded ceiling does not resound to the lute, when, in spite of this, men lie together on the soft grass near a stream of water beneath the branches of a lofty tree refreshing their bodies with joy and at no great cost, especially when the weather smiles and the season of the year spreads flowers all over the green grass. Nor do hot fevers leave the body more swiftly if you toss on embroidered tapestries and shimmering purple than if you have to lie on common drapery. Therefore, since riches are of no benefit in our body, nor social class nor a kingdom's glory, we should further suppose that they are of no benefit to the mind as well. . . .

The growth of society: from unbridled to enlightened self-interest [23]

But the human race at that time was much hardier on the land, as was fitting for creatures engendered by the hard earth. Supported from within on larger and more solid bones, they were fitted all over their flesh with powerful sinews, and were not easily capable of being harmed by heat or cold or unusual food or any damage to the body. And for many of the sun's cycles through the sky they dragged out their life in the roving manner of wild beasts. There was no sturdy director of the rounded plough, no one who knew how to work the land with iron or to dig young shoots into the soil or to cut down the old branches of tall trees with pruning knives. What sun and rain had given, what earth had created of its own accord, was gift sufficient to satisfy their hearts. . . . As yet they did not know how to manipulate things with fire, nor how to use skins and clothe their bodies in the spoils of wild beasts. They dwelt in woods and mountain caves and forests, and used to hide their rough limbs amid shrubs when forced to take shelter from the lash of winds and rains. Nor could they have the common good in view, nor did they know how to make mutual use of any customs or laws. Whatever prize fortune had provided to each man, he carried off, taught to apply his strength and live on his own account just for himself.

Then after they obtained huts and skins and fire, and woman united with man withdrew into a single marriage, and they saw offspring engendered from themselves, then the human race first began to soften. For fire saw to it that their chilly bodies could not now bear cold so well under the covering of the sky; sex sapped their strength, and children by their charm easily broke their parents' stern demeanor. Then too neighbors began to form friendships, eager not to harm one another and not to be harmed; and they gained protection for children and for the female sex, when with babyish noises and gestures they indicated that it is right for everyone to pity the weak. Yet harmony could not entirely be created; but a good and substantial number preserved their contracts honorably. Otherwise the human race would even then have been totally destroyed, and reproduction could not have maintained the generations down to the present day.

Day by day those of outstanding intellect and strength of mind would give increasing demonstrations of how to change the earlier mode of life by innovations and by fire. Kings began to found cities and to establish citadels for their own protection and refuge. They distributed cattle and lands, giving them to each man on the basis of his looks and strength and intellect; for good looks counted for much and strength was at a premium. Later came the invention of private property and the discovery of gold, which easily robbed the strong and handsome of their status; for in general people follow the wealthier man's party, however vigorous and handsome they may be by birth. But if someone should govern his life by true reasoning, a man's great wealth is to live sparingly with a tranquil mind; for there is never a shortage of little. But men wished to be famous and powerful, to secure a stable foundation for their fortune and the means of living out a peaceful life with wealth. To no purpose—in struggling to climb up to the pinnacle of status, they made their journey perilous. Even from the summit, resentment in a while, like a thunderbolt, strikes and hurls them down with ignominy into a foul abyss. For resentment, like a thunderbolt, generally scorches the heights and everything that is much higher than the rest. It is far better, then, to be obedient and quiet than to want imperial rule and the occupation of kingdoms. Let them accordingly toil in vain and sweat out their blood, as they fight along the narrow road of ambition. For the wisdom they savor is from another's mouth and they seek things from hearsay rather than from their own sensations. This was as much the case in the past as it is now and will be. And so the kings were killed; the ancient majesty of thrones and proud scepters lay overturned, and the illustrious badge of the sovereign head was stained with blood, mourning its great rank under the feet of the mob. For things are avidly stamped upon when they have previously roused extreme terror. Thus affairs were returning to the dregs of disorder, with each man seeking supreme power for himself.

Then some people taught how to institute magistrates and constitutional rights, with a view to the voluntary employment of laws. For the human race, worn out by its violent way of life, was enfeebled by feuds; all the more, then, of its own volition it submitted to laws and constraining rights. Each man had been ready out of passion to avenge himself more fiercely than is now permitted by equitable laws, and therefore people were nauseated by their violent way of life. Since then, fear of punishment spoils the prizes of life. Violence and wrongdoing entrap each person and generally recoil on their originator. It is not easy for one who infringes the common contracts of peace by his deeds to lead a calm and tranquil life. For even if he escapes notice by the race of gods and men, he must lack confidence that it will stay hidden for ever.

• • •

The Epicureans . . . say that the ancient legislators, after studying men's social life and their dealings with one another, pronounced murder a sacrilege and attached special penalties to it. Another factor may have been the existence of a certain natural affinity between man and man, deriving from their likeness in body and soul, which inhibited the destruction of this kind of creature as readily as that of others whom it is permitted to kill. But the principal reason for their refusal to tolerate murder and for pronouncing it sacrilegious was the belief that it is not useful to the general structure of human life. Thereafter, those who understood the utility of the law had no need of any further reason to restrain them from this act; the others, who were unable to take sufficient cognizance of this, refrained from readily killing one another through fear of the magnitude of the punishment. It is evident that each of these inhibitions is still operative today. . . . Originally no law, whether written or unwritten, among those that persist today and are naturally transmitted, was established by force, but only by agreement of the users themselves. For what distinguished the men who popularized such practices from the masses was not their physical strength and totalitarian power but their prudence. They established a rational calculation of utility in those whose previous perception of this was irrational and often forgetful, while terrifying others by the magnitude of the penalties. For the only remedy against the ignorance of utility was fear of the punishment fixed by the law. Today too this is the only check and deterrent on ordinary people from acting against public or private interest. But if everyone were equally able to observe and be mindful of utility, they would have no need of laws in addition; of their own volition, they would steer clear of what is forbidden and do what is prescribed. For the observation of what is useful and harmful is sufficient to secure avoidance of some things and choice of others. The threat of punishment is addressed to those who fail to take note of utility. For hanging over them, it compels them to master impulses which lead to inexpedient actions that are contrary to utility, and forcibly helps to constrain them to do what they should.

The importance of friendship to our well-being [24]

I notice that friendship has been discussed by our school in three ways. Some have said that the pleasures which belong to friends are not as desirable *per se* as those we desire as our own. This position is thought by certain people to make friendship unstable, though in my opinion its proponents are successful and easily defend themselves. They say that friendship is no more separable from pleasure than are the virtues we discussed previously. A lonely life without friends is packed with risks and anxieties. Therefore reason itself advises the formation of friendships; their acquisition strengthens the mind and gives it the absolutely secure expectation of generating pleasures. Moreover, just as enmities, resentments, and disparagements are opposed to pleasures, so friendships are creators of pleasures, as well as being their most reliable protectors, for friends and for ourselves alike. The pleasures they enjoy are not only of the present, but they are also elated by the hope of the near and distant future. Without friendship we are quite unable to secure a joy in life which is steady and lasting, nor can we preserve friendship itself unless we love our friends as much as ourselves. Therefore friendship involves both this latter and the link with pleasure. For we rejoice in our friends' joy as much as in our own and are equally pained by their distress. The wise man, therefore, will have just the same feelings towards his friend that he has for himself, and he will work as much for his friend's pleasure as he would for his own. . . . Some Epicureans, however, though intelligent enough, are a little more timid in facing the criticisms from you [Academics]: they are afraid that if we regard friendship as desirable just for our own pleasure, it will seem to be completely crippled, as it were. In their view, then, the first associations and unions and wishes to form relationships occur for the sake of pleasure; but when advancing familiarity has produced intimacy, affection blossoms to such an extent that friends come to be loved just for their own sake even if no advantage accrues from the friendship. If, at any rate, familiarity with places, temples, cities, gymnasia, playing-fields, dogs, horses, hunting, and other sports, gets us in the habit of loving them, how much more easily and rightly could this happen in human relationships! There are also some who say that wise men have a sort of contract to love their friends no less than themselves. We understand the possibility of this, and often observe it too. It is self-evident that no better means of living joyously can be found than such a relationship.

• • •

The [Epicureans] themselves in fact say that it is more pleasurable to confer a benefit than to receive one.

Stoicism was founded by Zeno of Citium (c. 336–c. 265 B.C.), who came to Athens following Aristotle's death, and gained a wide acceptance among later Roman thinkers. In what follows, the ideals of self-command and the universal harmony of interests are developed in the writings of both Greek and Roman Stoics.

STOICISM

Self-love as the primary impulse to action [25]

[Statement of Stoic ethics by Cato.] He began: It is the view of those whose system I adopt, that immediately upon birth (for that is the proper point to start from) a living creature feels an attachment for itself, and an impulse to preserve itself and to feel affection for its own constitution and for those things which tend to preserve that constitution; while on the other hand it conceives an antipathy to destruction and to those things which appear to threaten destruction. In proof of this opinion they urge that infants desire things conducive to their health and reject things that are the opposite before they have ever felt pleasure or pain; this would not be the case, unless they felt an affection for their own constitution and were afraid of destruction. But it would be impossible that they should feel desire at all unless they possessed self-consciousness, and consequently felt affection for themselves. This leads to the conclusion that it is love of self which supplies the primary impulse to action. . . .

• • •

A man naturally loves those things in which he is interested. Now do men take an interest in things evil? Certainly not. Do they take interest in what does not concern them? No, they do not. It follows then that they are interested in good things alone, and if interested in them, therefore love them too. Whoever then has knowledge of good things, would know how to love them; but how could one who cannot distinguish good things from evil and things indifferent from both have power to love? Therefore the wise man alone has power to love. . . .

[B]e not deceived, every creature, to speak generally, is attached to nothing so much as to its own interest. Whatever then seems to hinder his way to this, be it a brother or a father or a child, the object of his passion or his own lover, he hates him, guards against him, curses him. For his nature is to love nothing so much as his own interest; this is his father and brother and kinsfolk and country and god. At any rate, when the gods seem to hinder us in regard to this we revile even the gods and overthrow their statues and set fire to their temples, as Alexander ordered the shrines of Asclepius to be burnt when the object of his passion died. Therefore if interest, religion and honor, country, parents and friends are set in the same scale, then all are safe; but if interest is in one scale, and in the other friends and country and kindred and justice itself, all these are weighed down by interest and disappear. For the creature must needs incline to that side where 'I' and 'mine' are; if they are in the flesh, the ruling power must be there; if in the will, it must be there; if in external things, it must be there.

If then I identify myself with my will, then and only then shall I be a friend and son and father in the true sense. For this will be my interest—to guard my character for good faith, honor, forbearance, self-control, and service of others, to maintain my relations with others. But if I separate myself from what is noble, then Epicurus' statement is confirmed, which declares that "there is no such thing as the noble or at best it is but the creature of opinion."

It was this ignorance that made the Athenians and Lacedaemonians quarrel with one another, and the Thebans with both, and the Great King with Hellas, and the Macedonians with Hellas and the King, and now the Romans with the Getae; and yet earlier this was the reason of the wars with Ilion. Paris was the guest of Menelaus, and any one who had seen the courtesies they used to one another would not have believed one who denied that they were friends. But a morsel was thrown between them, in the shape of a pretty woman, and for that there was war! So now, when you see friends or brothers who seem to be of one mind, do not therefore pronounce upon their friendship, though they swear to it and say it is impossible for them to part with one another. The Governing Principle of the bad man is not to be trusted; it is uncertain, irresolute, conquered now by one impression, now by another. The question you must ask is, not what others ask, whether they were born of the same parents and brought up together and under the charge of the same slave; but this question only, where they put their interest—outside them or in the will. If they put it outside, do not call them friends, any more than you can call them faithful, or stable, or confident, or free; nay, do not call them even men, if you are wise. For it is no human judgment which makes them bite one another and revile one another and occupy deserts or marketplaces like wild beasts and behave like robbers in the lawcourts; and which makes them guilty of profligacy and adultery and seduction and the other offenses men commit against one another. There is one judgment and one only which is responsible for all this—that they set themselves and all their interests elsewhere than in their will. But if you hear that these men in very truth believe the good to lie only in the region of the will and in dealing rightly with impressions, you need trouble yourself no more as to whether a man is son or father, whether they are brothers, or have been familiar companions for years; I say, if you grasp this one fact and no more, you may pronounce with confidence that they are friends, as you may that they are faithful and just. For where else is friendship but where faith and honor are, where men give and take what is good, and nothing else?

Our natural affection for others [26]

Again, it is held by the Stoics to be important to understand that nature creates in parents an affection for their children; and parental affection is the source to which we trace the origin of the association of the human race in communities. This cannot but be clear in the first place from the conformation of the body and its members, which by themselves are enough to show that nature's scheme included the procreation of offspring. Yet it could not be consistent that nature should at once intend offspring to be born and make no provision for that offspring when born to be loved and cherished. Even in the lower animals nature's operation can be clearly discerned; when we observe the labor that they spend on bearing and rearing their young, we seem to be listening to the actual voice of nature. Hence as it is manifest that it is natural for us to shrink from pain, so it is clear that we derive from nature herself the impulse to love those to whom we have given birth. From this impulse is developed the sense of mutual attraction which unites human beings as such; this also is bestowed by nature. The mere fact of their common humanity requires that one man should feel another man to be akin to him. . . . [T]he ant, the bee, the stork, do certain actions for the sake of others besides themselves. With human beings this bond of mutual aid is far more intimate. It follows that we are by nature fitted to form unions.

Reflections on well-being [27]

Of all existing things some are in our power, and others are not in our power. In our power are thought, impulse, will to get and will to avoid, and, in a word, everything which is our own doing. Things not in our power include the body, property, reputation, office, and, in a word, everything which is not our own doing. Things in our power are by nature free, unhindered, untrammeled; things not in our power are weak, servile, subject to hindrance, dependent on others. Remember then that if you imagine that what is naturally slavish is free, and what is naturally another's is your own, you will be hampered, you will mourn, you will be put to confusion, you will blame gods and men; but if you think that only your own belongs to you, and that what is another's is indeed another's, no one will ever put compulsion or hindrance on you, you will blame none, you will accuse none, you will do nothing against your will, no one will harm you, you will have no enemy, for no harm can touch you.

Ask not that events should happen as you will, but let your will be that events should happen as they do, and you shall have peace.

The ignorant man's position and character is this: he never looks to himself for benefit or harm, but to the world outside him. The philosopher's position and character is that he always look to himself for benefit and harm.

The signs of one who is making progress are: he blames none, praises none, complains of none, accuses none, never speaks of himself as if he were somebody, or as if he knew anything. And if any one compliments him he laughs in himself at his compliment; and if one blames him, he makes no defense. He goes about like a convalescent, careful not to disturb his constitution on its road to recovery, until it has got firm hold. He has got rid of the will to get, and his will to avoid is directed no longer to what is beyond our power but only to what is in our power and contrary to nature. In all things he exercises his will without strain. If men regard him as foolish or ignorant he pays no heed. In one word, he keeps watch and guard on himself as his own enemy, lying in wait for him.

• • •

Never esteem as beneficial to yourself what will compel you to break faith, to abandon self-respect, to hate, suspect, or curse anyone, to dissemble, to long for anything which requires the privacy of walls and curtains. A man who has chosen the side of the mind and spirit within him and has become a worshipper of their excellence does not indulge in dramatics or lamentations; he needs neither solitude nor crowds; above all, he does not lead a life of pursuit and retreat. It does not matter at all to him whether he will have his soul within the body for a longer or a shorter time; if the time has come to depart, he will do so as easily as he would perform any other orderly and reverent action. His one care throughout life is that his mind should not adopt a way of life alien to a thinking and social being. . . .

Revere your faculty of thought; everything depends upon it, in order that there be no thought in your directing mind which is at odds with nature or incompatible with your status as a reasonable being. It is your faculty of thought which ensures that you be not prone to stumble into error, but at home among men and a follower of the gods. . . .

If you perform the task before you and follow the right rule of reason steadfastly, vigorously, with kindness; if you allow no distraction but preserve the spirit within you in its pure state as if you had to surrender it at any moment; if you concentrate on this, expecting nothing and shirking nothing, content to do any natural action which is at hand, heroically truthful in every word you utter, you will lead the good life. There is no one who could prevent you.

The natural coalescence of self-interest and the common good [28]

What is it then which disturbs and confounds the multitude? Is it the tyrant and his guards? Nay, God forbid! It is impossible for that which is free by nature to be disturbed or hindered by anything but itself. It is a man's own judgments which disturb him. For when the tyrant says to a man, "I will chain your leg," he that values his leg says, "Nay, have mercy," but he that values his will says, "If it seems more profitable to you, chain it."

"Do you pay no heed?"

No, I pay no heed.

"I will show you that I am master."

How can you? Zeus gave me my freedom. Or do you think that he was likely to let his own son be enslaved? You are master of my dead body, take it.

"Do you mean that when you approach me, you pay no respect to me?"

No, I only pay respect to myself: if you wish me to say that I pay respect to you too, I tell you that I do so, but only as I pay respect to my water-pot.

This is not mere self-love: for it is natural to man, as to other creatures, to do everything for his own sake; for even the sun does everything for its own sake, and in a word so does Zeus himself. But when he would be called "The Rain-giver" and "Fruit-giver" and "Father of men and gods," you see that he cannot win these names or do these works unless he does some good to the world at large: and in general he has so created the nature of the rational animal, that he can attain nothing good for himself, unless he contributes some service to the community. So it turns out that to do everything for his own sake is not unsocial. For what do you expect? Do you expect a man to hold aloof from himself and his own interest? No: we cannot ignore the one principle of action which governs all things—to be at unity with themselves.

Next, if you are a member of a city council, remember that you are a councilor; if young, that you are young; if old, that you are old; if a father, that you are a father. For each of these names, if properly considered, suggests the acts appropriate to it.

But if you go and disparage your brother, I tell you that you are forgetting who you are and what is your name. I say, if you were a smith and used your hammer wrong, you would have forgotten the smith; but if you forget the brother's part and turn into an enemy instead of a brother, are you going to imagine that you have undergone no change? If instead of man, a gentle and sociable creature, you have become a danger-ous, aggressive, and biting brute, have you lost nothing? Do you think you must lose cash in order to suffer damage? Does no other sort of loss damage man? If you lost skill in grammar or music you would count the loss as damage; if you are going to lose honor and dignity and gentleness, do you count it as nothing? Surely those other losses are due to some external cause outside our will, but these are due to ourselves. Those qualities it is no honor to have and no dishonor to lose, but these you cannot lack or lose without dishonor, reproach, and disaster.

• • •

Well then, for a man to take something from his neighbor and to profit by his neigh-bor's loss is more contrary to Nature than is death or poverty or pain or anything else that can affect either our person or our property. For, in the first place, injustice is fatal to social life and fellowship between man and man. For, if we are so disposed that each, to gain some personal profit, will defraud or injure his neighbor, then those bonds of human society, which are most in accord with Nature's laws, must of neces-sity be broken. Suppose, by way of comparison, that each one of our bodily members should conceive this idea and imagine that it could be strong and well if it should draw off to itself the health and strength of its neighboring member, the whole body would necessarily be enfeebled and die; so, if each one of us should seize upon the property of his neighbors and take from each whatever he could appropriate to his own use, the bonds of human society must inevitably be annihilated. For, without any conflict with Nature's laws, it is granted that everybody may prefer to secure for him-self rather than for his neighbor what is essential for the conduct of life; but Nature's laws do forbid us to increase our means, wealth, and resources by despoiling others.

But this principle is established not by Nature's laws alone (that is, by the common rules of equity), but also by the statutes of particular communities, in accordance with which in individual states the public interests are maintained. In all these it is with one accord ordained that no man shall be allowed for the sake of his own advantage to injure his neighbor. For it is to this that the laws have regard; this is their intent, that the bonds of union between citizens should not be impaired; and any attempt to destroy these bonds is repressed by the penalty of death, exile, imprisonment, or fine.

Again, this principle follows much more directly from the Reason which is in Nature, which is the law of gods and men. If anyone will hearken to that voice (and all will hearken to it who wish to live in accord with Nature's laws) he will never be guilty of coveting anything that is his neighbor's or of appropriating to himself what he has taken from his neighbor. Then, too, loftiness and greatness of spirit, and courtesy, justice, and generosity are much more in harmony with Nature than are selfish pleasure, riches, and life itself, but it requires a great and lofty spirit to despise these latter and count them as naught, when one weighs them over against the common weal. But for anyone to rob his neighbor for his own profit is more contrary to Nature than death, pain, and the like. In like manner it is more in accord with Nature to emulate the great Hercules and undergo the greatest toil and trouble for the sake of aiding or saving the world, if possible, than to live in seclusion, not only free from all care, but reveling in pleasures and abounding in wealth, while excelling others also in beauty and strength. Thus Hercules denied himself and underwent toil and tribulation for the world, and, out of gratitude for his services, popular belief has given him a place in the council of the gods.

The better and more noble, therefore, the character with which a man is endowed, the more does he prefer the life of service to the life of pleasure. Whence it follows that man, if he is obedient to Nature, cannot do harm to his fellow-man.

Finally, if a man wrongs his neighbor to gain some advantage for himself, he must either imagine that he is not acting in defiance of Nature or he must believe that death, poverty, pain, or even the loss of children, kinsmen, or friends, is more to be shunned than an act of injustice against another. If he thinks he is not violating the laws of Nature, when he wrongs his fellow-men, how is one to argue with the individual who takes away from man all that makes him man? But if he believes that, while such a course should be avoided, the other alternatives are much worse—namely, death, poverty, pain—he is mistaken in thinking that any ills affecting either his person or his property are more serious than those affecting his soul.

This, then, ought to be the chief end of all men, to make the interest of each individual and of the whole body politic identical. For, if the individual appropriates to selfish ends what should be devoted to the common good, all human fellowship will be destroyed.

And further, if Nature ordains that one man shall desire to promote the interests of a fellow-man, whoever he may be, just because he is a fellow-man, then it follows, in accordance with that same Nature, that there are interests that all men have in common. And, if this is true, we are all subject to one and the same law of Nature; and, if this also is true, we are certainly forbidden by Nature's law to wrong our neighbor. Now the first assumption is true; therefore the conclusion is likewise true. For that is an absurd position which is taken by some people, who say that they will not rob a parent or a brother for their own gain, but that their relation to the rest of their fellow-citizens is quite another thing. Such people contend in essence that they are bound to their fellow-citizens by no mutual obligations, social ties, or common interests. This attitude demolishes the whole structure of civil society.

Others again who say that regard should be had for the rights of fellow-citizens, but not of foreigners, would destroy the universal brotherhood of mankind; and, when this is annihilated, kindness, generosity, goodness, and justice must utterly perish; and those who work all this destruction must be considered as wickedly rebelling against the immortal gods. For they uproot the fellowship which the gods have established between human beings, and the closest bond of this fellowship is the conviction that it is more repugnant to Nature for man to rob a fellow-man for his own gain than to endure all possible loss, whether to his property or to his person . . . or even to his very soul—so far as these losses are not concerned with justice; for this virtue is the sovereign mistress and queen of all the virtues.

But, perhaps, someone may say, "Well, then, suppose a wise man were starving to death, might he not take the bread of some perfectly useless member of society?" Not at all; for my life is not more precious to me than that temper of soul which would keep me from doing wrong to anybody for my own advantage. "Or again; supposing a righteous man were in a position to rob the cruel and inhuman tyrant Phalalis of clothing, might he not do it to keep himself from freezing to death?"

These cases are very easy to decide. For, if merely for one's own benefit one were to take something away from a man, though he were a perfectly worthless fellow, it would be an act of meanness and contrary to Nature's law. But suppose one would be able, by remaining alive, to render signal service to the state and to human society—if from that motive one should take something from another, it would not be a matter for censure. But, if such is not the case, each one must bear his own burden of distress rather than rob a neighbor of his rights. We are not to say, therefore, that sickness or want or any evil of that sort is more repugnant to Nature than to covet and to appropriate what is one's neighbor's; but we do maintain that disregard of the common interests is repugnant to Nature; for it is unjust. And therefore Nature's law itself, which protects and conserves human interests, will surely determine that a man who is wise, good, and brave, should in emergency have the necessaries of life transferred to him from a person who is idle and worthless; for the good man's death would be a heavy loss to the common weal; only let him beware that self-esteem and self-love do not find in such a transfer of possessions a pretext for wrong-doing. But, thus guided in his decision, the good man will always perform his duty, promoting the general interests of human society on which I am so fond of dwelling.

II | MEDIEVAL ERA

𝒯he influence of the Judeo-Christian conception of self-interest—thought to be "contradictory" by some of its greatest defenders—can scarcely be exaggerated. On the one hand, the bible warns against excessive self-regard, which fosters the sinful attitude that one is self-sufficient without God. Since God alone brings salvation, such self-love is more properly described as self-loathing: "Who loveth iniquity, hateth his own soul" (*Psalms* 11:5). Yet, on the other hand, scripture models love-of-neighbor on self-love and promises bliss in the afterlife to those who commit themselves to God. The righteous may continue to be persecuted by the "self-seekers" in *this* world, but in heaven they are assured eternal happiness. Although the bible condemns self-interest, it also promises to promote it.

The two most important medieval philosophers, Augustine of Hippo (354–430) and Thomas Aquinas (1224–1274), take different approaches to interpreting biblical morality, but both embrace its ideal of neighborly love and locate the true interests of individuals in devotion to God.

It was Augustine's conviction that while classical philosophers had correctly identified *eudaimonia* as the end of humanity, they had utterly mischaracterized its nature, and therefore the true essence of self-interest. Whether they identified the interests of the self with virtue, pleasure, tranquillity, or some combination of these, he maintained, they all made the same fundamental error, namely, conceiving of the human good in temporal terms.

Our true interests lie, rather, in the eternal life we share with God. Our trespass through this life is merely a detour, a consequence of original sin, whereby Adam doomed his descendants to misery in the world to be followed by death. God has supplied some natural benefits in this realm, but it would be a serious mistake to treat these as anything more than a passing comfort. Both the necessaries of this life, as well as the general temporal welfare of both our friends and ourselves, must always be abandoned for the sake of eternal well-being. For Augustine, to prefer one's worldly to one's heavenly interests is nothing but the sign of an unsound mind.

Since most men do prefer their wordly interests to all else, mankind is a thoroughly corrupt lot, and one of the gravest consequences of this is that it fosters permanent conflicts of interests. In Augustine's view, all people possess a certain sense of fellowship insofar as they are human, but generally each individual pursues his self-interest to the detriment of his fellows. God has instituted temporal government primarily in order to control this tendency men have to harm and oppress one another for personal gain.

Yet, how futile man's attempt to secure his self-interest through oppression, or in any other way for that matter, declares Augustine. Since man's true interests are non-temporal, one quite literally cannot pursue one's self-interest in this world. Nor can one pursue one's heavenly interests while on earth. To attempt this is to treat oneself as "the end," rather than God, yet God alone is the end and our good, insofar as only he can grant salvation, in which our true self-interest lies. The only step we may take toward securing our advantage is thus to submit obediently to God. Since to do this requires that we forget ourselves, however, even in this sense we cannot directly pursue our own interests. For Augustine, self-fulfillment in any form entails "destruction."

Augustine's conception of self-interest is simple and straightforward: our interest lies in God, and we secure it, essentially, by not attempting to secure it; his conception of self-love, however, is complex. In fact, Augustine identifies three separate forms of self-love.

The first, which is associated with pride, is thoroughly negative. According to Augustine, evil self-love leads a man to glorify in himself and act as though he constitutes his own satisfaction, independently of God. Such pride is the origin of sin, and caused the downfall of Adam, who, rather than obeying God's injunction that he not eat from the tree of Knowledge, chose to "follow his own light."

Next there exists a natural, neutral form of self-love that is a feature of all animal life as such. This type of self-love is identifiable with the drive for self-preservation. It is on account of this that Augustine argues that there was no need for God to command love of self in addition to love of God and neighbor, which precepts form the cornerstone of all morality. For like the non-rational creatures, man loves himself "through a law of nature which has never been violated." Even when one falls into the depths of sin, a condition "more correctly called hate," this love persists, for we never hate ourselves, but only our corruption.

Positive love of self, the third and final form, is not really love of self at all, but love of God, or more precisely, love of self *through* love of God. It is never correct to love oneself simply and for one's own sake, according to Augustine. This follows from the natural "order of love," which places all possible objects of love in a hierarchy, depending on their proximity to God, who resides at the pinnacle. Nothing lower in the hierarchy can be loved before what is higher, nor can higher-placed entities be loved merely for the sake of things lower. Since man is manifestly beneath God, he is bound to love God before himself, and himself for the sake of God. Similarly with love of neighbor: to love another as oneself is to direct him toward love of God, too.

It seems odd that this third form should even be called self-love, and it is perhaps better described as self-forgetfulness in God. Augustine is quite at home in the biblical tradition juxtaposing love of self with self-overcoming, yet he is sensitive to the paradox this involves. What a "profound and strange" notion, he remarks, that the deepest form of self-love is ultimately a form of self-denial, and how "contradictory" seems the idea that "loftiness debases and lowliness exalts."

In specifying better and worse forms of self-love, Augustine is introducing nothing new to the Western tradition; what separates his account is his way of conceiving of the distinctions. Classical thinkers, who generally distinguish virtuous from vicious self-love in terms of commitment to the rational part of the soul, conceive of self-love in any form as in some sense a realization of the *self*. But for Augustine, true self-love transcends the self. The question is no longer one of the internal ordering of the soul, but of the relation of the soul to an external force. It is not that passion is subordinated to reason, but that the self is subordinated to God. Self-love is no longer the correlate of pride, but the vehicle of humility. Here we have a different conception of self-concern, indeed.

Thomas Aquinas's philosophical mission was to demonstrate the compatibility of Christian doctrine with Aristotelian natural philosophy, and in the area of self-concern this required two things: first, the establishment of a plausible link between the Aristotelian and Christian eudaimonism, and second, a modification of the Augustinian ideal of "self-overcoming."

Aquinas accomplished the first of these tasks by trading on Aristotle's ambiguity over the contemplative ideal. Augustine had rejected pagan eudaimonism on the grounds that it locates man's ultimate happiness in this world rather than in our eternal life with God. Aquinas agrees that it would be a mistake to conceive man's ultimate good temporally, but denies that a purely temporal idea of happiness is required by Aristotle's system. As we have seen, Aristotle states in *Nicomachean Ethics* X that man's greatest good lies in the contemplation of ultimate reality. What *is* ultimate reality, though, asks Aquinas, but God himself? And where shall we have the greatest opportunity to single-mindedly contemplate God but in the afterlife? For Aquinas, it is perfectly "Christian" to be an Aristotelian so far as man's final good is concerned.

Aquinas further aligns himself with Aristotle against Augustine by rejecting the view that man cannot achieve happiness in this world. Although man is fallen, he can in this life attain *human* happiness—an incomplete form of beatitude, but beatitude nonetheless. Not only can one achieve partial happiness in this life, moreover, but one can begin to have some share in the perfect happiness that awaits us in the next. For one can concern oneself minimally with worldly affairs and spend the bulk of one's time in the undistracted contemplation of God. The more single-minded our contemplative activity grows, the closer we approximate perfect bliss.

Aquinas's conception of self-love meets with far less success from the standpoint of Christian-Aristotelian synthesis than does his account of happiness and self-interest, a fact which suggests that the chasm separating classical from Judeo-Christian attitudes about self-concern may not be bridgeable. Following Augustine, Aquinas identifies three forms of self-love, the negative, the neutral, and the positive.

The first of these is associated with an excessive desire for temporal goods, and is referred to as "inordinate love of self." Self-love in this sense is said to be the cause of every sin, since it causes the desires that result in sin. It is also identified with pride, as in Augustine. Pride represents for Aquinas an excessive "desire to excel" by which man is "unduly lifted up"; its cause is apostasy from God. The connection between pride and sin, the two ideas most closely identified with negative self-love, is integral: that which turns one away from God is precisely that which of necessity must direct one toward evil.

Neutral self-love exists in two forms for Aquinas, "natural" and "from choice." Natural self-love is simply the drive for self-conservation. It involves desiring by natural appetite that which furthers one's own good and perfection. Rational beings also engage in another type of neutral self-love, though, that does not derive from appetite, but reason. This form of self-loving involves wishing by rational choice for that which will be of benefit to oneself.

A person can never fail to experience neutral self-love, according to Aquinas, because all that it involves is wishing oneself good, and everything that is capable of having desires necessarily desires the good. One can *accidentally* fail to wish oneself good, however, and in that sense be a self-hater. This can happen by two means: either by desiring something that one does not recognize to be evil, or by preferring the good of the nonessential to the essential parts of oneself. This latter form is of course the essence of self-hatred as identified by Aristotle. Aquinas transposes the distinction into Christian terminology, describing the difference as one of loving the outward, temporal self over the inward, spiritual one.

Positive self-love, the third form, consists in directing oneself toward God. Unlike Augustine, Aquinas does not see this as involving a paradox. Rather than viewing positive self-love as self-forgetfulness in God, he views it more along the lines of an organizing principle. Love of God is unifying, he says, directing all of a person's virtues and energies toward the divine. The life of the virtuous self-lover is thus goal-oriented and harmonious. Negative self-love creates the opposite effect, disuniting all of one's energies by generating conflicting desires for diverse temporal goods.

Despite the elements of Aristotelianism in his thought, Aquinas' ideas about self-concern are clearly more biblical than classical in nature. A certain measure of self-love is accepted as natural and necessary, but his discussion of self-interest focuses primarily on the after-life, and the concern throughout is more with man's relationship to God than with his relationship to himself. This is to be expected in theological discussions, of course, but it does not undermine the lasting importance of the questions they raise about self-concern, nor must we lose sight of the impact of these discussions upon the ensuing debate over self-interest—indeed, as will be seen, many modern problems are just medieval concerns reclothed in secular garb.

Augustine of Hippo was born in North Africa, and underwent a religious awakening in his early thirties, which he documented in his Confessions. *His views on self-interest are firmly rooted in the biblical ideals of brotherly love and self-renunciation in God.*

AUGUSTINE OF HIPPO
(354–430)

We must not love ourselves for our own sakes, but for God's [29]

Among all these things, then, those only are the true objects of enjoyment which we have spoken of as eternal and unchangeable. The rest are for use, that we may be able to arrive at the full enjoyment of the former. We, however, who enjoy and use other things are things ourselves. For a great thing truly is man, made after the image and similitude of God, not as respects the mortal body in which he is clothed, but as respects the rational soul by which he is exalted in honor above the beasts. And so it becomes an important question, whether men ought to enjoy, or to use, themselves, or to do both. For we are commanded to love one another: but it is a question whether man is to be loved by man for his own sake, or for the sake of something else. If it is for his own sake, we enjoy him; if it is for the sake of something else, we use him. It seems to me, then, that he is to be loved for the sake of something else. For if a thing is to be loved for its own sake, then in the enjoyment of it consists a happy life, the hope of which at least, if not yet the reality, is our comfort in the present time. But a curse is pronounced on him who places his hope in man.[30]

Neither ought any one to have joy in himself, if you look at the matter clearly, because no one ought to love even himself for his own sake, but for the sake of Him who is the true object of enjoyment. For a man is never in so good a state as when his whole life is a journey towards the unchangeable life, and his affections are entirely fixed upon that. If, however, he loves himself for his own sake, he does not look at himself in relation to God, but turns his mind in upon himself, and so is not occupied with anything that is unchangeable. And thus he does not enjoy himself at his best, because he is better when his mind is fully fixed upon, and his affections wrapped up in, the unchangeable good, than when he turns from that to enjoy even himself. Wherefore if you ought not to love even yourself for your own sake, but for His in whom your love finds its most worthy object, no other man has a right to be angry if you love him too for God's sake. For this is the law of love that has been laid down by Divine authority: "Thou shalt love thy neighbor as thyself"; but, "Thou shalt love God with all thy heart, and with all thy soul, and with all thy mind"[31]: so that you are to concentrate all your thoughts, your whole life, and your whole intelligence upon Him from whom you derive all that you bring. For when He says, "With all thy heart, and with all thy soul, and with all thy mind," He means that no part of our life is to be unoccupied, and to afford room, as it were, for the wish to enjoy some other object, but that whatever else may suggest itself to us as an object worthy of love is to be borne into the same channel in which the whole current of our affections flows. Whoever, then, loves his neighbor aright, ought to urge upon him that he too should love God with his whole heart, and soul, and mind. For in this way, loving his neighbor as himself, a man turns the whole current of his love both for himself and his neighbor into the channel of the love of God, which suffers no stream to be drawn off from itself by whose diversion its own volume would be diminished.

Individuals require no command to love themselves [32]

Those things which are objects of use are not all, however, to be loved, but those only which are either united with us in a common relation to God, such as a man or an angel, or are so related to us as to need the goodness of God through our instrumentality, such as the body. For assuredly the martyrs did not love the wickedness of their persecutors, although they used it to attain the favor of God. As, then, there are four kinds of things that are to be loved—first, that which is above us; second, ourselves; third, that which is on a level with us; fourth, that which is beneath us—no precepts need be given about the second and fourth of these. For, however far a man may fall away from the truth, he still continues to love himself, and to love his own body. The soul which flies away from the unchangeable Light, the Ruler of all things, does so that it may rule over itself and over its own body; and so it cannot but love both itself and its own body.

Moreover, it thinks it has attained something very great if it is able to lord it over its companions, that is, other men. For it is inherent in the sinful soul to desire above all things, and to claim as due to itself, that which is properly due to God only. Now such love of itself is more correctly called hate. For it is not just that it should desire what is beneath it to be obedient to it while itself will not obey its own superior; and most justly has it been said, "He who loveth iniquity hateth his own soul."[33] And accordingly the soul becomes weak, and endures much suffering about the mortal body. For, of course, it must love the body, and be grieved at its corruption; and the immortality and incorruptibility of the body spring out of the health of the soul. Now the health of the soul is to cling steadfastly to the better part, that is, to the unchangeable God. But when it aspires to lord it even over those who are by nature its equals—that is, its fellow-men—this is a reach of arrogance utterly intolerable. . . .

Man, therefore, ought to be taught the due measure of loving, that is, in what measure he may love himself so as to be of service to himself. For that he does love himself, and does desire to do good to himself, nobody but a fool would doubt. He is to be taught, too, in what measure to love his body, so as to care for it wisely and within due limits. For it is equally manifest that he loves his body also, and desires to keep it safe and sound. And yet a man may have something that he loves better than the safety and soundness of his body. For many have been found voluntarily to suffer both pains and amputations of some of their limbs that they might obtain other objects which they valued more highly. But no one is to be told not to desire the safety and health of his body because there is something he desires more. For the miser, though he loves money, buys bread for himself—that is, he gives away money that he is very fond of and desires to heap up, but it is because he values more highly the bodily health which the bread sustains. It is superfluous to argue longer on a point so very plain, but this is just what the error of wicked men often compels us to do. . . .

Seeing, then, that there is no need of a command that every man should love himself and his own body—seeing, that is, that we love ourselves, and what is beneath us but connected with us, through a law of nature which has never been violated, and which is common to us with the beasts (for even the beasts love themselves and their own bodies)—it only remained necessary to lay injunctions upon us in regard to God above us, and our neighbor beside us. "Thou shalt love," He says, "the Lord thy God with all thy heart, and with all thy soul, and with all thy mind; and thou shalt love thy neighbor as thyself; On these two commandments hang all the law and the prophets."[34] Thus the end of the commandment is love, and that twofold, the love of God and the love of our neighbor. Now, if you take yourself in your entirety—that is, soul and body together—and your neighbor in his entirety, soul and body together (for man is made up of soul and body), you will find that none of the classes of things that are to be loved is overlooked in these two commandments. For though, when the love of God comes first, and the measure of our love for Him is prescribed in such terms that it is evident all other things are to find their center in Him, nothing seems to be said about our love for ourselves; yet when it is said, "Thou shalt love thy neighbor as thyself," it at once becomes evident that our love for ourselves has not been overlooked. . . .

Now he is a man of just and holy life who forms an unprejudiced estimate of things, and keeps his affections also under strict control, so that he neither loves what he ought not to love, nor fails to love what he ought to love, nor loves that more which ought to be loved less, nor loves that equally which ought to be loved either less or more, nor loves that less or more which ought to be loved equally. No sinner is to be loved as a sinner; and every man is to be loved as a man for God's sake but God is to be loved for His own sake. And if God is to be loved more than any man, each man ought to love God more than himself. Likewise we ought to love another man better than our own body, because all things are to be loved in reference to God, and another man can have fellowship with us in the enjoyment of God, whereas our body cannot; for the body only lives through the soul, and it is by the soul that we enjoy God.

Self-love, pride, and sin [35]

The first destruction of man, was the love of himself. For if he had not loved himself, if he had preferred God to himself, he would have been willing to be ever subject unto God; and would not have been turned to the neglect of His will, and the doing his own will. For this is to love one's self, to wish to do one's own will. Prefer to this God's will; learn to love thyself by not loving thyself. For that ye may know that it is a vice to love one's self, the Apostle speaks thus, "For men shall be lovers of their own selves."[36] And can he who loves himself have any sure trust in himself? No; for he begins to love himself by forsaking God, and is driven away from himself to love those things which are beyond himself; to such a degree that when the aforesaid Apostle had said, "Men shall be lovers of their own selves," he subjoined immediately, "lovers of money." Already thou seest that thou art without. Thou hast begun to love thyself: stand in thyself if thou canst. Why goest thou without? Hast thou, as being rich in money, become a lover of money? Thou hast begun to love what is without thee, thou hast lost thyself. When a man's love then goes even away from himself to those things which are without, he begins to share the vanity of his vain desires, and prodigal as it were to spend his strength. He is dissipated, exhausted, without resource or strength, he feeds swine; and wearied with this office of feeding swine, he at last remembers what he was, and says, "How many hired servants of my Father's are eating bread, and I here perish with hunger!"[37] But when the son in the parable says this, what is said of him, who had squandered all he had on harlots, who wished to have in his own power what was being well kept for him with his father; he wished to have it at his own disposal, he squandered all, he was reduced to indigence: what is said of him? "And when he returned to himself." If "he returned to himself," he had gone away from himself. Because he had fallen from himself, had gone away from himself, he returns first to himself, that he may return to that state from which he had fallen away by falling from himself. For as by falling away from himself, he remained in himself; so by returning to himself, he ought not to remain in himself, lest he again go away from himself. Returning then to himself, that he might not remain in himself, what did he say? "I will arise and go to my Father."[38] See, whence he had fallen away from himself, he had fallen away from his Father; he had fallen away from himself, he had gone away from himself to those things which are without. He returns to himself, and goes to his Father, where he may keep himself in all security. If then he had gone away from himself, let him also in returning to himself, from whom he had gone away, that he may "go to his Father," deny himself. What is "deny himself"? Let him not trust in himself, let him feel that he is a man, and have respect to the words of the prophet, "Cursed is every one that putteth his hope in man."[39] Let him withdraw himself from himself but not towards things below. Let him withdraw himself from himself, that he may cleave unto God. Whatever of good he has, let him commit to Him by whom he was made; whatever of evil he has, he has made it for himself. The evil that is in him God made not; let him destroy what himself has done, who has been thereby undone. "Let him deny himself," He saith, "and take up his cross, and follow Me."

• • •

Our first parents fell into open disobedience because already they were secretly corrupted; for the evil act had never been done had not an evil will preceded it. And what is the origin of our evil will but pride? For "pride is the beginning of sin."[40] And what is pride but the craving for undue exaltation? And this is undue exaltation, when the soul abandons Him to whom it ought to cleave as its end, and becomes a kind of end to itself. This happens when it becomes its own satisfaction. And it does so when it falls away from that unchangeable good which ought to satisfy it more than itself. This falling away is spontaneous; for if the will had remained steadfast in the love of that higher and changeless good by which it was illumined to intelligence and kindled into love, it would not have turned away to find satisfaction in itself, and so become frigid and benighted; the woman would not have believed the serpent spoke the truth, nor would the man have preferred the request of his wife to the command of God, nor have supposed that it was a venial transgression to cleave to the partner of his life even in a partnership of sin. The wicked deed, then—that is to say, the transgression of eating the forbidden fruit—was committed by persons who were already wicked. That "evil fruit"[41] could be brought forth only by "a corrupt tree." But that the tree was evil was not the result of nature; for certainly it could become so only by the vice of the will, and vice is contrary to nature. Now, nature could not have been depraved by vice had it not been made out of nothing. Consequently, that it is a nature, this is because it is made by God; but that it falls away from Him, this is because it is made out of nothing. But man did not so fall away[42] as to become absolutely nothing; but being turned towards himself, his being became more contracted than it was when he clave to Him who supremely is. Accordingly, to exist in himself, that is, to be his own satisfaction after abandoning God, is not quite to become a nonentity, but to approximate to that. And therefore the holy Scriptures designate the proud by another name, "self-pleasers." For it is good to have the heart lifted up, yet not to one's self, for this is proud, but to the Lord, for this is obedient, and can be the act only of the humble. There is, therefore, something in humility which, strangely enough, exalts the heart, and something in pride which debases it. This seems, indeed, to be contradictory, that loftiness should debase and lowliness exalt. But pious humility enables us to submit to what is above us, and nothing is more exalted above us than God; and therefore humility, by making us subject to God, exalts us. But pride, being a defect of nature, by the very act of refusing subjection and revolting from Him who is supreme, falls to a low condition; and then comes to pass what is written: "Thou castedst them down when they lifted up themselves."[43] For He does not say, "when they had been lifted up," as if first they were exalted, and then afterwards cast down; but "when they lifted up themselves" even then they were cast down—that is to say, the very lifting up was already a fall. And therefore it is that humility is specially recommended to the city of God as it sojourns in this world, and is specially exhibited in the city of God, and in the person of Christ its King; while the contrary vice of pride, according to the testimony of the sacred writings, specially rules his adversary the devil. And certainly this is the great difference which distinguishes the two cities of which we speak, the one being the society of the godly men, the other of the ungodly, each associated with the angels that adhere to their party, and the one guided and fashioned by love of self, the other by love of God.

"He that loveth his life shall lose it" [44]

And now, by way of exhortation to follow in the path of His own passion, He adds, "He that loveth his life shall lose it," which may be understood in two ways: "He that loveth shall lose," that is, if thou lovest, be ready to lose; if thou wouldst possess life in Christ, be not afraid of death for Christ. Or otherwise, "He that loveth his life shall lose it." Do not love for fear of losing; love it not here, lest thou lose it in eternity. But what I have said last seems better to correspond with the meaning of the Gospel, for there follow the words, "And he that hateth his life in this world shall keep it unto life eternal." So that when it is said in the previous clause, "He that loveth," there is to be understood *in this world*, he it is that shall lose it. "But he that hateth," that is, in this world, is he that shall keep it unto life eternal. Surely a profound and strange declaration as to the measure of a man's love for his own life that leads to its destruction, and of his hatred to it that secures its preservation! If in a sinful way thou lovest it, then dost thou really hate it; if in a way accordant with what is good thou hast hated it then hast thou really loved it. Happy they who have so hated their life while keeping it, that their love shall not cause them to lose it. But beware of harboring the notion that thou mayest court self-destruction by any such understanding of thy duty to hate thy life in this world. For on such grounds it is that certain wrong-minded and perverted people, who, with regard to themselves, are murderers of a specially cruel and impious character, commit themselves to the flames, suffocate themselves in water, dash themselves against a precipice, and perish. This was no teaching of Christ's, who, on the other hand, met the devil's suggestion of a precipice with the answer, "Get thee behind me, Satan, for it is written, Thou shalt not tempt the Lord thy God."[45] To Peter also He said, signifying by what death he should glorify God, "When thou wast young, thou girdedst thyself, and walkedst whither thou wouldest: but when thou shalt be old, another shall gird thee, and carry thee whither thou wouldest not";[46]—where He made it sufficiently plain that it is not by Himself but by another that one must be slain who follows in the footsteps of Christ. And so, when one's case has reached the crisis that this condition is placed before him, either that he must act contrary to the divine commandment or quit this life, and that a man is compelled to choose one or other of the two by the persecutor who is threatening him with death, in such circumstances let him prefer dying in the love of God to living under His anger, in such circumstances let him hate his life in this world that he may keep it unto life eternal.

Our true interests do not lie in this life [47]

We know that both the competency of things necessary, and the well-being of ourselves and of our friends, so long as these concern this present world alone, are to be cast aside as dross in comparison with the obtaining of eternal life; for although the body may be in health, the mind cannot be regarded as sound which does not prefer eternal to temporal things; yea, the life which we live in time is wasted, if it be not spent in obtaining that by which we may be worthy of eternal life. Therefore all things which are the objects of useful and becoming desire are unquestionably to be viewed with reference to that one life which is lived with God, and is derived from Him. In so doing, we love ourselves if we love God; and we truly love our neighbors as ourselves, according to the second great commandment, if, so far as is in our power, we persuade them to a similar love of God. We love God, therefore, for what He is in Himself, and ourselves and our neighbors for His sake. Even when living thus, let us not think that we are securely established in that happy life, as if there was nothing more for which we should still pray. For how could we be said to live a happy life now, while that which alone is the object of a well-directed life is still wanting to us?

• • •

For our good, about which philosophers have so keenly contended, is nothing else than to be united to God. It is, if I may say so, by spiritually embracing Him that the intellectual soul is filled and impregnated with true virtues. We are enjoined to love this good with all our heart, with all our soul, with all our strength. To this good we ought to be led by those who love us, and to lead those we love. Thus are fulfilled those two commandments on which hang all the law and the prophets: "Thou shalt love the Lord thy God with all thy heart, and with all thy mind, and with all thy soul;" and "Thou shalt love thy neighbor as thyself."[48] For, that man might be intelligent in his self-love, there was appointed for him an end to which he might refer all his actions, that he might be blessed. For he who loves himself wishes nothing else than this. And the end set before him is "to draw near to God."[49] And so, when one who has this intelligent self-love is commanded to love his neighbor as himself, what else is enjoined than that he shall do all in his power to commend to him the love of God? This is the worship of God, this is true religion, this right piety, this the service due to God only. If any immortal power, then, no matter with what virtue endowed, loves us as himself, he must desire that we find our happiness by submitting ourselves to Him, in submission to whom he himself finds happiness. If he does not worship God, he is wretched, because deprived of God; if he worships God, he cannot wish to be worshipped in God's stead. On the contrary, these higher powers acquiesce heartily in the divine sentence in which it is written, "He that sacrificeth unto any god, save unto the Lord only, he shall be utterly destroyed."[50]

The "city of man" formed by self-love, the "city of God" by self-overcoming [51]

Accordingly, two cities have been formed by two loves: the earthly by the love of self, even to the contempt of God; the heavenly by the love of God, even to the contempt of self. The former, in a word, glories in itself, the latter in the Lord. For the one seeks glory from men; but the greatest glory of the other is God, the witness of conscience. The one lifts up its head in its own glory; the other says to its God, "Thou art my glory, and the lifter up of mine head."[52] In the one, the princes and the nations it sub-dues are ruled by the love of ruling; in the other, the princes and the subjects serve one another in love, the latter obeying, while the former take thought for all. The one delights in its own strength represented in the persons of its rulers; the other says to its God, "I will love Thee, O Lord, my strength."[53] And therefore the wise men of the one city, living according to man, have sought for profit to their own bodies or souls, or both, and those who have known God "glorified Him not as God, neither were thankful, but became vain in their imaginations, and their foolish heart was darkened; professing themselves to be wise"—that is, glorying in their own wisdom, and being possessed by pride—"they became fools, and changed the glory of the incorruptible God into an image made like to corruptible man, and to birds, and four-footed beasts, and creeping things." For they were either leaders or followers of the people in ador-ing images, "and worshipped and served the creature more than the Creator, who is blessed for ever."[54] But in the other city there is no human wisdom, but only godliness, which offers due worship to the true God, and looks for its reward in the society of the saints, of holy angels as well as holy men, "that God may be all in all."[55]

THOMAS AQUINAS
(1224–1274)

Is self-love the cause of all sin?[56]

THE FOURTH POINT:[57] 1. It would seem that self-love is not the source of all sin. A thing that is in itself good and obligatory cannot be called a source of sin. But self-love is good in itself and also obligatory, for in *Leviticus* it says that a man must love his neighbor as himself.[58] Therefore, self-love cannot be assigned as a proper cause of sin.

2. Moreover, St. Paul says, *Having thus found an occasion, sin worked in me by means of the commandment all manner of lust,*[59] and the *Gloss* comments that the *law is good, since by forbidding concupiscence, it forbids all evil,*[60] thus assuming that concupiscence is the cause of all sin. But concupiscence differs from love, as has been mentioned already.[61] Therefore, self-love is not the cause of all sin.

3. Furthermore, St. Augustine in commenting on, *Let those who would burn it with fire or cut it down,*[62] says that *every sin is due either to love arousing us to undue ardor or to fear inducing false humility.*[63] Therefore, self-love is not the only cause of sin.

4. Finally, just as man sometimes sins because of an inordinate love for someone else. Therefore, self-love is not the cause of every sin.

ON THE OTHER HAND, St. Augustine says that self-love, amounting to contempt of God builds up the city of Babylon.[64] But a man becomes a citizen of Babylon through whatever sin he commits. Therefore, self-love is the cause of every sin.

REPLY: Properly speaking, the cause of sin is assigned by reason of man's turning to the perishable good, and from this point of view every sin presupposes an inordinate desire for some temporal good.[65]

Man's inordinate love for a temporal good comes from an inordinate love of himself, for when we love someone we wish him good.

Quite clearly, then, it follows that inordinate self-love is the cause of all sin.

Hence: 1. A properly directed love of self is both obligatory and natural, so that a man might will for himself those things which are good for him. St. Augustine speaks of inordinate self-love, which leads to the contempt of God.[66]

2. Concupiscence, which is a desire for something good, presupposes love for self, as has been mentioned.[67]

3. A man loves both the good which he desires for himself and the self for whom he desires the good. Love for a thing, e.g., wine or money, is the very basis for fearing its loss, which makes evil a thing to be shunned. Every sin arises from an inordinate desire for something good or from an inordinate escape from evil. However, both of these presuppose love of the self. For a man desires a good thing or shuns an evil because he loves himself.

4. A friend is a *second self*,[68] thus when a man sins because of love for a friend, he sins for love of himself.

Are all sins connected? [69]

THE FIRST POINT: . . .

3. Moreover, all of the virtues which are based on one principle are connected.[70] But both virtues and sins are based on one principle, "for the love of God which builds the city of God" is the source and root of all good, and "the love of self which builds the city of Babylon" is the root of all sin, according to St. Augustine.[71] Therefore, all the sins and vices are connected, and whoever has one has all. . . .

ON THE OTHER HAND: Certain vices are mutually exclusive, as Aristotle says.[72] But mutually exclusive notes cannot co-exist in one subject. Therefore, it is impossible that all sins and vices be connected. . . .

REPLY: . . .

3. The love of God is an integrating force, for it centers a variety of affections on one central object. Accordingly, the virtues which flow from this love of God are mutually

connected. However, self-love dissipates human affection along many paths, for the temporal goods which man desires for himself are not only various but also diverse. Accordingly, the vices and sins which flow from self-love are not mutually connected.

Is pride the beginning of all sin? [73]

THE SECOND POINT: . . .

3. Further, the beginning of all sin would seem to be one which causes all sin. This is inordinate self-love, which, as Augustine declares, *builds the city of Babylon.*[74] Self-love, therefore, not pride is the beginning of all sin.

ON THE OTHER HAND, there is the text, *Pride is the beginning of all sin.*[75]

REPLY: Some authors maintain that pride has a three-fold significance.[76] It stands, first, for the disordered will for personal excellence. In this way it is a specific kind of sin.

In its second meaning it stands for a particular sort of explicit contempt for God, the refusal to be subject to his command. In this way, these authors maintain, pride is a general sin.

In a third sense it stands for the proclivity arising from fallen nature towards this contempt. And in this sense they say that it is the beginning of all sin, and differs from covetousness. For this concerns sin as a turning to a passing good, thus, as it were, it nourishes and fosters sin, and is consequently sin's 'root'. Pride, on the other hand, is rather concerned with sin as a turning away from God, whose command man refuses to obey. Because the nature of moral evil begins in turning away from God, pride is called sin's "beginning."

While this may be true, it is not according to the mind of the Wise Man,[77] who said, *The beginning of all sin is pride.* He obviously is speaking of pride as it is the inordinate desire to excel. This is clear from what he adds, *God has overturned the thrones of proud princes,*[78] and from the import of the whole chapter. . . .

HENCE:...

3. A man is loving himself when he wills his own prominence: to love yourself is to will good to yourself. Thus it amounts to the same thing whether pride or self-love be called the beginning of all sin.

Do sinners love themselves? [79]

THE SEVENTH POINT:[80] 1. Apparently sinners do love themselves. For it is above all in sinners that we find the very source of sin itself, namely, self-love, which as Augustine puts it *was the builder of Babylon.*[81]

2. Moreover, sin does not do away with nature. Now it is part of the nature of any-thing to love itself: even things without reason naturally seek their own good, such as their own self-preservation and so forth. Therefore sinners do love themselves.

3. Besides, as Dionysius observes,[82] goodness is something that all men love. Now many sinners are good in their own eyes, and so many of them love themselves.

ON THE OTHER HAND we have the words of the psalm, *He that loveth iniquity hateth his own soul.*[83]

REPLY: In one sense self-love is something that all men have in common; in another it is something peculiar to the good; and in still another, something peculiar to the wicked. For in common with everybody else, every man loves what he thinks he is.

Now when we are discussing what a man is, we are either talking about his very substance and nature, in which case we all know what we are, namely beings made up of soul and body; and in this way all, good or bad, love themselves to the extent that they love their own self-preservation.

Or else we are talking about what is most important in him, for example, we say that the ruler of a state is the state, and, accordingly, what a ruler does, the state is said to do. Here, however, all do not see themselves to be as they really are. For what chiefly makes a man what he is is his rational mind, the sensitive and bodily part of his nature being secondary, the former in the Apostle's language being called the *inner man*, the latter the *outer man.*[84] Now the good look upon their rational nature, or *inner man*, as being the most important thing they have, and so in this respect they think of themselves as they really are. But the wicked regard their sensitive and bodily part, that is the *outward man*, as having first place in their nature. And so, not rightly knowing themselves, they do not truly love themselves, but only what they imagine themselves to be. The good, on the other hand, truly knowing themselves, truly love themselves.

Aristotle proves this[85] from five characteristics of friendship. First, every friend wishes his friend to be and to live; secondly, he desires good things for him; thirdly, he does good to him; fourthly, he takes pleasure in his company; fifthly, he is of one mind with him, rejoicing and grieving over almost the same things. By these tests the good are shown to love themselves as to the *inner man*: they wish him to be preserved in his integrity; they desire good things, that is spiritual goods for him; they apply them-selves moreover to get them for him; they take pleasure in their own heart, for there they find good thoughts in the present, the memory of past blessings and the hope of future good, all of which bring them pleasure; in the same way they suffer no interior discord in their will because their whole soul is bent on the one thing. In contrast to all this, the wicked have no wish to preserve the *inner man* in his integrity, nor do they desire his spiritual good, nor work for this end, nor is it a pleasure for them to live with themselves by entering into their own hearts, because all they find there, past, present and future, is evil and fills them with disgust, nor are they even at one with themselves, on account of the gnawings of conscience as described in the psalm, *I will rebuke you and lay the charge before you.*[86] Likewise it may be shown that the wicked love themselves as regards the corruption that affects the *outward man*, which is quite contrary to the way the good love themselves.

HENCE: 1. The self-love referred to here which is the source of sin, is the kind peculiar to evil-doers, and which, as Augustine points out in the same passage,[87] *goes so far that they even despise God,* their desire for worldly goods being such that they hold spiritual things in contempt.

2. Granted that natural love is not entirely destroyed in the wicked, it is, all the same, something perverted as we have just shown.[88]

3. To the extent that the wicked think themselves good, they have some share of self-love. It is not, however, true self-love, but only apparent, and even this is not possible in the case of those who are far gone in wickedness.

Can one hate oneself? [89]

THE FOURTH POINT:[90] 1. It would seem that one can hate oneself. For the Psalmist says, *He that loves evil-doing hates his own soul.*[91] But there are many people who love evil-doing. Therefore many people hate themselves.

2. If we wish someone evil and do him harm, we hate him. But sometimes a person wishes himself evil, and does himself harm: e.g., a suicide. Therefore there are people who hate themselves.

3. Boëthius says, *Avarice makes a man hateful:*[92] which suggests that everyone hates a miser. But some men are misers. Therefore they hate themselves.

ON THE OTHER HAND St. Paul says, *No-one ever hated his own flesh.*[93]

REPLY: It is impossible for a person to hate himself, in the proper sense of the term. For everything, by its nature, wants what is good, and can want a thing for itself only in so far as it seems good from some point of view: as Dionysius says, evil lies outside the scope of the will.[94] Now to love someone is to want good things for him, as we have seen.[95] Of necessity, therefore, one must love oneself; and it is impossible to hate oneself, in the proper sense of that expression.

There are two less proper senses, however, in which a person may be said to hate himself. First, from the point of view of the good that he wants: for it sometimes happens that the thing which he wants because of some attractive appearance it presents is in fact harmful: in this sense, therefore, he wishes himself ill, and so "hates himself." Second, from the point of view of the part of himself for which he wants the good: for a thing "is," above all, its most important element; thus a state is said to do what its king does, as if the king were the state. Now clearly, a man is, above all, his mind. Some people, however, think that they are, above all, body and senses. They therefore do indeed love themselves under the description of what they take themselves to be; but they are hating themselves as they really are, wanting for themselves things that run counter to reason.

In these two senses, then, the man who loves evil-doing hates not only his soul, but himself.

1. This will make clear the answer to the first objection.

2. No one wills himself evil and does himself harm except in so far as it seems good from some point of view. Thus suicides see death as good, in so far as it puts an end to wretchedness and grief.

3. A miser hates something which is present in him, but he does not for that reason hate himself: just as a sick man hates his sickness precisely because he loves himself.

Alternatively, one might reply that avarice makes a person hateful to others, but not to himself. Indeed, it is a product of excessive self-love, leading one to want for oneself more temporal goods than one should.

Does an angel love himself both naturally and by choice? [96]

THE THIRD POINT:[97] 1. It would seem not; for we have seen[98] that while natural love goes directly to an end, choice-love is of a means to an end. But the same thing cannot be both end and means from the same point of view; nor then the same thing be object of both natural love and choice-love.

2. Besides, we have it from Dionysius that love is *a power uniting and holding together*:[99] but in that case a prior division is implied: so it seems an angel cannot love *himself* at all.

3. Again, love is a kind of movement, and all movement is towards an 'other'; hence again, no angel can love himself.

ON THE OTHER HAND we have Aristotle saying: *friendship with others springs from the friendship one has with oneself.*[100]

REPLY: Since love is always of some good, and goodness is found both in substances and in inherent properties, as Aristotle says,[102] it follows that love can be either for a thing as existing in itself or for a thing as inhering in another. We love in the first way when we love a thing as willing good for *it*; in the second way when we love a thing as willing it for another—as I love knowledge, not as wanting it to be good, but as wanting to have its goodness. And some have called the latter sort of loving "desire" and the former sort "friendship."

Now it is clear that things that lack knowledge all tend by nature towards some good for themselves, as fire always flies upward to the place natural to it. And so it is with natural appetition both in angels and man: each seeks his own good and fulfilment; that is, each loves himself. By nature then—driven by natural appetition—angels and men love themselves: but also love by choice, in choosing their own good.

Hence: 1. As we have explained,[102] it is not in the same respect, but in different respects, that an angel or a man loves himself by nature and by choice.

2. As being simply one implies more unity than being in union with another, so a subject's self-love is more of a unity than his union, through love, with another. And Dionysius spoke of love as uniting and holding together precisely in order to show that love of the not-self derives from love of the self—as the term "uniting" derives from "one."

3. As love, considered as an activity, is immanent in the lover, so is it if considered as a movement; that is, it remains in the lover and does not of necessity stretch out to anything else. But it can turn back to the lover so that he loves himself, just as knowledge can turn back on the knower so that he knows himself.

Does an angel naturally love God more than self? [103]

THE FIFTH POINT:[104] 1. It would seem not: for, as we have seen,[105] natural loving implies union in nature, but the divine nature is very far removed from the angelic; hence by nature an angel must love God less than himself; indeed, less even than other angels.

2. Moreover, it is in its source and principle that a thing exists at its maximum. Now the source and principle of natural love is love of self; one thing naturally loves another only as good for itself. No angel, then, can naturally love God more than himself.

3. Again, nature circles upon itself; the activity of everything in our experience is directed by nature to self-preservation. But this would not be so if anything naturally tended towards another more than itself. No angel, then, loves God more than self.

4. Besides, if anyone loves God more than self, this can only be due to charity. Now the love of charity is not natural to angels; it is *poured into their hearts by the Holy Spirit that is given them*, as Augustine says.[106] So no angel naturally loves God more than himself.

5. Further, natural love remains while nature remains; but a sinful man or angel no longer loves God more than himself; as Augustine says, *Two loves have built two cities, the city of self-love implying contempt for God, and that of God-love, implying contempt for self.*[107] It follows that to love God more than oneself was never natural.

ON THE OTHER HAND, all the moral commandments of the Law come under natural law, and one of them is the command to love God more than oneself.[108] Therefore this love is part of the law of nature; consequently it is by nature that the angels love God more than themselves.

REPLY: Some theologians say that an angel by nature loves God more than himself with the love of desire, in the sense that he desires for himself the divine good more than his own good; and that in a certain sense he also loves God thus with the love of friendship, inasmuch as he naturally desires for God a greater good than for himself—for he desires God to be God and himself to be himself. But they add nevertheless that absolutely speaking an angel by nature loves himself more than God, for his natural self-love is more basic and more intense than his natural love for God.

But this is clearly false if we consider the natural inclination of things, and if we take—as we may—the innate tendencies of non-rational being as a pointer to the way the intellectual nature itself moves to its ends by appetition and will. For nature shows us that everything which, precisely in virtue of its nature, belongs to something else, is primarily and principally inclined towards that to which it belongs rather than towards itself. Consider the way things naturally behave; it is as Aristotle said,[109] *each natural thing is adapted to act for an end by the nature moving it to act*: thus we see the parts of a whole going into action for the sake of the whole, whatever the result to themselves; a hand instinctively moves to ward off a blow that would harm the body as a whole. And since reason follows the model of nature, we find a like tendency, for example, in good citizens; they are disposed to face death for the well-being of their city; and if man were made by nature part of a city, this disposition would be purely instinctive.

Since then the good, taken quite universally, is God himself, and since all angels, all men and all other creatures exist as contained within that good—because every creature, precisely in respect of what it is by nature, belongs to God—it follows that the instinctive natural love of each angel and each man is for God first of all and for God more than for self. Otherwise, if this were not true, if creatures by nature loved themselves more than God, then natural loving would be perverse; and would not be perfected, but destroyed, by charity.

Hence: 1. This is a good argument when applied to things that stand on an equal footing and of which one is not the ground of the other's existence and goodness. Among such things certainly natural love goes to the self more than to others, each thing being more one with itself than with anything else. But as between two things of which one is the entire reason why there is any being or goodness in the other, then of its nature the latter must love the former more than itself: every part, as we have said,[110] by nature loves the whole more than itself. And so too each individual of a species tends naturally to the good of the species more than to its own private good. Now God is not just the good of this or that species; he is the universal good, simply and absolutely. Hence each and every being, each in the way appropriate to it, by nature loves God more than itself.

2. The statement that God is loved by an angel as good for the angel himself can be understood in two senses, one false, the other true. If the "as" indicates the objective end of the angel's loving, the statement is false; for no angel naturally loves God for the sake of the end which is his own good, but for the sake of the end which is God himself.[111] But if it indicates the motive of the love from the lover's point of view, then it is true; for what makes any nature love God is that it derives from God all the goodness that it has.

3. It is true that each nature circles upon itself, but it does so, not only in respect of what is particular to itself, but also, and much more, in respect of what it has in common with other things. Each individual thing tends not only to keep itself in being, but to keep its species going also. And far more does it tend of its nature towards the good that is absolutely universal.

4. God as the universal good on whom depends all the goodness found in nature is loved by all things with natural love; but as the good which of its nature beatifies all with supernatural bliss, he is loved with the love of charity.

5. Since in the godhead the divine being itself and the divine being that is the general good towards which all creatures tend is one and the same thing, it follows that all creatures who see his very essence are impelled by identically the same love both to love him as he is other than creatures and to love him as creation's general good. And because he is this general good, the term of all natural appetition, then whoever has the immediate vision of what he is cannot help but love him. But those who do not see God in this way know him only through this or that of his effects; and sometimes such effects go contrary to their will. This is how creatures can sometimes be said to hate God; though it remains true that, as the common good, the term of all appetition, God is naturally loved by each thing more than itself.

Is the following enumeration of the four we are bound to love out of charity an adequate one: God, our neighbor, our body, and ourselves? [112]

THE TWELFTH POINT:[113] 1. It would not appear so. For Augustine says, *He who does not love God, does not love himself.*[114] Love of oneself, therefore, is included in love of God. Hence love of oneself and love of God are not two distinct things.

2. Moreover, in any division, part must not be set over against whole. Now our body is a part of us. We should not therefore divide it from ourselves as a distinct object of our love.

3. Besides, just as we have a body, so has our neighbor. Therefore in the same way as the love we have for him is distinct from the love we have for ourselves, so our love for his body is distinct from the love of our own. It is not right, then, to set out only four things as objects of charity.

ON THE OTHER HAND Augustine says, *There are four a man must love, one is above him,* namely God; *another is himself; the third is close by him,* namely his neighbor; *and the fourth is beneath him,* namely his own body.[115]

REPLY: As we said earlier,[116] the friendship we call charity rests on a fellowship of eternal happiness. Now in this fellowship we can distinguish three elements. One, which actively communicates this happiness to us, namely, God; another, which directly shares in it, men and angels; and a third, to which eternal happiness comes by a kind of overflow namely, the human body. Now what communicates happiness to us is lovable because it is the cause of our happiness. But what shares in happiness can be lovable for two reasons: either because it is identified with us, or because it is associated with us. And in this way we have two things to be loved by charity, according as a man loves both himself and his neighbor.

Hence: 1. Love has as many different objects as there are different relations between a lover and the various things he loves. Now a man's relationship to God is not the same as his relationship to himself and because of this we say that his love has two distinct objects, the love of one in this case being the cause of his loving the other. Accordingly remove one, and you remove the other.

2. The rational soul, capable of eternal happiness is where charity is rooted, and man's body cannot share directly in this happiness, but only by a kind of overflow. Since, therefore, it is his rational soul that counts for most in man, his charity makes him love himself in one way and his body in another.

3. A man loves his neighbor, body and soul because he is his partner, potentially or actually in the same eternal happiness. In other words, in what concerns one's neighbor there is only one reason for loving him in charity. And so his body should not be singled out as a special object of love.

Does charity demand that a man love God more than himself? [117]

THE TWELFTH POINT: [118] 1. It would not seem to be so. For Aristotle says, that *friendliness towards others springs from friendliness towards oneself.*[119] Now a cause is stronger than its effect. Therefore a man's friendship for himself is greater than his friendship for anyone else, and so he is bound to love himself more than God.

2. Moreover, we love something to the extent that it is our own good. But that which is the reason for loving is loved more than that which is loved because of it. Just as in knowledge premises are known more than what is derived from them. Therefore a man loves himself more than any other good whatsoever, and consequently does not love God more than himself.

3. Besides, in so far as a man loves God he desires to enjoy him. But to the extent that he desires this, he is loving himself, since enjoying God is the highest good any-

one could wish for himself. Therefore charity does not mean that a man love God more than himself.

ON THE OTHER HAND Augustine says, *If you are bound to love yourself not for your own sake, but for his, where your love's purest motive is to be found, let no one take offense if you love him, too, for God's sake.*[120] Now what is found in the effect is found to an even greater degree in its cause. Therefore a man should love God more than himself.

REPLY: Two good things we get from God, the good of nature and the good of grace. Now God, by giving us natural goods, provides the basis for that natural love by which man, when he is whole and unspoiled, loves God above all things including himself. This holds not only for man but for each and every creature in its own way, according as the love in question is intellectual, rational, animal, or even, as with stones and other things that lack knowledge, what we call 'natural' love. The reason for this is that a part naturally loves the common good of the whole more than its own particular good. The way things behave is evidence of this, for every part displays a dominant inclination for some action conducive to the good of the whole. The same is to be seen with the civic virtues, which make the citizens put up with losses in their own property and persons when the common good is at stake. How much more then is this realized in the friendship of charity, which is based on a common sharing of the gifts of grace. Accordingly man is bound in charity to love God, who is the common good of all things, more than himself; for eternal happiness is to be found in God as in the common principle and source of all things which are capable of sharing such happiness.

Hence: 1. Aristotle is talking about friendliness towards someone in whom the good, which is the object of friendship, is of a partial nature, not about friendliness towards a person in whom such a good is the good of the whole universe.

2. The part does indeed love the good of the whole as something congenial to itself; not however as subordinating the good of the whole to itself, but itself to the good of the whole.

3. The will to enjoy God is to love him with what we call a love of concupiscence. But in loving him it is not this, but rather love of friendship which predominates, because in itself his good is greater than any we can derive by enjoying it. Therefore, simply speaking, by charity, man loves God more than himself.

Ought a man in charity to love himself more than his neighbor?[121]

THE FOURTH POINT:[122] 1. It would seem not. For as stated earlier,[124] the principal object of charity is God. But sometimes a man's neighbor is more closely united to God than he himself is, and therefore he ought to love him more than himself.

2. Again, the more we love a person the more we avoid hurting him. Now if a man has charity, he willingly endures harm for his neighbor's sake; *he that neglects a loss for the sake of a friend is just.*[124] And so a man in charity should love his neighbor more than himself.

3. Besides, we read that charity *seeks not her own.*[125] Now we love those most whose good we are most concerned to seek. Consequently charity does not require us to love ourselves more than our neighbor.

ON THE OTHER HAND we read in *Leviticus* and in *Matthew, You shall love your neighbor as yourself;*[126] from which we see that a man's love for himself is, so to speak, the paradigm of his love for others. Now the paradigm is more than what takes after it. Therefore a man is bound in charity to love himself more than his neighbor.

REPLY: There are two realities in man: the spiritual and the corporal. Now, as stated earlier on,[127] when we talk about loving ourselves, it is our spiritual nature that we have in mind. And here we are bound to love ourselves more than anyone else, God alone excepted. This is obvious from the very motive of our love. For, as we said above,[128] we love God as the fount of that good which forms the basis of charity, then ourselves as sharing in it, and our neighbors as partners. But the motive for loving which this partnership provides implies a certain union with reference to God. Hence as unity is stronger than union, so the fact that a man himself participates in the divine good is a more powerful reason for loving than the fact that another is associated with him in this participation. Consequently a man ought in charity to love himself more than his neighbor, as is indicated by the fact that, as sin is incompatible with eternal happiness, he may not incur such an evil, even to free another from it.

Hence: 1. It is not merely its object, God, that gives charity its quantity, but the one who loves as well, that is, the man who possesses charity, just as the quantity of any action depends, in a sense, on the subject who performs it. Thus, granted that the better man is closer to God, he is not, for all that, as close to me as I am to myself. And so it does not follow that one should love one's neighbor more than oneself.

2. We ought to put up with bodily harm for a friend's sake: in fact by so doing we show that what we love most is our own spiritual self, because to act like this is a mark of perfect virtue, the very good of the soul itself. But as already stated,[129] to incur spiritual loss by committing sin is never lawful, even to save one's neighbor.

3. As Augustine says in his *Rule* the phrase, *charity seeks not her own, means that she puts the common good before her own private interests.*[130] Now the common good is always more lovable than one's own private good, just as for each part the good of the whole is more lovable than its own partial good, as already noted.[131]

Should a man's charity include himself? [132]

THE FOURTH POINT: [133] 1. It seems not. For in one of his homilies Gregory says that *charity is not possible where there are less than two.* [134] No one, therefore, has charity for himself.

2. Moreover, the very nature of friendship, according to Aristotle, [135] implies a return of love, as well as a certain equality, which is not possible for a man with regard to himself. But, as stated earlier, [136] charity is a kind of friendship, and consequently no one can have charity towards himself.

3. Besides, there can be nothing blameworthy about charity, for, as St. Paul says, *charity does not deal perversely.* [137] But loving oneself is blameworthy, for he warns Timothy that *in the last days there will come times of stress, for men will be lovers of self.* [138] Therefore man cannot love himself out of charity.

ON THE OTHER HAND *Leviticus* teaches, *Thou shalt love thy friend as thyself.* [139] But we love a friend out of charity. Therefore we must love ourselves also out of charity.

REPLY: Since, as we have said, [140] charity is a kind of friendship, we can talk about it in two ways: First, as friendship in a general sense. And here we must concede that, strictly speaking, we do not have friendship for ourselves, but something more, because friendship implies a union of some kind, love being, as Dionysius puts it, a *unifying force*, [141] whereas, with regard to himself, man possesses unity, which is something more than union. Accordingly, as unity is presupposed to union, so our love for ourselves is the model and root of friendship; for our friendship for others consists precisely in the fact that our attitude to them is the same as to ourselves. Aristotle remarks that *friendly feelings towards others flow from a man's own feelings towards himself.* [142] In somewhat the same way with regard to principles we do not have science, strictly speaking, but something more, namely an intuitive grasp or understanding.

Or we can discuss charity in terms of its special character, in other words according as it is friendship, for God chiefly, and consequently for whatever belongs to him. Now included among these is man himself who possesses charity. So, among other things which, as belonging to God he loves out of charity, man also loves himself.

Hence: 1. Gregory is speaking about charity in terms of the general character of all friendship.

2. The same is to be said with regard to the second objection.

3. People who love themselves are censured for a self-love which fastens on the fleshly part of their nature only, and makes them follow its lead. This is not that true love of self as rational beings by which we desire whatever makes for the perfection of reason. And it is in this latter way, especially, that love of self belongs to charity.

III | EARLY MODERN ERA

$\mathcal{T}$homas Hobbes (1588–1679) ushered in the early modern era of thought on the subject of self-concern, rejecting Judeo-Christian supernaturalism in favor of a wholly natural conception of self-interest. We have no philosophical grounds for conceiving of our interests atemporally, he says, since it is impossible to reason about what, if anything, happens once we die. Gone is the "eternal life" conception of happiness, as well as the view that self-love is evil insofar as it constitutes an impediment to love of God. There are not three forms of self-love, but one, and insofar as love of self is an entirely natural phenomenon—its essential purpose being self-preservation—there is nothing sinful about it. On the contrary, it constitutes the "first right of nature."

Hobbes's account of self-concern hinges upon his psychology of man, which itself rests upon two crucial premises—first, that all voluntary action is egoistically motivated, and, second, that reason is simply the instrument we use to satisfy our desires. Stripped of its end-conferring power, reason is now impotent to determine self-interest, which is instead established by passion. In fact, our "good" consists entirely in whatever we happen to desire at a given moment. Since our desires constantly change, self-interest is in perpetual flux. This of course implies the non-existence of a *summum bonum*, which Hobbes regards as a mere philosopher's fiction.

There are interesting epistemological consequences of Hobbes' account of self-interest. Human beings normally consult reason in their efforts to best satisfy their desires. Sometimes, though, reason makes observations contrary to desire—for instance, that an undesirable result will attend the pursuit of a particular passion. When the initial desire is sufficiently strong, it will not want to accept this, however, and so will abandon reason in favor of some alternate guide, such as custom. Since human beings are motivated by passion, passion has the power to check reason in this way. And since self-interest is constituted by passion, rationality is entirely beholden to self-interest. Hobbes goes so far as to say that man would abandon even mathematical truths if for some reason he perceived them as contrary to his good.

Insofar as individual lives are run by passion, Hobbes concludes that people are bound to suffer conflicts of interest. Prior to the institution of government, human beings existed in a state of de facto war, he claims, without any safety or security. Recognizing the advantages of peace, they form a covenant for mutual self-protection.

What if one can secretly violate the covenant, though? This is the question of fools, according to Hobbes. When one enters the social contract, one voluntarily agrees to abide by its terms, yet "voluntarily to undo that, which from the beginning he had voluntarily done" is an "absurdity." Further, one who commits an unjust act cannot possibly foresee whether he will get caught, or therefore whether the act will actually result in his advantage. To act under such conditions cannot be consistent with self-interest.

In his defense of justice, as much else, Hobbes' relation to previous thinkers on the subject of self-concern is quite complex. Though he has moved away from the medieval tradition in certain respects, two crucial similarities remain. First, although Hobbes represents a dramatic shift from the other-worldliness of medieval philosophy, his own model of human nature is strongly influenced by the Augustinian conception of temporal man. The idea of man as passion-driven, the rhetoric of interpersonal war, and the view of government as arising to curb self-interest, are all present in the *City of God*. It might not be amiss to say that the *natural* self-love of Hobbes corresponds to the *negative* self-love of Augustine, at least in its antisocial tendencies.

Second, Hobbes follows the medieval, against the Platonic-Aristotleliean, view in representing the harm associated with wrongdoing as being of external origin. As we have seen, the ancients had conceived of injustice as an affliction of the soul, for which the primary punishment arose from within. Medieval thinkers removed the tribunal to an external location, discovering it in God. Hobbes follows this externalism, but—in the tradition of the Sophists—secularizes it, relocating the tribunal in the civil government.

The concept of God reappears in our next philosopher, Baruch Spinoza's (1632–1677), discussion of self-interest, but Spinoza identifies God not with a supreme being who stands above the world, but with the whole of Nature. In Spinoza's view, the natural world is a single substance of which everything we observe, including ourselves, is an aspect. Inasmuch as substance is fully determinate, all that occurs does so necessarily. This entails that human beings possess no free will in the ordinary sense of the term, but Spinoza believes that we attain freedom, and so happiness, to the extent we eradicate our confused ideas and form an "adequate," i.e., true, understanding of the world, and especially of the causes of our own actions. This releases us from the "bondage" of passion, and thus from control by external forces. The greater our understanding, the more we move ourselves from within.

At the heart of our understanding of our own nature lies the recognition that, like all animate things, we are driven by an inner force—a *conatus*—to preserve our own being or activity. This is the ultimate principle of our nature. Since human beings exist and are active to the extent they understand, the *conatus* seeks after that which fosters wisdom. The mind accordingly judges "nothing else to be to its advantage except what conduces to understanding." Since the greater the object of knowledge, the greater the wisdom, Spinoza argues that man's highest good is the knowledge of God.

Spinoza defines virtue in terms of acting in accordance with the laws of human nature, and since the essence of our nature is to strive for self-preservation, the *conatus* forms the basis of all virtue. "To act in absolute conformity with virtue is nothing else in us but to act, to live, to preserve one's own being (these three mean the same) under the guidance of reason, on the basis of seeking one's own advantage." Spinoza is aware that it may sound paradoxical to define virtue in terms of self-interest, but he specifically aims to "gain the attention of those who believe [falsely] that the principle that every man is bound to seek his own advantage is the basis, not of virtue or piety, but of impiety."

It is in striving for greater activity through understanding that an individual experiences both happiness and self-love. We feel pleasure and self-approval to the extent we are conscious of our own rational activity, and, conversely, experience pain at the awareness of our own passivity. Self-contentment is in this sense a deliverance of reason, that is, of the rational appraisal of our success in realizing our nature.

Spinoza believes that the individual who practices virtue—i.e., who lives in accordance with his nature, rationally seeking his own advantage—will be a great social asset, for several reasons. For one thing, he will take pleasure in pleasing others. This is because he will experience pleasure at the thought of his own active role in fostering their enjoyment. Further, he will live by principles that are beneficial to mankind—such as justice. That is, he will seek to discover principles of conduct that accord with his own nature and foster his own advantage, and, inasmuch as he shares a nature in common with other men, the principles he adopts will accord with *their* nature—and thus benefit *them*—as well. In addition, he will not be captive to passive emotions, which are the source of all interpersonal conflict. To the extent men live under the direction of reason and are guided by the dictates of human nature, they will enjoy a shared and mutually advantageous good. Thus Spinoza remarks—again, paradoxically in the view of some philosophers—that it is precisely when each individual seeks his own advantage that he is of the greatest advantage to his fellows.

In spite of his belief in the harmony of interests, however, Spinoza's political discussion closes on a note of realism. In the ordinary course of things, he says, individuals tend not to run their lives strictly rationally, and are prone to being overcome by passive emotions. Thus, they are "pulled in different directions" while at the same time needing one another's help. Recognizing the advantages to be had from cooperation, however, they form a protective agreement which leads them to refrain from harming one another out of fear of suffering greater harm as a result. In this way, the state is formed, and the foundation for conventional morality is laid.

Bernard Mandeville (1670–1733), one of the lesser-known philosophers of the early modern age, embraces a similar diagnosis of political society, though ultimately he offers two differing accounts of the role of self-interest therein. In some of his writings, he portrays the pursuit of self-interest as socially harmful. Agreeing with Hobbes that self-interest must somehow be enlightened, however, he thinks that Hobbes went wrong in viewing the threat of punishment sufficient for this end; force subdues the problem but does not correct it. What is necessary in addition is to effect a change of *belief*: individuals must somehow be convinced that their true interests lie in public service, rather than in self-pursuit. The way to accomplish this, according to Mandeville, is to appeal to peoples' pride. Convince people of the supreme importance of honor, and then persuade them that honorable action is that which conquers self-interested passion and promotes the common weal. Vanity will do the rest.

The idea that pride leads men to curb self-interest to the benefit of society appears at odds, though, with the view developed by Mandeville in *The Grumbling Hive: Or, Knaves turn'd Honest*. Previous philosophers had assumed that a society of passion-driven egoists must self-destruct, and had conceived government as a means of curbing the harmful effects of the pursuit of self-interest. In *The Grumbling Hive* Mandeville rejects the idea that self-interest entails social misery; quite the contrary, within the context of a stable government, a great and happy society "without great Vices, is a vain Eutopia seated in the brain." It is only from "private vices" that comes "public virtue."

Mandeville does not demonstrate this thesis with an argument, but by means of a sprightly piece of verse in which he chronicles the downfall of the "grumbling hive," a prosperous society of vicious bees which, having become virtuous, is left destitute and unhappy. Mandeville's explanation for this is that self-interest alone propels industry and progress, insofar as it breeds ever-changing patterns of desire. In order to satisfy his desires, an individual is led to various forms of activity that create profitable opportunities for others. A society of strictly public-minded individuals would quickly stagnate, since everyone would be content with what he already had.

Whether Mandeville's two conceptions of self-interest may be reconciled is not a question which can satisfactorily be addressed here. Suffice it to say that Mandeville represents the ambiguity felt over self-concern in the modern age. On the one hand, many were convinced that a society is healthiest and happiest in which each citizen pursues his own interests. Yet, at the same time they were beholden to the deeply implanted the idea that self-interest is fundamentally at odds with virtue and morality.

Bishop Joseph Butler (1692–1752), the next figure we consider, continued the debate in a set of sermons he delivered at the Rolls Chapel in 1726. Regarding self-love, he had two central questions: first, how does it relate to self-interest?, and, second, does it oppose benevolence? Despite his theological orientation, Butler felt these questions could be answered solely by attending to human nature.

Butler begins by distinguishing sharply between self-love and our particular affections for external things. Self-love is simply our general desire for personal happiness. As such it is not equivalent to happiness, nor does it determine this or that to constitute our interest. Our interests are determined, rather, on the basis of our nature, which gives rise to our various affections for external things. These affections are directed outwardly and their satisfaction requires that we take a genuine interest and delight in their objects. For instance, were there no inherent connection between our culinary desires and fine food, we would derive no more enjoyment from partaking of a feast than we would from swallowing a stone. Gratification requires "disengagement."

Self-love sets us on the path of gratifying our desires, but that is all. Those who make self-love itself, rather than particular external goods, their objective, make themselves miserable, as they fail to find satisfaction in the things that make life enjoyable.

As for benevolence, Butler argues that our affection for other people is no more or less connected to self-love than our affection for food, honor, or anything else. All affections are equally interested or disinterested because all have precisely the same relation to the self.

We conclude our reading in Butler with a passage that considers the relation between self-love and morality. Human beings pursue various courses of action, some of which reflect their rational principle, and others which violate it. Our true interests, in Butler's view, coincide with the former. Conscience and reasonable self-love ultimately point us in the same direction, and this ensures the perfect coincidence of duty and interest.

Francis Hutcheson (1694–1746) rejects this conclusion; in his view, it is simply a mistake to try to reconcile duty and happiness. Morality is about benefiting other people, he claims, and is both approved of and motivated by "benevolence"—a principle of action that is utterly distinct from self-interest.

Self-love, Hutcheson concedes, is a basic human impulse that influences much that we do. In fact, sometimes it even directs us to benevolent action. However, it is not action that counts but *motivation*: if a virtuous action is selfishly motivated, we do not give it moral approbation, and if it is motivated jointly by self-interest and benevolence, we subtract the input made by self-interest to calculate its moral worth.

Hutcheson considers and rejects various arguments which attempt to show that benevolence itself is grounded in self-interest. He denies, for instance, that we can summon up benevolent impulses whenever we find it would be in our interest to do so, and he argues that even if we experience pleasure upon sincerely benefiting others, this consequence must not be confused with our initial intention, which was simply to benefit them.

Hutcheson also repudiates the efforts by Hobbes and others to demonstrate that we are rational to the extent we pursue our self-interest. Self-love and benevolence are equally primitive instincts, he says, and each is equally distinct from reason. Reason is simply man's faculty for discovering the most efficient means to his chosen ends. The ends themselves are dictated by his affections, and these are by no means exclusively self-regarding.

David Hume (1711–1776), a student and friend of Hutcheson, agrees that people can and do display genuine benevolence. Hume considers it absurd to assert with the Hobbesians that disinterested benevolence is impossible. As he observes, philosophers who reduce all human motivation to egoism often do so with the thought that simple explanations are preferable to complex ones, and that egoism is the simplest possible account of our motives. Yet, Hume argues that psychological egoism is far from a simple hypothesis. To the casual observer, a good deal of human action appears disinterested, and in denying the appearance of things, psychological egoism is forced to postulate a hidden egoistic mechanism lurking behind surface benevolence. But why not take things at face value? As Hume mocks, we might as well postulate that a wagon moves by the operation of minute wheels and springs as attempt to explain every apparently benevolent action in terms of hidden egoistic impulses.

That said, Hume is ambivalent about how far-reaching our benevolent instincts go. In his discussion of justice, he suggests that selfishness, which leads to competition for scarce resources, would force the breakdown of society if it weren't for the fact that selfishness itself leads us to see the advantage of just institutions. Justice could never be supported by benevolence, which is incapable of regulating our love of gain. Among friends and family our disinterested affections ensure sharing and sacrifice, but in the wider society they lose their strength.

Though he denies that individuals have direct concern for the happiness of mankind, Hume finds our benevolent impulses strong enough to concern us with strangers' good when our own interests are not at stake. Other things being equal, we would never inflict harm on another—for instance, tread on another's "gouty toes"—when we could just as easily avoid doing so, and we would approve disinterestedly of one moral system over another if we judged the one to be more favorable to the general interest.

Our ultimate sanction for obeying morality is not disinterest, though, but a regard to personal happiness. And Hume believes it takes little argument to show that a person will be better-off practicing the various personal and social virtues than their corresponding vices. Who needs elaborate demonstration to be convinced that he will ultimately be happier by, say, practicing temperance and avoiding excessive pleasure? Similarly, the benefits to the self attendant upon humanity and kindness — peace of mind and perception of our own integrity — far exceed those attained through the immoral treatment of others. This may not be evident to everyone, says Hume, but all those of an "ingenuous" nature cannot fail to see that it is so.

The movement away from psychological egoism continues with Adam Smith (1723–1790), who, though best known today for his work in political economy, spent a large part of his academic career as a professor of moral philosophy. Smith based his ethics on the twin pillars of sympathy and self-command. The former he viewed as the affection by means of which men become able to identify disinterestedly with the feelings of others. Sympathy operates not merely by allowing us to imagine what we should feel like if another's circumstances were to befall us, but by allowing us to imaginatively place ourselves in his situation and come to feel his pain. It is thus in no sense a "selfish" principle. Indeed, sympathy can lead to self-hatred by enabling us to experience the ill will harbored towards us by those we have offended or wronged.

The primary function of self-command, in contrast — an ideal which Smith borrows from Stoicism — is to regulate our passions and help us maintain our dignity. Self-command promotes self-love by providing us with a difficult moral challenge — that of conquering our "natural sensibility" — which nature rewards with self-approbation.

Both sympathy and self-command issue from a common principle, the "impartial spectator." The spectator is the judge within our breast that enables us to view both our own interests and those of others from the third-person point of view. We tend naturally to over-emphasize the importance of our own concerns, and to de-emphasize those of others, but the spectator enables us to place both concerns in their proper perspective, and so generates the appropriate affections with respect to each.

Nonetheless, self-interest remains for Smith a central motive in human nature. Self-concern, for instance, is cited as a major impetus to virtue. Following Hume, Smith finds that people are most frequently moved to act morally out of respect for the dignity of their own characters and from dread of inward disgrace. Smith devotes a good deal of attention to the phenomenon of remorse, explaining how it makes wrong-doing unprofitable solely from the self-regarding standpoint. Self-interest is also cited by Smith as the engine which drives the marketplace. We do not approach our fellow businessmen with appeals to their sympathy, but, rather, to their self-love. We must convince our trading-partners that a particular deal is to *their* advantage; it does no good to cite its benefit to ourselves.

In comparing Smith's remarks on the impartial spectator and on the marketplace, one begins to suspect that he is of two minds about self-interest—a tension referred to in the secondary literature as "Das Adam Smith problem." The spectator's stance is lauded for the way it raises us above narrow self-preference, and enables us to perceive our own concerns disinterestedly. Smith goes so far as to describe the restraining of selfishness and flowering of benevolence as the "perfection of human nature." However, Smith condemns those who neglect their own interests, and he seems to follow Mandeville in assuming that a society which operates on the principle of self-interest will flourish. In Smith's view, this is because when individuals pursue their own good, they tend inadvertently to promote the public interest. In his memorable phrase, it is as though an "invisible hand" enters the scene and directs self-interested endeavors toward the common good.

The final figure we consider from the Early Modern Era is Immanuel Kant (1724–1804), who sharpens the long-standing dichotomy between self-interest and morality. Kant grants that happiness—on his definition, the summation of all our inclinations—is a necessary end for all rational beings. Yet, although it is sought by all, happiness is such a vague and indefinite concept that individuals can neither state consistently what their happiness consists in, nor, to the extent they can form a coherent conception of it, successfully employ reason toward its attainment. The best that can be done in the realm of happiness is to follow the dictates of instinct.

Seeing how ill-equipped Reason is to secure Happiness, and assuming that nature suits each faculty to an appropriate purpose, Reason must have some alternative function in our lives, and this, Kant ascertains, is to guide moral action. Moral, unlike merely prudential, actions, are undertaken not in order to achieve this or that subjective end, but for the sake of the rational principle they embody. Reason establishes in us the only faculty capable of enabling us to override inclination and act strictly for principle's—or duty's—sake, and this is the good will.

Because of the omnipresence of inclination, Kant believes it impossible to determine on empirical grounds whether anyone ever actually succeeds in acting wholly from duty. This is certainly the case where duty and inclination prompt us to the same action, but it even obtains where an individual acts on principle despite the opposition of his inclinations. "We come everywhere upon the dear self, which is always turning up. . . ." The best we can do is *try* to make duty the determining ground of the will, even though we shall never know the extent of our success.

Among our moral duties Kant includes various duties toward the self, though he distinguishes these sharply from self-love. Self-love is defined as the inclination to be satisfied with one's perfections—to, as it were, morally pat oneself on the back. Kant finds self-love detestable inasmuch as it leads us to twist the moral law to our own advantage, and make exceptions for ourselves. Our concern should not be with loving ourselves in this sense, but with acting in such a way as to merit self-esteem. We esteem something to the extent it has intrinsic worth, and we ourselves have intrinsic worth to the extent that we obey the dictates of our rational nature and perform our duty.

Our primary duty to the self, then, is fundamentally negative: it is to conscientiously restrict the pursuit of our natural inclinations and interests in the name of morality and human dignity. Of course, the motive in this, as in all moral action, must be duty; to the extent we attempt to esteem ourselves from inclination, we engage in a self-defeating—indeed, in a self-contradictory—enterprise.

With Kant ends what we are here loosely calling the "early modern" era, a period of inquiry which is truly remarkable for the array of viewpoints its offers on self-interest. Here we find everything espoused from psychological egoism to its contrary, from the equation of virtue with morality to the statement of their utter opposition. The arguments of the classical and medieval philosophers are taken up, but new questions are raised and the overall debate is advanced in such significant ways that this era's ideas about self-interest continue to be more closely studied than those of any other.

THOMAS HOBBES
(1588–1679)

Happiness is the satisfaction of desire [143]

But whatsoever is the object of any man's Appetite or Desire; that is it, which he for his part calleth *Good*: And the object of his Hate, and Aversion, *Evil*; And of his Contempt, *Vile*, and *Inconsiderable*. For these words of Good, Evil, and Contemptible, are ever used with relation to the person that useth them: There being nothing simply and absolutely so; . . .

Continual success in obtaining those things which a man from time to time desireth, that is to say, continual prospering, is that men call FELICITY; I mean the Felicity of this life. For there is no such thing as perpetual Tranquillity of mind, while we live here; because Life itself is but Motion, and can never be without Desire, nor without Fear, no more than without Sense.

[T]he Felicity of this life, consisteth not in the repose of a mind satisfied. For there is no such *Finis ultimus*, (utmost Aim,) nor *Summum Bonum*, (greatest Good,) as is spoken of in the Books of the old Moral Philosophers. Nor can a man any more live, whose Desires are at an end, than he, whose Senses and Imaginations are at a stand. Felicity is a continual progress of the desire, from one object to another; the attaining of the former, being still but the way to the latter. The cause whereof is, That the object of man's desire, is not to enjoy once only, and for one instant of time; but to assure for ever, the way of his future desire. And therefore the voluntary actions and inclinations of all men, tend, not only to the procuring, but also to the assuring of a contented life; and differ only in the way: which ariseth partly from the diversity of passions, in diverse men; and partly from the difference of the knowledge, or opinion each one has of the causes, which produce the effect desired.

So that in the first place, I put for a general inclination of all mankind, a perpetual and restless desire of Power after power, that ceaseth only in Death. And the cause of this, is not always that a man hopes for a more intensive delight, than he has already attained to; or that he cannot be content with a moderate power: but because he cannot assure the power and means to live well, which he hath present, without the acquisition of more.

The pursuit of self-interest places human beings in a condition of universal war [144]

NATURE hath made men so equal, in the faculties of body, and mind; as that though there be found one man sometimes manifestly stronger in body, or of quicker mind then another; yet when all is reckoned together, the difference between man, and man, is not so considerable, as that one man can thereupon claim to himself any benefit, to which another may not pretend, as well as he. For as to the strength of body, the weakest has strength enough to kill the strongest, either by secret machination, or by confederacy with others, that are in the same danger with himself. . . .

From this equality of ability, ariseth equality of hope in the attaining of our Ends. And therefore if any two men desire the same thing, which nevertheless they cannot both enjoy, they become enemies; and in the way to their End, (which is principally their own conservation, and sometimes their delectation only,) endeavor to destroy, or subdue one another. And from hence it comes to pass, that where an Invader hath no more to Fear, than another man's single power; if one plant, sow, build, or possess a convenient Seat, others may probably be expected to come prepared with forces united, to dispossess, and deprive him, not only of the fruit of his labor, but also of his life, or liberty. And the Invader again is in the like danger of another.

And from this diffidence of one another, there is no way for any man to secure himself, so reasonable, as Anticipation; that is, by force, or wiles, to master the persons of all men he can, so long, till he see no other power great enough to endanger him: And this is no more than his own conservation requireth, and is generally allowed. Also because there be some, that taking pleasure in contemplating their own power in the acts of conquest, which they pursue farther than their security requires; if others, that otherwise would be glad to be at ease within modest bounds, should not by invasion increase their power, they would not be able, long time, by standing only on their defence, to subsist. And by consequence, such augmentation of dominion over men, being necessary to a man's conservation, it ought to be allowed him.

Again, men have no pleasure, (but on the contrary a great deal of grief) in keeping company, where there is no power able to over-awe them all. For every man looketh that his companion should value him, at the same rate he sets upon himself: And upon all signs of contempt, or undervaluing, naturally endeavors, as far as he dares (which amongst them that have no common power, to keep them in quiet, is far enough to make them destroy each other,) to extort a greater value from his contemners, by dommage; and from others, by the example.

So that in the nature of man, we find three principal causes of quarrel. First, Competition; Secondly, Diffidence; Thirdly, Glory.

The first, maketh men invade for Gain; the second, for Safety; and the third, for Reputation. The first use Violence, to make themselves Masters of other men's persons, wives, children, and cattle; the second, to defend them; the third, for trifles, as a word, a smile, a different opinion, and any other sign of undervalue, either direct in their Persons, or by reflection in their Kindred, their Friends, their Nation, their Profession, or their Name.

Hereby it is manifest, that during the time men live without a common Power to keep them all in awe, they are in that condition which is called War; and such a war, as is of every man, against every man. For WAR, consisteth not in Battle only, or the act of fighting; but in a tract of time wherein the Will to contend by Battle is sufficiently known: and therefore the notion of TIME, is to be considered in the nature of War; as it is in the nature of Weather. For as the nature of Foul weather, lieth not in a shower or two of rain but in an inclination thereto of many days together: So the nature of War, consisteth not in actual fighting; but in the known disposition thereto, during all the time there is no assurance to the contrary. All other time is PEACE.

Whatsoever therefore is consequent to a time of War, where every man is Enemy to every man; the same is consequent to the time, wherein men live without other security, than what their own strength, and their own invention shall furnish them withal. In such condition, there is no place for Industry; because the fruit thereof is uncertain: and consequently no Culture of the Earth; no Navigation, nor use of the commodities that may be imported by Sea; no commodious Building; no Instruments of moving, and removing such things as require much force; no Knowledge of the face of the Earth; no account of Time; no Arts; no Letters; no Society; and which is worst of all, continual fear, and danger of violent death; And the life of man, solitary, poor, nasty, brutish, and short.

It may seem strange to some man, that has not well weighed these things; that Nature should thus dissociate, and render men apt to invade, and destroy one another: and he may therefore, not trusting to this Inference, made from the Passions, desire perhaps to have the same confirmed by Experience. Let him therefore consider with himself, when taking a journey, he arms himself, and seeks to go well accompanied; when going to sleep, he locks his doors; when even in his house he locks his chests; and this when he knows there be Laws, and public Officers, armed, to revenge all injuries shall be done him; what opinion he has of his fellow subjects, when he rides armed; of his fellow Citizens, when he locks his doors; and of his children, and servants, when he locks his chests. Does he not there as much accuse mankind by his actions, as I do by my words? But neither of us accuse man's nature in it. The Desires, and other Passions of man, are in themselves no Sin. No more are the Actions, that proceed from those Passions, till they know a Law that forbids them: which till Laws be made they cannot know: nor can any Law be made, till they have agreed upon the Person that shall make it.

Human beings protect their self-interest renouncing certain rights [145]

THE RIGHT OF NATURE, which Writers commonly call *Jus Naturale,* is the Liberty each man hath, to use his own power, as he will himself, for the preservation of his own Nature, that is to say, of his own Life; and consequently, of doing any thing which in his own Judgment, and Reason, he shall conceive to be the aptest means thereunto.

By LIBERTY, is understood, according to the proper signification of the word, the absence of external Impediments: which Impediments, may oft take away part of a man's power to do what he would; but cannot hinder him from using the power left him, according as his judgment, and reason shall dictate to him.

A LAW OF NATURE, (*Lex Naturalis,*) is a Precept, or general Rule, found out by Reason, by which a man is forbidden to do, that, which is destructive of his life, or taketh away the means of preserving the same; and to omit, that, by which he thinketh it may be best preserved. For though they that speak of this subject, used to confound *Jus,* and *Lex, Right* and *Law;* yet they ought to be distinguished; because RIGHT, consisteth in liberty to do, or to forbear; Whereas LAW, determineth, and bindeth to one of them: so that Law, and Right differ as much, as Obligation, and Liberty; which in one and the same matter are inconsistent.

And because the condition of Man, (as hath been declared in the precedent Chapter) is a condition of War of every one against every one; in which case every one is governed by his own Reason; and there is nothing he can make use of, that may not be a help unto him, in preserving his life against his enemies; It followeth, that in such a condition, every man has a Right to every thing; even to one another's body. And therefore, as long as this natural Right of every man to every thing endureth, there can be no security to any man, (how strong or wise soever he be) of living out the time, which Nature ordinarily alloweth men to live. And consequently it is a precept, or general rule of Reason, *That every man, ought to endeavor Peace, as far as he has hope of obtaining it; and when he cannot obtain it, that he may seek, and use, all helps, and advantages of War.* The first branch of which Rule, containeth the first, and Fundamental Law of Nature; which is, *to seek Peace, and follow it.* The Second, the sum of the Right of Nature; which is, *By all means we can, to defend our selves.*

From this Fundamental Law of Nature, by which men are commanded to endeavor Peace, is derived this second Law; *That a man be willing, when others are so too, as far-forth, as for Peace, and defense of himself he shall think it necessary, to lay down this right to all things; and be contented with so much liberty against other men, as he would allow other men against himself.* For as long as every man holdeth this Right, of doing any thing he liketh; so long are all men in the condition of War. But if other men will not lay down their Right, as well as he, then there is no Reason for any one, to divest himself of his: For that were to expose himself to Prey, (which no man is bound to) rather than to dispose himself to Peace. This is that Law of the Gospel, *Whatsoever you require that others should do to you, that do ye to them.* And that Law of all men, *Quod tibi fieri non vis, alteri ne feceris.*

Violating the social contract is contrary to self-interest [146]

FROM that law of Nature, by which we are obliged to transfer to another, such Rights, as being retained, hinder the peace of Mankind, there followeth a Third; which is this, *That men perform their Covenants made:* without which, Covenants are in vain, and but Empty words; and the Right of all men to all things remaining, we are still in the condition of War.

And in this law of Nature, consisteth the Fountain and Original of JUSTICE. For where no Covenant hath preceded, there hath no Right been transferred, and every man has right to every thing; and consequently, no action can be Unjust. But when a Covenant is made, then to break it is *Unjust:* And the definition of INJUSTICE, is no other than *the not Performance of Covenant.* And whatsoever is not Unjust, is *Just.*

But because Covenants of mutual trust, where there is a fear of not performance on either part, (as hath been said in the former Chapter,) are invalid, though the Original of Justice be the making of Covenants; yet Injustice actually there can be none, till the cause of such fear be taken away; which while men are in the natural condition of War, cannot be done. Therefore before the names of Just, and Unjust can have place, there must be some coercive Power, to compel men equally to the performance of their Covenants, by the terror of some punishment, greater than the benefit they expect by the breach of their Covenant; and to make good that Propriety, which by mutual Contract men acquire, in recompense of the universal Right they abandon: and such power there is none before the erection of a Commonwealth. And this is also to be gathered out of the ordinary definition of Justice in the Schools: For they say, that *Justice is the constant Will of giving to every man his own.* And therefore where there is no *Own,* that is, no Propriety, there is no Injustice; and where there is no coercive Power erected, that is, where there is no Commonwealth, there is no Propriety; all men having Right to all things: Therefore where there is no Commonwealth, there nothing is Unjust. So that the nature of Justice, consisteth in keeping of valid Covenants: but the Validity of Covenants begins not but with the Constitution of a Civil Power, sufficient to compel men to keep them: And then it is also that Propriety begins.

The Fool hath said in his heart, there is no such thing as justice; and sometimes also with his tongue seriously alleging, that every man's conservation and contentment, being committed to his own care, there could be no reason, why every man might not do what he thought conduced thereunto: and therefore also to make, or not make; keep, or not keep Covenants, was not against Reason, when it conduced to ones benefit. He does not therein deny that there be Covenants; and that they are sometimes broken, sometimes kept; and that such breach of them may be called Injustice, and the observance of them Justice: but he questioneth, whether Injustice, taking away the fear of God, (for the same Fool hath said in his heart there is no God,) may not sometimes stand with that Reason, which dictateth to every man his own good; and particularly then, when it conduceth to such a benefit, as shall put a man in a condition, to neglect not only the dispraise, and revilings, but also the power of other men. The Kingdom of God is gotten by violence: but what if it could be gotten by unjust violence? Were it against Reason so to get it, when it is Impossible to receive hurt by it? And if it be not against Reason, it is not against Justice: or else Justice is not to be approved for good. From such reasoning as this, Successful wickedness hath obtained the name of Virtue: and some that in all other things have disallowed the violation of Faith yet have allowed it, when it is for the getting of a Kingdom. And the Heathen that believed that *Saturn* was deposed by his son *Jupiter*, believed nevertheless the same *Jupiter* to be the avenger of Injustice: Somewhat like to a piece of Law in *Cokes* Commentaries on *Litleton*; where he says, If the right Heir of the Crown be attainted of Treason; yet the Crown shall descend to him, and *eo instante* the Attainder be void: From which instances a man will be very prone to infer; that when the Heir apparent of a Kingdom, shall kill him that is in possession, though his father; you may call it Injustice, or by what other name you will; yet it can never be against Reason, seeing all the voluntary actions of men tend to the benefit of themselves; and those actions are most Reasonable, that conduce most to their ends. This specious reasoning is nevertheless false.

For the question is not of promises mutual, where there is no security of performance on either side; as when there is no Civil Power erected over the parties promising; for such promises are no Covenants: But either where one of the parties has performed already; or where there is a Power to make him perform; there is the question whether it be against reason, that is, against the benefit of the other to perform, or not. And I say it is not against reason. For the manifestation whereof, we are to consider; First, that when a man doth a thing which notwithstanding any thing can be foreseen and reckoned on, tendeth to his own destruction, howsoever some accident which he could not expect, arriving may turn it to his benefit; yet such events do not make it reasonably or wisely done. Secondly, that in a condition of War, wherein every man to every man, for want of a common Power to keep them all in awe, is an Enemy, there is no man can hope by his own strength, or wit, to defend himself from destruction, without the help of Confederates; where every one expects the same defense by the Confederation, that any one else does: and therefore he which declares he thinks it reason to deceive those that help him, can in reason expect no other means of safety than what can be had from his own single Power. He therefore that breaketh his Covenant, and consequently declareth that he thinks he may with reason do so, cannot be received into any Society, that unite themselves for Peace and Defense, but by the error of them that receive him, nor when he is received, be retained in it, without seeing the danger of their error; which errors a man cannot reasonably reckon upon as the means of his security: and therefore if he be left, or cast out of Society, he perisheth; and if he live in Society, it is by the errors of other men, which he could not foresee, nor reckon upon; and consequently against the reason of his preservation; and so, as all men that contribute not to his destruction, forbear him only out of ignorance of what is good for themselves.

Baruch Spinoza was born in Amsterdam, Holland, and at age twenty-four was excommunicated from the Dutch Jewish community for his unorthodox views. By vocation he was a lens-grinder, but in his quiet hours developed one of the most profound philosophical systems in Western thought. The ethical component of that system is grounded in the concept of conatus — *the drive for self-preservation exhibited by every animate thing.*

BARUCH SPINOZA
(1632–1677)

Conatus *as the foundation of self-regard* [147]

III, PROPOSITION 6

Each thing, in so far as it is in itself, endeavors to persist in its own being.

Proof

Particular things are modes whereby the attributes of God are expressed in a definite and determinate way (Cor.Pr.25, I[148]), that is (Pr.34, I), they are things which express in a definite and determinate way the power of God whereby he is and acts, and no thing can have in itself anything by which it can be destroyed, that is, which can annul its existence (Pr.4, III). On the contrary, it opposes everything that can annul its existence (preceding Pr.); and thus, as far as it can and as far as it is in itself, it endeavors to persist in its own being.

93

III, PROPOSITION 7

The conatus [149] *with which each thing endeavors to persist in its own being is nothing*
but the actual essence of the thing itself.

Proof

From the given essence of a thing certain things necessarily follow (Pr.36, I), nor do
things effect anything other than that which necessarily follows from their determinate
nature (Pr.29, I). Therefore, the power of any thing, or the conatus with which it acts
or endeavors to act, alone or in conjunction with other things, that is (Pr.6,III), the
power or conatus by which it endeavors to persist in is own being, is nothing but the
given, or actual, essence of the thing.

III, PROPOSITION

The mind, both in so far as it has clear and distinct ideas and in so far as it has confused ideas,
endeavors to persist in its own being over an indefinite period of time, and is conscious of this conatus.

Proof

The essence of the mind is constituted by adequate and inadequate ideas [150] (as we
showed in Pr.3,III), and so (Pr.7, III) it endeavors to persist in its own being in so far as
it has both these kinds of ideas, and does so (Pr.8, III) over an indefinite period of
time. Now since the mind (Pr.23, II) is necessarily conscious of itself through the
ideas of the affections of the body, therefore the mind is conscious of its conatus.

Scholium

When this conatus is related to the mind alone, it is called Will (*voluntas*); when it is
related to mind and body together, it is called Appetite (*appetitus*), which is therefore
nothing else but man's essence, from the nature of which there necessarily follow
those things that tend to his preservation, and which man is thus determined to perform. Further, there is no difference between appetite and Desire (*cupiditas*) except
that desire is usually related to men in so far as they are conscious of their appetite.
Therefore it can be defined as follows: desire is appetite accompanied by the consciousness thereof.

It is clear from the above considerations that we do not endeavor, will, seek after or
desire because we judge a thing to be good. On the contrary, we judge a thing to be
good because we endeavor, will, seek after and desire it.

III, PROPOSITION 30

If anyone has done something which he imagines affects others with pleasure, he will be affected with
pleasure accompanied by the idea of himself as cause; that is, he will regard himself with pleasure.

If, on the other hand, he imagines he has done something which affects others with pain,
he will regard himself with pain.

Proof

He who imagines he affects others with pleasure or pain will by that very fact be affected with pleasure or pain (Pr.27, III). Now since man (Prs. 19 and 23, II) is conscious of himself through the affections by which he is determined to act, he who has done something which he thinks affects others with pleasure will be affected with pleasure along with the consciousness of himself as cause; that is, he will regard himself with pleasure. The contrary likewise follows.

PROPOSITION 53
When the mind regards its own self and its power of activity, it feels pleasure, and the more
so the more distinctly it imagines itself and its power of activity.

Proof

Man knows himself only through the affections of his body and their ideas (Prs. 19 and 23, II). When therefore it happens that the mind can regard its own self, by that very fact it is assumed to pass to a state of greater perfection, that is, (Sch.Pr. 11, III), to be affected with pleasure, and the more so the more distinctly it is able to imagine itself and its power of activity.

Corollary

The more a man imagines he is praised by others, the more this pleasure is fostered. For the more he thinks he is praised by others, the more he thinks that others are affected with pleasure by him, and this accompanied by the idea of himself (Sch.Pr.29, III). So (Pr.27, III) he is affected with greater pleasure, accompanied by the idea of himself.

III, PROPOSITION 54
The mind endeavors to think only of the things that affirm its power of activity.

Proof

The mind's conatus, or power, is the very essence of the mind (Pr.7, III). But the essence of the mind affirms only what the mind is and can do (as is self-evident), and not what the mind is not and cannot do. So the mind endeavors to think only of what affirms, or posits, its power of activity.

III, PROPOSITION 55

When the mind thinks of its own impotence, by that very fact it feels pain

Proof

The essence of the mind affirms only what the mind is and can do; that is, it is of the nature of the mind to think only of those things that affirm its power of activity (preceding Pr.). Therefore, when we say that the mind, in regarding itself, thinks of its own impotence, we are simply saying that while the mind is endeavoring to think of something that affirms its power of activity, this conatus is checked; that is, it feels pain (Sch.Pr. II, III).

Corollary

This pain is fostered all the more if one thinks he is blamed by others. The proof is on the same lines as Cor.Pr. 53, III.

Scholium

This pain, accompanied by the idea of our own impotence, is called Humility (*humilitas*). The pleasure that arises from regarding ourselves is called Self-love (*philautia*) or Self-contentment (*acquiescentia in se ipso*). And since this pleasure is repeated whenever a man regards his own capabilities, that is, his power of activity, the result is again that everyone is eager to tell of his exploits and to boast of his strength both of body and mind, and for this reason men bore one another. From this it again follows that men are by nature envious (see Sch.Pr.24, and Sch.Pr.32, III), that is, they rejoice at the weakness of their fellows and are pained at their accomplishments. For whenever a man imagines his own actions he is affected with pleasure (Pr.53, III), and the more so as his actions express greater perfection and he imagines them more distinctly; that is (by what was said in Sch.I, Pr.40, II), the more he can distinguish them from the actions of others and regard them as something special. Therefore everybody will most enjoy regarding himself when he regards in himself something that he denies of others. But if what he affirms of himself belongs to the universal idea of man or animal, he will derive no such great joy therefrom, and he will on the other hand feel pain if he thinks of his actions as inferior, compared with the actions of others. This pain (Pr.28, III) he will endeavor to remove by wrongly interpreting the actions of his fellows or by embellishing his own as much as he can. It is therefore clear that men are prone to hatred and envy, and this is accentuated by their upbringing. . . .

Virtue, community, and advantage [151]

IV, SCHOLIUM, PROPOSITION 18

. . . Since reason demands nothing contrary to nature, it therefore demands that every man should love himself, should seek his own advantage (I mean his real advantage), should aim at whatever really leads a man towards greater perfection, and, to sum it all up, that each man, as far as in him lies, should endeavor to preserve his own being. This is as necessarily true as that the whole is greater than its parts (Pr.4, III).

Again, since virtue (Def.8, IV) is nothing other than to act from the laws of one's own nature, and since nobody endeavors to preserve his own being (Pr.7, III) except from the laws of his own nature, it follows firstly that the basis of virtue is the very conatus to preserve one's own being, and that happiness consists in a man's being able to preserve his own being. Secondly, it follows that virtue should be sought for its own sake, and that there is nothing preferable to it or more to our advantage, for the sake of which it should be sought. Thirdly, it follows that those who commit suicide are of weak spirit and are completely overcome by external causes opposed to their own nature. Further, it follows from Post.4, II that we can never bring it about that we should need nothing outside ourselves to preserve our own being and that we should live a life quite unrelated to things outside ourselves. Besides, if we consider the mind, surely our intellect would be less perfect if the mind were in solitude and understood nothing beyond itself. Therefore there are many things outside ourselves which are advantageous to us and ought therefore to be sought. Of these none more excellent can be discovered than those which are in complete harmony with our own nature. For example, if two individuals of completely the same nature are combined, they compose an individual twice as powerful as each one singly.

Therefore nothing is more advantageous to man than man. Men, I repeat, can wish for nothing more excellent for preserving their own being than that they should all be in such harmony in all respects that their minds and bodies should compose, as it were, one mind and one body, and that all together should endeavor as best they can to preserve their own being, and that all together they should aim at the common advantage of all. From this it follows that men who are governed by reason, that is, men who aim at their own advantage under the guidance of reason, seek nothing for themselves that they would not desire for the rest of mankind; and so are just, faithful, and honorable.

These are the dictates of reason, which I have decided to set forth in brief at this point before embarking upon their more detailed demonstration. This I have done so that I may, if possible, gain the attention of those who believe that the principle that every man is bound to seek his own advantage is the basis, not of virtue or piety, but of impiety. Now that I have briefly shown that the contrary is the case, I proceed to its proof, using the same method as hitherto.

PROPOSITION 20

The more every man endeavors and is able to seek his own advantage, that is, to preserve his own being, the more he is endowed with virtue. On the other hand, in so far as he neglects to preserve what is to his advantage, that is, his own being, to that extent he is weak.

Proof

Virtue is human power, which is defined solely by man's essence (Def.8, IV); that is, it is defined solely by the conatus whereby man endeavors to persist in his own being (Pr.7, III). Therefore the more every man endeavors and is able to preserve his own being, the more he is endowed with virtue, and consequently (Prs.4 and 6, III) in so far as he neglects to preserve his own being, to that extent he is weak.

Scholium

Therefore nobody, unless he is overcome by external causes contrary to his own nature, neglects to seek his own advantage, that is, to preserve his own being. Nobody, I repeat, refuses food or kills himself from the necessity of his own nature, but from the constraint of external causes. This can take place in many ways. A man kills himself when he is compelled by another who twists the hand in which he happens to hold a sword and makes him turn the blade against his heart; or when, in obedience to a tyrant's command, he, like Seneca, is compelled to open his veins, that is, he chooses a lesser evil to avoid a greater. Or it may come about when unobservable external causes condition a man's imagination and affect his body in such a way that the latter assumes a different nature contrary to the previously existing one, a nature whereof there can be no idea in mind (Pr.10, III). But that a man from the necessity of his own nature should endeavor to cease to exist or to be changed into another form, is as impossible as that something should come from nothing, as anyone can see with a little thought.

IV, PROPOSITION 22

No virtue can be conceived as prior to this one, namely, the conatus to preserve oneself.

Proof

The conatus to preserve itself is the very essence of a thing (Pr.7, III). Thus if any virtue could be conceived as prior to this one—namely this conatus—then (Def.8. IV) the essence of a thing would be conceived as prior to itself, which is obviously absurd. Therefore no virtue . . . etc.

Corollary

The conatus to preserve oneself is the primary and sole basis of virtue. For no other principle can be conceived as prior to this one (preceding Pr.), and no virtue can be conceived independently (Pr.21, IV).

IV, PROPOSITION 24

To act in absolute conformity with virtue is nothing else in us but to act, to live, to preserve one's own being (these three mean the same) under the guidance of reason, on the basis of seeking one's own advantage.

Proof

To act in absolute conformity with virtue is nothing else (Def.8, IV) but to act according to the laws of one's own nature. But we are active only in so far as we understand (Pr.3, III). Therefore to act from virtue is nothing else in us but to act, to live, and to preserve one's own being under the guidance of reason, on the basis (Cor.Pr.22, IV) of seeking one's own advantage.

IV, PROPOSITION 26

Whatever we endeavor according to reason is nothing else but to understand; and the mind, in so far as it exercises reason, judges nothing else to be to its advantage except what conduces to understanding.

Proof

The conatus to preserve itself is nothing but the essence of a thing (Pr.7, III), which, in so far as it exists as such, is conceived as having a force to persist in existing (Pr.6, III) and to do those things that necessarily follow from its given nature (see Definition of Appetite in Sch Pr.9, III). But the essence of reason is nothing other than our mind in so far as it clearly and distinctly understands (see its Definition in Sch.2,Pr.40, II). Therefore (Pr.40, II) whatever we endeavor according to reason is nothing else but to endeavor to understand. Again, since this conatus of the mind wherewith the mind, in so far as it exercises reason, endeavors to preserve its own being is nothing else but a conatus to understand (by the first part of this proof), this conatus to understand (Cor.Pr.22, IV) is therefore the primary and only basis of virtue, and it is not for some further purpose that we endeavor to understand things (Pr.25, IV). On the contrary, the mind, in so far as it exercises reason, cannot conceive any good for itself except what is conducive to understanding.

PROPOSITION 28

The mind's highest good is the knowledge of God, and the mind's highest virtue is to know God.

Proof

The highest object that the mind can understand is God, that is (Def.6, I), an absolutely infinite being, and one without whom (Pr.15, I) nothing can be or be conceived. Thus (Prs.26 and 27, IV) the mind's utmost advantage or (Def.1, IV) its highest good is knowledge of God. Again, the mind is active only to the extent that it understands (Prs.1 and 3, III), and to that extent only (Pr.23, IV) can it be said without qualification to act from virtue. So the absolute virtue of the mind is to understand. But the highest thing the mind can understand is God (as we have just proved). Therefore the highest virtue of the mind is to understand or to know God.

IV, PROPOSITION 31

In so far as a thing is in agreement with our nature, to that extent it is necessarily good.

Proof

In so far as a thing is in agreement with our nature, it cannot be bad (preceding Pr.). Therefore it is necessarily good or indifferent. If we make the latter assumption, namely, that it is neither good nor bad, then nothing will follow from its nature (Ax.3, IV) which serves to preserve our nature; that is, (by hypotheses) which serves to preserve the nature of the thing itself. But this is absurd (Pr.6, III). Therefore, in so far as it is in agreement with our nature, it is necessarily good.

Corollary

Hence it follows that the more a thing is in agreement with our nature, the more advantageous it is to us, that is, the more it is good; and, conversely, the more advantageous a thing is to us, to that extent it is in more agreement with our nature. For in so far as it is not in agreement with our nature, it is necessarily either different from our nature or contrary to it. If it is different (Pr.29, IV), it can be neither good nor bad but if contrary, it will therefore be contrary also to that which is in agreement with our nature, that is (preceding Pr.), contrary to our good; that is, it will be evil. So nothing can be good save in so far as it is in agreement with our nature. So the more a thing is in agreement with our nature, the more advantageous it is to us, and vice versa.

IV, PROPOSITION 35

In so far as men live under the guidance of reason, to that extent only
do they always necessarily agree in nature.

Proof

In so far as men are assailed by passive emotions, they can be different in nature (Pr.33, IV) and contrary to one another (preceding Pr.). But we say that men are active only in so far as they live under the guidance of reason (Pr.3, III). Thus whatever follows from human nature, in so far as it is defined by reason, must be understood (Def.2, III) through human nature alone as its proximate cause. But since everyone, in accordance with the laws of his own nature, aims at what he judges to be good and endeavors to remove what he judges to be evil (Pr.19, IV), and since furthermore what we judge from the dictates of reason to be good or evil is necessarily good or evil (Pr.41, II), it follows that in so far as men live under the guidance of reason, to that extent only do they necessarily do the things which are necessarily good for human nature and consequently for every single man; that is (Cor.Pr.31, IV), which agree with the nature of every single man. So men also are necessarily in agreement with one another in so far as they live under the guidance of reason.

Corollary 1

There is no individual thing in the universe more advantageous to man than a man who lives by the guidance of reason. For the most advantageous thing to man is that which agrees most closely with his nature (Cor.Pr.31, IV); that is (as is self-evident), man. But man acts absolutely according to the laws of his own nature when he lives under the guidance of reason (Def.2, III), and only to that extent is he always necessarily in agreement with the nature of another man (preceding Pr.). Therefore among individual things there is nothing more advantageous to man than a man who . . . etc.

Corollary 2

It is when every man is most devoted to seeking his own advantage that men are of most advantage to one another. For the more every man seeks his own advantage and endeavors to preserve himself, the more he is endowed with virtue (Pr.20, IV), or (and this is the same thing [Def.8, IV]) the greater the power with which he is endowed for acting according to the laws of his own nature; that is (Pr.3, III), for living by the guidance of reason. But it is when men live by the guidance of reason that they agree most in nature (preceding Pr.). Therefore (preceding Cor.) it is when each is most devoted to seeking his own advantage that men are of most advantage to one another.

Scholium

What we have just demonstrated is also confirmed by daily experience with so many convincing examples as to give rise to the common saying: "Man is a God to man." Yet it is rarely the case that men live by the guidance of reason; their condition is such that they are generally disposed to envy and mutual dislike. Nevertheless they find solitary life scarcely endurable, so that for most people the definition "man is a social animal" meets with strong approval. And the fact of the matter is that the social organization of man shows a balance of much more profit than loss. So let satirists deride as much as they like the doings of mankind, let theologians revile them, and let the "misanthropists" (*melancholici*) heap praise on the life of rude rusticity, despising men and admiring beasts. Men will still discover from experience that they can much more easily meet their needs by mutual help and can ward off ever-threatening perils only by joining forces, not to mention that it is a much more excellent thing and worthy of our knowledge to study the deeds of men than the deeds of beasts. . . .

PROPOSITION 37

The good which every man who pursues virtue aims at for himself he will also desire
for the rest of mankind, and all the more as he acquires a greater knowledge of God.

Proof

In so far as men live by the guidance of reason, they are most useful to man (Cor. 1,
Pr.35, IV), and so (Pr. 19, IV) by the guidance of reason we shall necessarily endeavor to
bring it about that men should live by the guidance of reason. But the good that every
man who lives according to the dictates of reason, that is (Pr.24, IV), who pursues
virtue, seeks for himself is to understand (Pr.26, IV). Therefore the good which every
man who pursues virtue seeks for himself he will also desire for the rest of mankind.
Again, desire, in so far as it is related to mind, is the very essence of mind (Def. of
Emotions 1). Now the essence of mind consists in knowledge (Pr.11, II) which involves
the knowledge of God (Pr.47, II), without which (Pr.15, I) it can neither be nor be conceived. So the more the essence of the mind involves knowledge of God, the greater
the desire with which he who pursues virtue desires for another the good which he
seeks for himself.

Another Proof

The good which a man seeks for himself, and loves, he will love with greater con-
stancy if he sees others loving the same thing (Pr.31, III). Thus (Cor.Pr.31, III) he will
endeavor that others should love the same thing. And because this good (preceding
Pr.) is common to all, and all can enjoy it, he will therefore endeavor (by the same reasoning) that all should enjoy it, and the more so (Pr.37, III) the more he enjoys this
good. . . .

Scholium 2

. . . Every man exists by the sovereign right of his nature, and consequently by the sovereign right of his nature every man does what follows from the necessity of his
nature. So it is by the sovereign right of his nature that every man judges what is good
and what is bad, and has regard for his own advantage according to his own way of
thinking (Prs.19 and 20, IV), and seeks revenge (Cor.2,Pr.40, III), and endeavors to preserve what he loves and to destroy what he hates (Pr.28, III). Now if men lived by the
guidance of reason, every man would possess this right of his (Cor.1,Pr.35, IV) without
any harm to another. But since men are subject to passive emotions (Cor.Pr.4, IV)
which far surpass the power or virtue of men (Pr.6, IV), they are therefore often pulled
in different directions (Pr.33, IV) and are contrary to one another (Pr.34, IV), while
needing each other's help (Sch.Pr.35, IV).

Therefore, in order that men may live in harmony and help one another, it is necessary for them to give up their natural right and to create a feeling of mutual con-

fidence that they will refrain from any action that may be harmful to another. The way to bring this about, (that men who are necessarily subject to passive emotions [Cor.Pr.4, IV] and are inconstant and variable [Pr.33, IV] should establish a mutual confidence and should trust one another) is obvious from Pr.7, IV and Pr.39, III. There it was demonstrated that no emotion can be checked except by a stronger emotion contrary to the emotion which is to be checked, and that every man refrains from inflicting injury through fear of greater injury. On these terms, then, society can be established, provided that it claims for itself the right that every man has of avenging himself and deciding what is good and what is evil; and furthermore if it has the power to prescribe common rules of behavior and to pass laws to enforce them, not by reason, which is incapable of checking the emotions (Sch.Pr.17, IV), but by threats.

Now such a society, strengthened by law and by the capacity to preserve itself, is called a State (*civitas*): and those who are protected by its rights are called Citizens (*cives*). From this it can readily be understood that in a state of nature there is nothing that is universally agreed upon as good or evil, since every man in a state of nature has regard only to his own advantage and decides what is good and what is bad according to his own way of thinking and only in so far as he has regard to his own advantage, and is not bound by any law to obey anyone but himself. Thus in a state of nature wrong-doing cannot be conceived, but it can be in a civil state where good and bad are decided by common agreement and everyone is bound to obey the state. Wrong-doing is therefore nothing other than disobedience, which is therefore punishable only by the sovereign right of the state, and obedience is held to be merit in a citizen because he is thereby deemed to deserve to enjoy the advantages of the state. . . .

IV, PROPOSITION 52

Self-contentment (acquiescentia in se ipso) *can arise from reason and only that self-contentment which arises from reason is the highest there can be.*

Proof

Self-contentment is the pleasure arising from a man's contemplation of himself and his power of activity (Def. of Emotions 25). Now man's true power of activity, or his virtue, is reason itself (Pr.3, III), which man regards clearly and distinctly (Prs. 40 and 43, II). Therefore self-contentment arises from reason. Again, in contemplating himself a man perceives clearly and distinctly, that is, adequately, only what follows from his power of activity (Def.2, III), that is (Pr.3, III) what follows from his power of understanding. So the greatest self-contentment there can be arises only from this contemplation.

Scholium

In fact self-contentment is the highest good we can hope for. For (as we proved in Pr.25, IV) nobody endeavors to preserve his own being for the sake of something else. And because this self-contentment is increasingly fostered and strengthened by praise (Cor.Pr.53, III), and on the other hand is increasingly disturbed by blame (Cor.Pr. 55, III) honor (*gloria*) is the greatest incentive, and we can scarcely endure life in disgrace.

IV, PROPOSITION 53

Humility is not a virtue; that is, it does not arise from reason.

Proof

Humility is the pain arising from a man's contemplation of his own weakness (Def. of Emotions 26). Now in so far as a man knows himself by true reason, to that extent he is assumed to understand his own essence, that is (Pr.7, III), his own power. Therefore if a man, in contemplating himself, perceives some weakness in himself, this does not arise from his understanding himself but (Pr.55, III) from the checking of his power of activity. Now if we suppose that a man conceives his own weakness from understanding something more powerful than himself, by the knowledge of which he measures his own power of activity, we are conceiving only that the man understands himself distinctly; that is (Pr.26, IV), that his power of activity is assisted. Therefore the humility or the pain, that arises from a man's contemplation of his own weakness does not arise from true contemplation or reason, and is not a virtue but a passive emotion.

BERNARD MANDEVILLE
(c. 1670—1733)

How private vice promotes public benefit [152]

The Grumbling Hive: or, Knaves turn'd Honest

    A Spacious Hive well stocked with Bees,
That liv'd in Luxury and Ease;
And yet as fam'd for Laws and Arms,
As yielding large and early Swarms;
Was counted the great Nursery
Of Sciences and Industry.
No Bees had better Government,
More Fickleness, or less Content:
They were not Slaves to Tyranny,
Nor rul'd by wild Democracy;
But Kings, that could not wrong, because
Their Power was circumscrib'd by Laws.

THESE Insects liv'd like Men, and all
Our Actions they perform'd in small:
They did whatever's done in Town,
And what belongs to Sword or Gown:
Tho' th' Artful Works, by nimble Slight
Of minute Limbs, 'scap'd Human Sight;
Yet we've no Engines, Laborers,
Ships, Castles, Arms, Artificers,
Craft, Science, Shop, or Instrument,
But they had an Equivalent:
Which, since their Language is unknown,
Must be call'd, as we do our own.
As grant, that among other Things,
They wanted Dice, yet they had Kings;
And those had Guards; from whence we may
Justly conclude, they had some Play;
Unless a Regiment be shewn
Of Soldiers, that make use of none.

VAST Numbers throng'd the fruitful Hive;
Yet those vast Numbers made 'em thrive;
Millions endeavoring to supply
Each other's Lust and Vanity;
While other Millions were employ'd,
To see their Handy-works destroy'd;
They furnish'd half the Universe;
Yet had more Work than Laborers.
Some with vast Stocks, and little Pains,
Jump'd into Business of great Gains;
And some were damn'd to Scythes and Spades,
And all those hard laborious Trades;
Where willing Wretches daily sweat,
And wear out Strength and Limbs to eat:
While others follow'd Mysteries,
To which few Folks bind 'Prentices;
That want no Stock, but that of Brass,
And may set up without a Cross;
As Sharpers, Parasites, Pimps, Players,
Pick-pockets, Coiners, Quacks, Sooth-sayers,
And all those, that in Enmity,

With downright Working, cunningly
Convert to their own Use the Labor
Of their good-natur'd heedless Neighbor.
These were call'd Knaves, but bar the Name,
The grave Industrious were the same:
All Trades and Places knew some Cheat,
No Calling was without Deceit.

    THE Lawyers, of whose Art the Basis
Was raising Feuds and splitting Cases,
Oppos'd all Registers, that Cheats
Might make more Work with dipt Estates;
As wer't unlawful, that one's own,
Without a Law-Suit, should be known.
They kept off Hearings willfully,
To finger the refreshing Fee;
And to defend a wicked Cause,
Examin'd and survey'd the Laws,
As Burglars Shops and Houses do,
To find out where they'd best break through.

    PHYSICIANS valu'd Fame and Wealth
Above the drooping Patient's Health,
Or their own Skill: The greatest Part
Study'd, instead of Rules of Art,
Grave pensive Looks and dull Behavior,
To gain th' Apothecary's Favor;
The Praise of Midwives, Priests, and all
That serv'd at Birth or Funeral.
To bear with th' ever-talking Tribe,
And hear my Lady's Aunt prescribe;
With formal Smile, and kind How d'ye,
To fawn on all the Family;
And, which of all the greatest Curse is,
T' endure th' Impertinence of Nurses.

    AMONG the many Priests of *Jove*,
Hir'd to draw Blessings from Above,
Some few were Learn'd and Eloquent,
But thousands Hot and Ignorant:

Yet all pass'd Muster that could hide
Their Sloth, Lust, Avarice and Pride;
For which they were as fam'd as Tailors
For Cabbage, or for Brandy Sailors:
Some, meager-look'd, and meanly clad,
Would mystically pray for Bread,
Meaning by that an ample Store,
Yet lit'rally received no more;
And, while these holy Drudges starv'd,
The lazy Ones, for which they serv'd,
Indulg'd their Ease, with all the Graces
Of Health and Plenty in their Faces.

    THE Soldiers, that were forc'd to fight,
If they surviv'd, got Honor by't;
Tho' some, that shunn'd the bloody Fray,
Had Limbs shot off, that ran away:
Some valiant Gen'rals fought the Foe;
Others took Bribes to let them go:
Some ventur'd always where 'twas warm,
Lost now a Leg, and then an Arm;
Till quite disabled, and put by,
They liv'd on half their Salary;
While others never came in Play,
And staid at Home for double Pay.

    THEIR Kings were serv'd, but Knavishly,
Cheated by their own Ministry;
Many, that for their Welfare slaved,
Robbing the very Crown they saved:
Pensions were small, and they liv'd high,
Yet boasted of their Honesty.
Calling, whene'er they strain'd their Right,
The slipp'ry Trick a Perquisite;
And when Folks understood their Cant,
They chang'd that for Emolument;
Unwilling to be short or plain,
In any thing concerning Gain;
For there was not a Bee but would
Get more, I won't say, than he should;

But than he dar'd to let them know,
That pay'd for't; as your Gamesters do,
That, tho' at fair Play, ne'er will own
Before the Losers what they've won.

    BUT who can all their Frauds repeat?
The very Stuff, which in the Street
They sold for Dirt t'enrich the Ground,
Was often by the Buyers found
Sophisticated with a quarter
Of good-for-nothing Stones and Mortar;
Tho' *Flail* had little Cause to mutter,
Who sold the other Salt for Butter.

    JUSTICE her self, fam'd for fair Dealing,
By Blindness had not lost her Feeling;
Her Left Hand, which the Scales should hold,
Had often dropt 'em, brib'd with Gold;
And, tho' she seem'd Impartial,
Where Punishment was corporal,
Pretended to a reg'lar Course,
In Murder, and all Crimes of Force;
Tho' some, first pillory'd for Cheating,
Were hang'd in Hemp of their own beating;
Yet, it was thought, the Sword she bore
Check'd but the Desp'rate and the Poor;
That, urg'd by mere Necessity,
Were ty'd up to the wretched Tree
For Crimes, which not deserv'd that Fate,
But to secure the Rich and Great.

    THUS every Part was full of Vice,
Yet the whole Mass a Paradise;
Flatter'd in Peace, and fear'd in Wars,
They were th' Esteem of Foreigners,
And lavish of their Wealth and Lives,
The Balance of all other Hives.
Such were the Blessings of that State;
Their Crimes conspir'd to make them Great:
And Virtue, who from Politicks

Had learn'd a Thousand Cunning Tricks,
Was, by their happy Influence,
Made Friends with Vice: And ever since,
The worst of all the Multitude
Did something for the Common Good.

    THIS was the State's Craft, that maintain'd
The Whole of which each Part complain'd:
This, as in Music Harmony,
Made Jarrings in the main agree;
Parties directly opposite,
Assist each other, as 'twere for Spite;
And Temp'rance with Sobriety,
Serve Drunkenness and Gluttony.

    THE Root of Evil, Avarice,
That damn'd ill-natur'd baneful Vice,
Was Slave to Prodigality,
That noble Sin; whilst Luxury
Employ'd a Million of the Poor,
And odious Pride a Million more:
Envy it self, and Vanity,
Were Ministers of Industry;
Their darling Folly, Fickleness,
In Diet, Furniture and Dress,
That strange ridic'lous Vice, was made
The very Wheel that turn'd the Trade.
Their Laws and Clothes were equally
Objects of Mutability;
For, what was well done for a time,
In half a Year became a Crime;
Yet while they alter'd thus their Laws,
Still finding and correcting Flaws,
They mended by Inconstancy
Faults, which no Prudence could foresee.

    THUS Vice nurs'd Ingenuity,
Which join'd with Time and Industry,
Had carry'd Life's Conveniencies,
Its real Pleasures, Comforts, Ease,

To such a Height, the very Poor
Liv'd better than the Rich before,
And nothing could be added more.

    HOW Vain is Mortal Happiness!
Had they but known the Bounds of Bliss;
And that Perfection here below
Is more than Gods can well bestow;
The Grumbling Brutes had been content
With Ministers and Government.
But they, at every ill Success,
Like Creatures lost without Redress,
Curs'd Politicians, Armies, Fleets;
While every one cry'd, *Damn the Cheats*,
And would, tho' conscious of his own,
In others barb'rously bear none.

    ONE, that had got a Princely Store,
By cheating Master, King and Poor,
Dar'd cry aloud, *The Land must sink*
For all its Fraud; And whom d'ye think
The Sermonizing Rascal chid?
A Glover that sold Lamb for Kid.

    THE least thing was not done amiss,
Or cross'd the Public Business;
But all the Rogues cry'd brazenly,
Good Gods, Had we but Honesty!
Merc'ry smil'd at th' Impudence,
And others call'd it want of Sense,
Always to rail at what they lov'd:
But *Jove* with Indignation mov'd,
At last in Anger swore, *He'd rid*
The bawling Hive of Fraud; and did.
The very Moment it departs,
And Honesty fills all their Hearts;
There shews 'em, like th' Instructive Tree,
Those Crimes which they're asham'd to see;
Which now in Silence they confess,
By blushing at their Ugliness:

Like Children, that would hide their Faults,
And by their Color own their Thoughts:
Imag'ning, when they're look'd upon,
That others see what they have done.

     BUT, Oh ye Gods! What Consternation,
How vast and sudden was th' Alteration!
In half an Hour, the Nation round,
Meat fell a Penny in the Pound.
The Mask Hypocrisy's flung down,
From the great Statesman to the Clown:
And some in borrow'd Looks well known,
Appear'd like Strangers in their own.
The Bar was silent from that Day;
For now the willing Debtors pay,
Ev'n what's by Creditors forgot;
Who quitted them that had it not.
Those, that were in the Wrong, stood mute,
And dropt the patch'd vexatious Suit:
On which since nothing less can thrive,
Than Lawyers in an honest Hive,
All, except those that got enough,
With Inkhorns by their sides troop'd off.

     JUSTICE hang'd some, set others free;
And after Goal delivery,
Her Presence being no more requir'd,
With all her Train and Pomp retir'd.
First march'd some Smiths with Locks and Grates,
Fetters, and Doors with Iron Plates:
Next Goalers, Turnkeys and Assistants:
Before the Goddess, at some distance,
Her chief and faithful Minister,
'Squire CATCH the Law's great Finisher,
Bore not th' imaginary Sword,
But his own Tools, an Ax and Cord:
Then on a Cloud the Hood-wink'd Fair,
JUSTICE her self was push' d by Air:
About her Chariot, and behind,
Were Sergeants, Bums of every kind,

Tip-staffs, and all those Officers,
That squeeze a Living out of Tears.

THO' Physic liv'd, while Folks were ill,
None would prescribe, but Bees of skill,
Which through the Hive dispers'd so wide,
That none of them had need to ride;
Wav'd vain Disputes, and strove to free
The Patients of their Misery;
Left Drugs in cheating Countries grown,
And us'd the Product of their own;
Knowing the Gods sent no Disease
To Nations without Remedies.

THEIR Clergy rous'd from Laziness,
Laid not their Charge on Journey-Bees;
But serv'd themselves, exempt from Vice,
The Gods with Pray'r and Sacrifice;
All those, that were unfit, or knew
Their Service might be spar'd, withdrew:
Nor was there Business for so many,
(If th' Honest stand in need of any,)
Few only with the High-Priest staid,
To whom the rest Obedience paid:
Himself employ'd in Holy Cares,
Resign'd to others State-Affairs.
He chas'd no Starv'ling from his Door,
Nor pinch'd the Wages of the Poor;
But at his House the Hungry's fed,
The Hireling finds unmeasur'd Bread,
The needy Trav'ler Board and Bed.

AMONG the King's great Ministers,
And all th' inferior Officers
The Change was great; for frugally
They now liv'd on their Salary:
That a poor Bee should ten times come
To ask his Due, a trifling Sum,
And by some well-hir'd Clerk be made
To give a Crown, or ne'er be paid,

Would now be call'd a downright Cheat,
Tho' formerly a Perquisite.
All Places manag'd first by Three,
Who watch'd each other's Knavery,
And often for a Fellow-feeling,
Promoted one another's stealing,
Are happily supply'd by One,
By which some thousands more are gone.

    NO Honor now could be content,
To live and owe for what was spent;
Liv'ries in Brokers Shops are hung,
They part with Coaches for a Song;
Sell stately Horses by whole Sets;
And Country-Houses, to pay Debts.

    VAIN Cost is shunn'd as much as Fraud;
They have no Forces kept Abroad;
Laugh at th' Esteem of Foreigners,
And empty Glory got by Wars;
They fight, but for their Country's sake,
When Right or Liberty's at Stake.

    NOW mind the glorious Hive, and see
How Honesty and Trade agree.
The Shew is gone, it thins apace;
And looks with quite another Face.
For 'twas not only that They went,
By whom vast Sums were Yearly spent;
But Multitudes that liv'd on them,
Were daily forc'd to do the same.
In vain to other Trades they'd fly;
All were o'er-stock'd accordingly.

    THE Price of Land and Houses falls;
Mirac'lous Palaces, whose Walls,
Like those of *Thebes*, were rais'd by Play,
Are to be let; while the once gay,
Well-seated Household Gods would be
More pleas'd to expire in Flames, than see

The mean Inscription on the Door
Smile at the lofty ones they bore.
The building Trade is quite destroy'd,
Artificers are not employ'd;
No Limner for his Art is fam'd,
Stone-cutters, Carvers are not nam'd.

    THOSE that remain'd, grown temp'rate, strive,
Not how to spend, but how to live,
And, when they paid their Tavern Score,
Resolv'd to enter it no more
No Vintner's Jilt in all the Hive
Could wear now Cloth of Gold, and thrive;
Nor *Torcol* such vast Sums advance,
For *Burgundy* and *Ortelans*;
The Courtier's gone, that with his Miss
Supp'd at his House on Christmas Peas;
Spending as much in two Hours stay,
As keeps a Troop of Horse a Day.

    THE haughty *Chloe*, to live Great,
Had made her Husband rob the State:
But now she sells her Furniture,
Which th' *Indies* had been ransack'd for;
Contracts th' expensive Bill of Fare,
And wears her strong Suit a whole Year:
The slight and fickle Age is past;
And Clothes, as well as Fashions, last.
Weavers, that join'd rich Silk with Plate,
And all the Trades subordinate,
Are gone. Still Peace and Plenty reign,
And every Thing is cheap, tho' plain:
Kind Nature, free from Gard'ners Force,
Allows all Fruits in her own Course;
But Rarities cannot be had,
Where Pains to get them are not paid.

    AS Pride and Luxury decrease,
So by degrees they leave the Seas.
Not Merchants now, but Companies

Remove whole Manufactories.
All Arts and Crafts neglected lie;
Content, the Bane of Industry,
Makes 'em admire their homely Store,
And neither seek nor covet more.

   so few in the vast Hive remain,
The hundredth Part they can't maintain
Against th' Insults of numerous Foes;
Whom yet they valiantly oppose:
Till some well-fenc'd Retreat is found,
And here they die or stand their Ground.
No Hireling in their Army's known;
But bravely fighting for their own,
Their Courage and Integrity
At last were crown'd with Victory.
They triumph'd not without their Cost,
For many Thousand Bees were lost.
Hard'ned with Toils and Exercise,
They counted Ease it self a Vice;
Which so improv'd their Temperance;
That, to avoid Extravagance,
They flew into a hollow Tree,
Blest with Content and Honesty.

THE MORAL

   THEN leave Complaints: Fools only strive
To make a Great an Honest Hive
T' enjoy the World's Conveniencies,
Be fam'd in War, yet live in Ease,
Without great Vices, is a vain
UTOPIA seated in the Brain.
Fraud, Luxury and Pride must live,
While we the Benefits receive:
Hunger's a dreadful Plague, no doubt,
Yet who digests or thrives without?
Do we not owe the Growth of Wine
To the dry shabby crooked Vine?
Which, while its Shoots neglected stood,
Chok'd other Plants, and ran to Wood;

But blest us with its noble Fruit,
As soon as it was ty'd and cut:
So Vice is beneficial found,
When it's by Justice lopt and bound;
Nay, where the People would be great,
As necessary to the State,
As Hunger is to make 'em eat.
Bare Virtue can't make Nations live
In Splendor; they, that would revive
A Golden Age, must be as free,
For Acorns, as for Honesty.

Moral virtue is basis in pride [153]

All untaught Animals are only solicitous of pleasing themselves, and naturally follow the bent of their own Inclinations, without considering the good or harm that from their being pleased will accrue to others. This is the Reason, that in the wild State of Nature those Creatures are fittest to live peaceably together in great Numbers, that discover the least of Understanding, and have the fewest Appetites to gratify; and consequently no Species of Animals is, without the Curb of Government, less capable of agreeing long together in Multitudes than that of Man; yet such are his Qualities, whether good or bad, I shall not determine, that no Creature besides himself can ever be made sociable: But being an extraordinary selfish and headstrong, as well as cunning Animal, however he may be subdued by superior Strength, it is impossible by Force alone to make him tractable, and receive the Improvements he is capable of.

The Chief Thing, therefore, which Lawgivers and other wise Men, that have labored for the Establishment of Society, have endeavor'd, has been to make the People they were to govern, believe, that it was more beneficial for every Body to conquer than indulge his Appetites, and much better to mind the Public than what seem'd his private Interest. As this has always been a very difficult Task, so no Wit or Eloquence has been left untried to compass it; and the Moralists and Philosophers of all Ages employed their utmost Skill to prove the Truth of so useful an Assertion. But whether Mankind would have ever believ'd it or not, it is not likely that any Body could have persuaded them to disapprove of their natural Inclinations, or prefer the good of others to their own, if at the same time he had not shew'd them an Equivalent to be enjoy'd as a Reward for the Violence, which by so doing they of necessity must commit upon themselves. . . .

They thoroughly examin'd all the Strength and Frailties of our Nature, and observing that none were either so savage as not to be charm'd with Praise, or so despicable as patiently to bear Contempt, justly concluded, that Flattery must be the most powerful

Argument that could be used to Human Creatures. Making use of this bewitching Engine, they extoll'd the Excellency of our Nature above other Animals, and setting forth with unbounded Praises the Wonders of our Sagacity and Vastness of Under-standing, bestow'd a thousand Encomiums on the Rationality of our Souls, by the Help of which we were capable of performing the most noble Achievements. Having by this artful way of Flattery insinuated themselves into the Hearts of Men, they began to instruct them in the Notions of Honor and Shame; representing the one as the worst of all Evils, and the other as the highest Good to which Mortals could aspire: Which being done, they laid before them how unbecoming it was the Dignity of such sublime Creatures to be solicitous about gratifying those Appetites, which they had in common with Brutes, and at the same time unmindful of those higher Qualities that gave them the preeminence over all visible Beings. They indeed con-fess'd, that those impulses of Nature were very pressing; that it was troublesome to resist, and very difficult wholly to subdue them. But this they only used as an Argu-ment to demonstrate, how glorious the Conquest of them was on the one hand, and how scandalous on the other not to attempt it.

To introduce, moreover, an Emulation amongst Men, they divided the whole Species into two Classes, vastly differing from one another: The one consisted of abject, low-minded People, that always hunting after immediate Enjoyment, were wholly incapable of Self-denial, and without regard to the good of others, had no higher Aim than their private Advantage; such as being enslaved by Voluptuousness, yielded without Resistance to every gross desire, and made no use of their Rational Faculties but to heighten their Sensual Pleasure. These vile grov'ling Wretches, they said, were the Dross of their Kind, and having only the Shape of Men, differ'd from Brutes in nothing but their outward Figure. But the other Class was made up of lofty high-spirited Creatures, that free from sordid Selfishness, esteem'd the Improvements of the Mind to be their fairest Possessions; and setting a true value upon themselves, took no Delight but in embellishing that Part in which their Excellency consisted; such as despising whatever they had in common with irrational Creatures, opposed by the Help of Reason their most violent Inclinations; and making a continual War with themselves to promote the Peace of others, aim'd at no less than the Public Welfare and the Conquest of their own Passion. . . . These they call'd the true Representatives of their sublime Species, exceeding in worth the first Class by more degrees, than that it self was superior to the Beasts of the Field.

As in all Animals that are not too imperfect to discover Pride, we find, that the finest and such as are the most beautiful and valuable of their kind, have generally the greatest Share of it; so in Man, the most perfect of Animals, it is so inseparable from his very Essence (how cunningly soever some may learn to hide or disguise it) that without it the Compound he is made of would want one of the chiefest Ingredients: Which, if we consider, it is hardly to be doubted but Lessons and Remonstrances, so skillfully adapted to the good Opinion Man has of himself, as those I have mentioned, must, if scatter'd amongst a Multitude not only gain the assent of most of them, as to the Speculative part, but likewise induce several, especially the fiercest, most resolute, and best among them, to endure a thousand Inconveniences, and undergo as many Hardships, that they may have the pleasure of counting themselves men of the second Class, and consequently appropriating to themselves all the Excellences they have heard of it. . . .

It being the Interest then of the very worst of them, more than any, to preach up Public-spiritedness, that they might reap the Fruits of the Labor and Self-denial of others, and at the same time indulge their own Appetites with less disturbance, they agreed with the rest, to call every thing, which, without Regard to the Public, Man should commit to gratify any of his Appetites, VICE; if in that Action there cou'd be observed the least prospect, that it might either be injurious to any of the Society, or ever render himself less serviceable to others: And to give the Name of VIRTUE to every Performance, by which Man, contrary to the impulse of Nature, should endeavor the Benefit of others, or the Conquest of his own Passions out of a Rational Ambition of being good.

It shall be objected, that no Society was ever any ways civiliz'd before the major part had agreed upon some Worship or other of an over-ruling Power, and consequently that the Notions of Good and Evil, and the Distinction between *Virtue* and *Vice*, were never the Contrivance of Politicians, but the pure Effect of Religion. Before I answer this Objection, I must repeat what I have said already, that in this *Enquiry into the Origin of Moral Virtue*, I speak neither of *Jews* or *Christians*, but Man in his State of Nature and Ignorance of the true Deity; and then I affirm, that the Idolatrous Superstitions of all other Nations, and the pitiful Notions they had of the Supreme Being, were incapable of exciting Man to Virtue, and good for nothing but to awe and amuse a rude and unthinking Multitude. . . .

It is visible . . . that it was not any Heathen Religion or other Idolatrous Superstition, that first put Man upon crossing his Appetites and subduing his dearest Inclinations, but the skillful Management of wary Politicians; and the nearer we search into human Nature, the more we shall be convinced, that the Moral Virtues are the Political Offspring which Flattery begot upon Pride.

Bishop Joseph Butler was born at Wantage, Berkshire, educated at Oriel College, Oxford, and ordained a priest a few years thereafter. His most important reflections on self-interest appear in a set of sermons he delivered at the Rolls Chapel in 1726, in which he tried to reconcile self-regard with both benevolence and morality.

JOSEPH BUTLER
(1692–1752)

other love

self-love = private interest

On the relationship between self-love and particular affections [154]

[I]t seems worth while to inquire, whether private interest is likely to be promoted in proportion to the degree in which self-love engrosses us, and prevails over all other principles; or whether the contracted affection may not possibly be so prevalent as to disappoint itself, and even contradict its own end, private good.

And since, further, there is generally thought to be some peculiar kind of contrariety between self-love and the love of our neighbor, between the pursuit of public and of private good; insomuch that when you are recommending one of these, you are supposed to be speaking against the other; and from hence arises a secret prejudice against, and frequently open scorn of all talk of public spirit, and real goodwill to our fellow-creatures; it will be necessary to inquire what respect benevolence hath to self-love, and the pursuit of private interest to the pursuit of public: or whether there be anything of that peculiar inconsistence and contrariety between them, over and above what there is between self-love and other passions and particular affections, and their respective pursuits.

These inquiries, it is hoped, may be favorably attended to: for there shall be all possible concessions made to the favorite passion, which hath so much allowed to it, and whose cause is so universally pleaded: it shall be treated with the utmost tenderness and concern for its interests.

In order to do this, as well as to determine the forementioned questions, it will be necessary to consider the nature, the object, and end of that self-love, as distinguished from other principles or affections in the mind, and their respective objects.

Every man hath a general desire of his own happiness; and likewise a variety of particular affections, passions, and appetites to particular external objects. The former proceeds from, or is self-love; and seems inseparable from all sensible creatures, who can reflect upon themselves and their own interest or happiness, so as to have that interest an object to their minds: what is to be said of the latter is, that they proceed from, or together make up that particular nature according to which man is made. The object the former pursues is somewhat internal, our own happiness, enjoyment, satisfaction; whether we have, or have not, a distinct particular perception what it is, or wherein it consists: the objects of the latter are this or that particular external thing, which the affections tend towards, and of which it hath always a particular idea or perception. The principle we call self-love never seeks anything external for the sake of the thing, but only as a means of happiness or good: particular affections rest in the external things themselves. One belongs to man as a reasonable creature reflecting upon his own interest or happiness. The other, though quite distinct from reason, are as much a part of human nature.

That all particular appetites and passions are towards *external things themselves*, distinct from the *pleasure arising from them*, is manifested from hence; that there could not be this pleasure, were it not for that prior suitableness between the object and the passion: there could be no enjoyment or delight from one thing more than another, from eating food more than from swallowing a stone, if there were not an affection or appetite to one thing more than another.

Every particular affection, even the love of our neighbor, is as really our own affection, as self-love; and the pleasure arising from its gratification is as much my own pleasure, as the pleasure self-love would have, from knowing I myself should be happy some time hence, would be my own pleasure. And if, because every particular affection is a man's own, and the pleasure arising from its gratification his own pleasure, or pleasure to himself, such particular affection must be called self-love; according to this way of speaking, no creature whatever can possibly act but merely from self-love; and every action and every affection whatever is to be resolved up into this one principle. But then this is not the language of mankind: or if it were, we should want words to express the difference, between the principle of an action, proceeding from cool consideration that it will be to my own advantage; and an action, suppose of revenge, or of friendship, by which a man runs upon certain ruin, to do evil or good to another. It is manifest the principles of these actions are totally different, and so want different words to be distinguished by: all that they agree in is, that they both proceed from, and are done to gratify an inclination in a man's self. But the principle or inclination in one case is self-love; in the other, hatred or love of another. There is then a distinction between the cool principle of self-love, or general desire of our happiness, as one part of our nature, and one principle of action; and the particular affections towards particular external objects, as another part of our nature, and another principle of action. How much soever therefore is to be allowed to self-love, yet it cannot be allowed to be the whole of our inward constitution; because, you see, there are other parts or principles which come into it.

Further, private happiness or good is all which self-love can make us desire, or be concerned about: in having this consists its gratification: it is an affection to ourselves; a regard to our own interest, happiness, and private good: and in the proportion a man hath this, he is interested, or a lover of himself. Let this be kept in mind; because there is commonly, as I shall presently have occasion to observe, another sense put upon these words. On the other hand, particular affections tend towards particular external things: these are their objects; having these is their end: in this consists their gratification: no matter whether it be, or be not, upon the whole, our interest or happiness. An action done from the former of these principles is called an interested action. An action proceeding from any of the latter has its denomination of passionate, ambitious, friendly, revengeful, or any other, from the particular appetite or affection from which it proceeds. Thus self-love as one part of human nature, and the several particular principles as the other part, are, themselves, their objects and ends, stated and shown.

From hence it will be easy to see, how far, and in what ways, each of these can contribute and be subservient to the private good of the individual. Happiness does not consist in self-love. The desire of happiness is no more the thing itself, than the desire of riches is the possession or enjoyment of them. People may love themselves with the most entire and unbounded affection, and yet be extremely miserable. Neither can self-love any way help them out, but by setting them on work to get rid of the causes of their misery, to gain or make use of those objects which are by nature adapted to afford satisfaction. Happiness or satisfaction consists only in the enjoyment of those objects, which are by nature suited to our several particular appetites, passions, and affections. So that if self-love wholly engrosses us, and leaves no room for any other principle, there can be absolutely no such thing at all as happiness, or enjoyment of any kind whatever; since happiness consists in the gratification of particular passions, which supposes the having of them. Self-love then does not constitute *this* or *that* to be our interest or good; but, our interest or good being constituted by nature and supposed, self-love only puts us upon obtaining and securing it. Therefore, if it be possible, that self-love may prevail and exert itself in a degree or manner which is not subservient to this end; then it will not follow, that our interest will be promoted in proportion to the degree in which that principle engrosses us, and prevails over others. Nay further, the private and contracted affection, when it is not subservient to this end, private good, may, for anything that appears, have a direct contrary tendency and effect. And if we will consider the matter, we shall see that it often really has. *Disengagement* is absolutely necessary to enjoyment; and a person may have so steady and fixed an eye upon his own interest, whatever he places it in, as may hinder him from *attending* to many gratifications within his reach, which others have their minds free and open to. Over-fondness for a child is not generally thought to be for its advantage: and, if there be any guess to be made from appearances, surely that character we call selfish is not the most promising for happiness. Such a temper may plainly be, and exert itself in a degree and manner which may give us unnecessary and useless solicitude and anxiety, in a degree and manner which may prevent obtaining the means and materials of enjoyment, as well as the making use of them. Immoderate self-love does very ill consult its own interest: and, how much soever a paradox it may appear, it is certainly true, that even from self-love we should endeavor to get over all inordinate regard to, and consideration of ourselves. Every one of our passions and affections hath its natural stint and bound, which may easily be exceeded; whereas our enjoyments can possibly be but in a determinate measure and degree. Therefore such excess of the affection, since it cannot procure any enjoyment, must in all cases be useless; but is generally attended with inconveniences, and often is downright pain and misery. This holds as much with regard to self-love as to all other affections. The natural degree of it, so far as it sets us on work to gain and make use of the materials of satisfaction, may be to our real advantage; but beyond or besides this, it is in several respects an inconvenience and disadvantage. Thus it appears, that private interest is so far from being likely to be promoted in proportion to the degree in which self-love engrosses us, and prevails over all other principles; that the contracted affection may be so prevalent as to disappoint itself, and even contradict its own end, private good.

Self-love is no more contrary to benevolence than to any other affection [155]

"But who, except the most sordidly covetous, ever thought there was any rivalship between the love of greatness, honor, power, or between sensual appetites and self-love? No, there is a perfect harmony between them. It is by means of these particular appetites and affections that self-love is gratified in enjoyment, happiness, and satisfaction. The competition and rivalship is between self-love and the love of our neighbor: that affection which leads us out of ourselves, makes us regardless of our own interest, and substitute that of another in its stead." Whether then there be any peculiar competition and contrariety in this case, shall now be considered.

Self-love and interestedness was stated to consist in or be an affection to ourselves, a regard to our own private good: it is therefore distinct from benevolence, which is an affection to the good of our fellow-creatures. But that benevolence is distinct from, that is, not the same thing with self-love, is no reason for its being looked upon with any peculiar suspicion; because every principle whatever, by means of which self-love is gratified, is distinct from it; and all things which are distinct from each other are equally so. A man has an affection or aversion to another: that one of these tends to, and is gratified by doing good, that the other tends to, and is gratified by doing harm, does not in the least alter the respect which either one or the other of these inward feelings has to self-love. We use the word *property* so as to exclude any other persons having an interest in that of which we say a particular man has the property. And we often use the word *selfish* so as to exclude in the same manner all regards to the good of others. But the cases are not parallel: for though that exclusion is really part of the idea of property; yet such positive exclusion, or bringing this peculiar disregard to the good of others into the idea of self-love, is in reality adding to the idea, or changing it from what it was before stated to consist in, namely, an affection to ourselves. This being the whole idea of self-love, it can no otherwise exclude good-will or love of others, than merely by not including it, no otherwise, than it excludes love of arts or reputation, or of anything else. Neither on the other hand does benevolence, any more than love of arts or of reputation, exclude self-love. Love of our neighbor then has just the same respect to, is no more distant from, self-love, than hatred of our neighbor, or than love or hatred of anything else. Thus the principles, from which men rush upon certain ruin for the destruction of an enemy, and for the preservation of a friend, have the same respect to the private affection, and are equally interested, or equally disinterested: and it is of no avail, whether they are said to be one or the other. Therefore, to those who are shocked to hear virtue spoken of as disinterested, it may be allowed that it is indeed absurd to speak thus of it; unless hatred, several particular instances of vice, and all the common affections and aversions in mankind, are acknowledged to be disinterested too. Is there any less inconsistence, between the love of inanimate things, or of creatures merely sensitive, and self-love; than between self-love and the love of our neighbor? Is desire of and delight in the happiness of another any more a diminution of self-love, than desire of and delight in the esteem of another? They are both equally desire of and delight in somewhat external to ourselves: either both or neither are so. The object of self-love is expressed in the term *self*: and every appetite of sense, and every particular affection of the heart, are equally interested or disinterested, because the objects of them are all equally self or somewhat else. Whatever ridicule therefore the mention of a disinterested principle or action may be supposed to lie open to, must, upon the matter being thus stated, relate to ambition, and every appetite and particular affection, as much as to benevolence. And indeed all the ridicule, and all the grave perplexity, of which this subject hath had its full share, is merely from words. The most intelligible way of speaking of it seems to be this: that self-love and the actions done in consequence of it (for these will presently appear to be the same as to this question) are interested; that particular affections towards external objects, and the actions done in consequence of those affections, are not so. But every one is at liberty to use words as he pleases. All that is here insisted upon is, that ambition, revenge, benevolence, all particular passions whatever, and the actions they produce, are equally interested or disinterested.

Thus it appears that there is no peculiar contrariety between self-love and benevolence; no greater competition between these, than between any other particular affections and self-love. . . .

Conscience and "cool self-love" always point us in the same direction [156]

The apostle asserts, that the Gentiles *do by* nature *the things contained in the law.* . . . What that is in man by which he is *naturally a law to himself*, is explained in the following words: "which shew the work of the law written in their hearts, their conscience also bearing witness, and their thoughts the meanwhile accusing or else excusing one another" [*Rom.* ii.15]. If there be a distinction to be made between the *works written in their hearts*, and the witness of conscience; by the former must be meant the natural disposition to kindness and compassion, to do what is of good report, to which this apostle often refers: that part of the nature of man, treated of in the foregoing discourse, which with very little reflection and, of course, leads him to society, and by means of which he naturally acts a just and good part in it, unless other passions or interest lead him astray. Yet since other passions, and regards to private interest, which lead us (though indirectly, yet they lead us) astray, are themselves in a degree equally natural, and often most prevalent; and since we have no method of seeing the particular degrees in which one or the other is placed in us by nature; it is plain the former, considered merely as natural, good and right as they are, can no more be a law to us than the latter. But there is a superior principle of reflection or conscience in every man, which distinguishes between the internal principles of his heart, as well as his external actions: which passes judgment upon himself and them; pronounces determinately some actions to be in themselves just, right, good; others to be in themselves evil, wrong, unjust: which, without being consulted, without being advised with, magisterially exerts itself, and approves or condemns him the doer of them accordingly: and which, if not forcibly stopped, naturally and always, of course, goes on to anticipate a higher and more effectual sentence, which shall hereafter second and affirm its own. . . .

Man may act according to that principle or inclination which for the present happens to be strongest, and yet act in a way disproportionate to, and violate his real proper nature. Suppose a brute creature by any bait to be allured into a snare, by which he is destroyed. He plainly followed the bent of his nature, leading him to gratify his appetite: there is an entire correspondence between his whole nature and such an action: such action therefore is natural. But suppose a man, foreseeing the same danger of certain ruin, should rush into it for the sake of a present gratification; he in this instance would follow his strongest desire, as did the brute creature: but there would be as manifest a disproportion, between the nature of a man and such an action, as between the meanest work of art and the skill of the greatest master in that art: which disproportion arises, not from considering the action singly in *itself*, or in its *consequences*; but from comparison of it with the nature of the agent. And since such an action is utterly disproportionate to the nature of man, it is in the strictest and most proper sense unnatural; this word expressing that disproportion. Therefore instead of the words *disproportionate to his nature*, the word *unnatural* may now be put; this being more familiar to us: but let it be observed, that it stands for the same thing precisely.

Now what is it which renders such a rash action unnatural? Is it that he went against the principle of reasonable and cool self-love, considered *merely* as a part of his nature? No: for if he had acted the contrary way, he would equally have gone against a principle, or part of his nature, namely, passion or appetite. But to deny a present appetite, from foresight that the gratification of it would end in immediate ruin or extreme misery, is by no means an unnatural action: whereas to contradict or go against cool self-love for the sake of such gratification, is so in the instance before us. Such an action then being unnatural; and its being so not arising from a man's going against a principle or desire barely, nor in going against that principle or desire which happens for the present to be strongest; it necessarily follows, that there must be some other difference or distinction to be made between these two principles, passion and cool self-love, than what I have yet taken notice of. And this difference, not being a difference in strength or degree, I call a difference in *nature* and in *kind*. And since, in the instance still before us, if passion prevails over self-love, the consequent action is unnatural; but if self-love prevails over passion, the action is natural: it is manifest that self-love is in human nature a superior principle to passion. This may be contradicted without violating that nature; but the former cannot. So that if we will act conformably to the economy of man's nature, reasonable self-love must govern. Thus, without particular consideration of conscience, we may have a clear conception of the *superior nature* of one inward principle to another; and see that there really is this natural superiority, quite distinct from degrees of strength and prevalency.

But allowing that mankind hath the rule of right within himself, yet it may be asked, "What obligations are we under to attend to and follow it?" I answer: it has been proved that man by his nature is a law to himself, without the particular distinct consideration of the positive sanctions of that law; the rewards and punishments which we feel, and those which from the light of reason we have ground to believe are annexed to it. The question then carries its own answer along with it. Your obligation to obey this law, is its being the law of your nature. That your conscience approves of and attests to such a course of action, is itself alone an obligation. . . .

However, let us hear what is to be said against obeying this law of our nature. And the sum is no more than this: "Why should we be concerned about anything out of and beyond ourselves? If we do find within ourselves regards to others, and restraints of we know not how many different kinds; yet these being embarrassments, and hindering us from going the nearest way to our own good, why should we not endeavor to suppress and get over them?"

Thus people go on with words, which, when applied to human nature, and the condition in which it is placed in this world, have really no meaning. For does not all this kind of talk go upon supposition, that our happiness in this world consists in somewhat quite distinct from regards to others; and that it is the privilege of vice to be without restraint or confinement? Whereas, on the contrary, the enjoyments, in a manner all the common enjoyments of life, even the pleasures of vice, depend upon these regards of one kind or another to our fellow-creatures. Throw off all regards to others, and we should be quite indifferent to infamy and to honor; there could be no such thing at all as ambition; and scarce any such thing as covetousness; for we should likewise be equally indifferent to the disgrace of poverty, the several neglects and kinds of contempt which accompany this state; and to the reputation of riches, the regard and respect they usually procure. Neither is restraint by any means peculiar to one course of life: but our very nature, exclusive of conscience and our condition, lays us under an absolute necessity of it. We cannot gain any end whatever without being confined to the proper means, which is often the most painful and uneasy confinement. And in numberless instances a present appetite cannot be gratified without such apparent and immediate ruin and misery, that the most dissolute man in the world chooses to forego the pleasure, rather than endure the pain. . . .

Reasonable self-love and conscience are the chief or superior principles in the nature of man: because an action may be suitable to this nature, though all other principles be violated; but becomes unsuitable, if either of those are. Conscience and self-love, if we understand our true happiness, always lead us the same way. Duty and interest are perfectly coincident; for the most part in this world, but entirely and in every instance if we take in the future, and the whole; this being implied in the notion of a good and perfect administration of things. Thus they who have been so wise in their generation as to regard only their own supposed interest, at the expense and to the injury of others, shall at last find, that he who has given up all the advantages of the present world, rather than violate his conscience and the relations of life, has infinitely better provided for himself, and secured his own interest and happiness.

Francis Hutcheson, a leading figure of the Scottish Enlightenment, was born in Ulster and educated at the University of Glasgow. He repudiated psychological egoism and argued for morality's basis in other-regard.

FRANCIS HUTCHESON
(1694–1746)

Virtuous action flows from affection for others, never from self-love [157]

Every action, which we apprehend as either morally good or evil, is always supposed to flow from some affection toward sensitive natures; and whatever we call virtue or vice is either some such affection, or some action consequent upon it. Or it may perhaps be enough to make an action or omission appear vicious, if it argues the want of such affection toward rational agents as we expect in characters counted morally good. All the actions counted religious in any country are supposed, by those who count them so, to flow from some affections toward the deity; and whatever we call social virtue we still suppose to flow from affections toward our fellow creatures. For in this all seem to agree, that external motions, when accompanied with no affections toward God or man, or evidencing no want of the expected affections toward either, can have no moral good or evil in them.

Ask, for instance, the most abstemious hermit, if temperance of itself would be morally good, supposing it showed no obedience toward the deity, made us no fitter for devotion, or the service of mankind, or the search after truth, than luxury; and he will easily grant that it would be no moral good, though still it might be naturally good or advantageous to health. And mere courage, or contempt of danger, if we conceive it to have no regard to the defense of the innocent, or repairing of wrongs, or self-interest, would only entitle its possessor to Bedlam. When such sort of courage is sometimes admired, it is upon some secret apprehension of a good intention in the use of it, or as a natural ability capable of a useful application. Prudence, if it was only employed in promoting private interest, is never imagined to be a virtue: and justice, or observing a strict equality, if it has no regard to the good of mankind, the preservation of rights, and securing peace, is a quality properer for its ordinary gestamen, a beam and scales, than for a rational agent. So that these four qualities, commonly called cardinal virtues, obtain that name because they are dispositions universally necessary to promote public good, and denote affections toward rational agents; otherwise there would appear no virtue in them.

Now if it can be made appear that none of these affections which we approve as virtuous, are either self-love, or desire of private interest; since all virtue is either some such affections, or actions consequent upon them, it must necessarily follow that virtue springs from some other affection than self-love, or desire of private advantage. And where self-interest excites to the same action, the approbation is given only to the disinterested principle.

The affections which are of most importance in morals are commonly included under the names love and hatred. Now in discoursing of love, we need not be cautioned not to include that love between the sexes, which, when no other affections accompany it, is only a desire of pleasure, and is never counted a virtue. Love toward rational agents is subdivided into love of complacence or esteem, and love of benevolence. And hatred is subdivided into hatred of displicence or contempt, and hatred of malice. Complacence denotes approbation of any person by our moral sense, and is rather a perception than an affection, though the affection of good will is ordinarily subsequent to it. Benevolence is the desire of the happiness of another. Their opposites are called dislike and malice. Concerning each of these separately we shall consider whether they can be influenced by motives of self-interest.

Complacence, esteem, or good-liking, at first view appears to be disinterested, and so displicence or dislike; and are entirely excited by some moral qualities, good or evil, apprehended to be in the objects, which qualities the very frame of our nature determines us to approve or disapprove, according to the moral sense[158] above explained. Propose to a man all the rewards in the world, or threaten all the punishments, to engage him to esteem and complacence toward a person entirely unknown, or if known, apprehended to be cruel, treacherous, ungrateful. You may procure external obsequiousness, or good offices, or dissimulation, but real esteem no price can purchase. And the same is obvious as to contempt, which no motive of advantage can prevent. On the contrary, represent a character as generous, kind, faithful, humane, though in the most distant parts of the world, and we cannot avoid esteem and complacence. A bribe may possibly make us attempt to ruin such a man, or some strong motive of advantage may excite us to oppose his interest, but it can never make us disapprove him while we retain the same opinion of his temper and intentions. Nay, when we consult our own hearts, we shall find that we can scarce ever persuade ourselves to attempt any mischief against such persons from any motive of advantage, nor execute it without the strongest reluctance and remorse, until we have blinded ourselves into a false opinion about his temper.

Benevolence is contrary to self-interest [159]

As to the love of benevolence, the very name excludes self-interest. We never call that man benevolent who is in fact useful to others, but at the same time only intends his own interest, without any ultimate desire of the good of others. If there be any benevolence at all, it must be disinterested; for the most useful action imaginable loses all appearance of benevolence, as soon as we discern that it only flowed from self-love or interest. Thus, never were any human actions more advantageous than the inventions of fire and iron, but if these were casual, or if the inventor only intended his own interest in them, there is nothing which can be called benevolent in them. Wherever then benevolence is supposed, there it is imagined disinterested and designed for the good of others. To raise benevolence, no more is required than calmly to consider any sensitive nature not pernicious to others. Gratitude arises from benefits conferred from good will on ourselves or those we love; complacence is a perception of the moral sense. Gratitude includes some complacence, and complacence still raises a stronger good will than that we have toward indifferent characters, where there is no opposition of interests.

But it must be here observed that as all men have self-love as well as benevolence, these two principles may jointly excite a man to the same action, and then they are to be considered as two forces impelling the same body to motion; sometimes they conspire, sometimes are indifferent to each other, and sometimes are in some degree opposite. Thus if a man has such strong benevolence as would have produced an action without any views of self-interest, that such a man has also in view private advantage, along with public good, as the effect of his action, does no way diminish the benevolence of the action. When he would not have produced so much public good had it not been for the prospect of self-interest, then the effect of self-love is to be deducted, and his benevolence is proportioned to the remainder of good, which pure benevolence would have produced. When a man's benevolence is hurtful to himself, then self-love is opposite to benevolence, and the benevolence is proportioned to the sum of the good produced added to the resistance of self-love surmounted by it. In most cases it is impossible for men to know how far their fellows are influenced by the one or other of these principles, but yet the general truth is sufficiently certain, that this is the way in which the benevolence of actions is to be computed.

Refutation of two arguments for the view that benevolence is based on self-love [160]

There are two ways in which some may deduce benevolence from self-love, the one supposing that we voluntarily bring this affection upon ourselves whenever we have an opinion that it will be for our interest to have this affection, either as it may be immediately pleasant, or may afford pleasant reflection afterwards by our moral sense, or as it may tend to procure some external reward from God or man. The other scheme alleges no such power in us of raising desire or affection of any kind by our choice or volition, but supposes our minds determined by the frame of their nature to desire whatever is apprehended as the means of any private happiness, and that the observation of the happiness of other persons, in many cases is made the necessary occasion of pleasure to the observer, as their misery is the occasion of his uneasiness: and in consequence of this connection, as soon as we have observed it, we begin to desire the happiness of others as the means of obtaining this happiness to ourselves which we expect from the contemplation of others in a happy state. They allege it to be impossible to desire either the happiness of another, or any event whatsoever, without conceiving it as the means of some happiness or pleasure to ourselves, but own at the same time that desire is not raised in us directly by any volition, but arises necessarily upon our apprehending any object or event to be conducive to our happiness.

That the former scheme is not just may appear from this general consideration, that neither benevolence nor any other affection or desire can be directly raised by volition. If they could, then we could be bribed into any affection whatsoever toward any object, even the most improper. We might raise jealousy, fear, anger, love toward any sort of persons indifferently by a hire, even as we engage men to external actions, or to the dissimulation of passions, but this every person will by his own reflection find to be impossible. The prospect of any advantage to arise to us from having any affection may indeed turn our attention to those qualities in the object which are naturally constituted the necessary causes or occasions of the advantageous affection, and if we find such qualities in the object the affection will certainly arise. Thus indirectly the prospect of advantage may tend to raise any affection, but if these qualities be not found or apprehended in the object, no volition of ours nor desire will ever raise any affection in us.

But more particularly, that desire of the good of others which we approve as virtuous, cannot be alleged to be voluntarily raised from prospect of any pleasure accompanying the affection itself. For it is plain that our benevolence is not always accompanied with pleasure; nay it is often attended with pain when the object is in distress. Desire in general is rather uneasy than pleasant. It is true, indeed, all the passions and affections justify themselves; while they continue . . . we generally approve our being thus affected on this occasion as an innocent disposition or a just one, and condemn a person who would be otherwise affected on the like occasion. So the sorrowful, the angry, the jealous, the compassionate approve their several passions on the apprehended occasion, but we should not therefore conclude that sorrow, anger, jealousy, or pity are pleasant, or chosen for their concomitant pleasure. The case is plainly thus: the frame of our nature on the occasions which move these passions determines us to be thus affected, and to approve our affection at least as innocent. Uneasiness generally attends our desires of any kind, and this sensation tends to fix our attention and to continue the desire. But the desire does not terminate upon the removal of the pain accompanying the desire, but upon some other event. The concomitant pain is what we seldom reflect upon, unless when it is very violent. Nor does any desire or affection terminate upon the pleasure which may accompany the affection; much less is it raised by an act of will with a view to obtain this pleasure.

The same reflection will show that we do not by an act of our will raise in ourselves that benevolence which we approve as virtuous, with a view to obtain future pleasures of self-approbation by our moral sense. Could we raise affections in this manner, we should be engaged to any affection by the prospect of an interest equivalent to this of self-approbation, such as wealth or sensual pleasure, which with many tempers are more powerful; and yet we universally own that that disposition to do good offices to others which is raised by these motives is not virtuous. How can we then imagine that the virtuous benevolence is brought upon us by a motive equally selfish?

But what will most effectually convince us of the truth on this point is reflection upon our own hearts, whether we have not a desire of the good of others, generally without any consideration or intention of obtaining these pleasant reflections on our own virtue. Nay, often this desire is strongest where we least imagine virtue, in natural affection toward offspring, and in gratitude to a great benefactor; the absence of which is indeed the greatest vice, but the affections themselves are not esteemed in any considerable degree virtuous. The same reflection will also convince us that these desires or affections are not produced by choice, with a view to obtain this private good.

In like manner, if no volition of ours can directly raise affections from the former prospects of interest, no more can any volition raise them from prospects of eternal rewards, or to avoid eternal punishments. The former motives differ from these only as smaller from greater, shorter from more durable. If affections could be directly raised by volition, the same consideration would make us angry at the most innocent or virtuous character, and jealous of the most faithful and affectionate, or sorrowful for the prosperity of a friend; which we all find to be impossible. The prospect of a future state may, no doubt, have a greater indirect influence, by turning our attention to the qualities in the objects naturally apt to raise the required affection, than any other consideration.[161]

It is indeed probably true in fact, that those who are engaged by prospect of future rewards to do good offices to mankind, have generally the virtuous benevolence jointly exciting them to action. Because, as it may appear hereafter, benevolence is natural to mankind, and still operates where there is no opposition of apparent interest, or where any contrary apparent interest is overbalanced by a greater interest. Men conscious of this do generally approve good offices, to which motives of a future state partly excited the agent. But that the approbation is founded upon the apprehension of a disinterested desire partly exciting the agent, is plain from this, that not only obedience to an evil deity in doing mischief, or even in performing trifling ceremonies, only from hope of reward or prospect of avoiding punishment, but even obedience to a good deity only from the same motives, without any love or gratitude towards him, and with a perfect indifference about the happiness or misery of mankind, abstracting from this private interest, would meet with no approbation. We plainly see that a change of external circumstances of interest under an evil deity, without any change in the disposition of the agent, would lead him into every cruelty and inhumanity.

Gratitude toward the deity is indeed disinterested, as it will appear hereafter. This affection therefore may obtain our approbation, where it excites to action, though there were no other benevolence exciting the agent. But this case scarce occurs among men. But where the sanction of the law is the only motive of action, we could expect no more benevolence, nor no other affection, than those in one forced by the law to be curator to a person for whom he has not the least regard. The agent would so manage as to save himself harmless if he could, but would be under no concern about the success of his attempts, or the happiness of the person whom he served, provided he performed the task required by law; nor would any spectator approve this conduct.

Benevolence cannot be reduced to a desire for pleasure [162]

The other scheme is more plausible: that benevolence is not raised by any volition upon prospect of advantage, but that we desire the happiness of others, as conceiving it necessary to procure some pleasant sensations which we expect to feel upon seeing others happy; and that for like reason we have aversion to their misery. This connection between the happiness of others and our pleasure, say they, is chiefly felt among friends, parents, and children, and eminently virtuous characters. But this benevolence flows as directly from self-love as any other desire.

To show that this scheme is not true in fact, let us consider that if in our benevolence we only desired the happiness of others as the means of this pleasure to ourselves, whence is it that no man approves the desire of the happiness of others as the means of procuring wealth or sensual pleasure to ourselves? If a person had wagered concerning the future happiness of a man of such veracity that he would sincerely confess whether he were happy or not, would this wagerer's desire of the happiness of another, in order to win the wager, be approved as virtuous? If not, wherein does this desire differ from the former, except that in one case there is one pleasant sensation expected, and in the other case other sensations? For by increasing or diminishing the sum wagered, the interest in this case may be made either greater or less than that in the other.

Reflecting in our minds again will best discover the truth. Many have never thought upon this connection; nor do we ordinarily intend the obtaining of any such pleasure when we do generous offices. We all often feel delight upon seeing others happy, but during our pursuit of their happiness we have no intention of obtaining this delight. We often feel the pain of compassion, but were our sole ultimate intention or desire the freeing ourselves from this pain, would the deity offer to us either wholly to blot out all memory of the person in distress, or to take away this connection, so that we should be easy during the misery of our friend on the one hand, or on the other would relieve him from his misery, we should be as ready to choose the former way as the latter, since either of them would free us from our pain, which upon this scheme is the sole end proposed by the compassionate person. Don't we find in ourselves that our desire does not terminate upon the removal of our own pain? Were this our sole intention we would run away, shut our eyes, or divert our thoughts from the miserable object, as the readiest way of removing our pain. This we seldom do, nay we crowd about such objects, and voluntarily expose ourselves to this pain, unless calm reflection upon our inability to relieve the miserable, countermand our inclination, or some selfish affection as fear of danger overpower it.

To make this yet clearer, suppose that the deity should declare to a good man that he should be suddenly annihilated, but at this instant of his exit it should be left to his choice whether his friend, his children, or his country should be made happy or miserable for the future, when he himself could have no sense of either pleasure or pain from their state. Pray would he be any more indifferent about their state now that he neither hoped or feared anything to himself from it, than he was in any prior period of his life? Nay, is it not a pretty common opinion among us, that after our decease we know nothing of what befalls those who survive us? How comes it then that we do not lose at the approach of death all concern for our families, friends, or country? Can there be any instance given of our desiring anything only as the means of private good as violently when we know that we shall not enjoy this good many minutes, as if we expected the possession of this good for many years? Is this the way we compute the value of annuities?

How the disinterested desire of the good of others should seem inconceivable, it is hard to account. Perhaps it is owing to the attempts of some great men to give definitions of simple ideas. Desire, say they, is uneasiness, or uneasy sensation upon the absence of any good. Whereas desire is as distinct from uneasiness as volition is from sensation. Don't they themselves often speak of our desiring to remove uneasiness? Desire then is different from uneasiness, however a sense of uneasiness accompanies it, as extension does the idea of color, which yet is a very distinct idea. Now wherein lies the impossibility of desiring the happiness of another without conceiving it as the means of obtaining anything farther, even as we desire our own happiness without farther view? If any allege that we desire our own happiness as the means of removing the uneasiness we feel in the absence of happiness, then at least the desire of removing our own uneasiness is an ultimate desire. And why may we not have other ultimate desires?

But can any being be concerned about the absence of an event which gives it no uneasiness? Perhaps superior natures desire without uneasy sensation. But what if we cannot? We may be uneasy while a desired event is in suspense, and yet not desire this event only as the means of removing this uneasiness. Nay, if we did not desire the event without view to this uneasiness, we should never have brought the uneasiness upon ourselves by desiring it. So likewise we may feel delight upon the existence of a desired event, when yet we did not desire the event only as the means of obtaining this delight, even as we often receive delight from events which we had an aversion to.

Proof of the possibility of disinterest [163]

Having removed these false springs of virtuous action, let us next establish the true one, namely some determination of our nature to study the good of others, or some instinct, antecedent to all reason from interest, which influences us to the love of others, even as the moral sense . . . determines us to approve the actions which flow from this love in ourselves or others. This disinterested affection may appear strange to men impressed with notions of self-love as the sole spring of action, from the pulpit, the schools, the systems, and conversations regulated by them. But let us consider it in its strongest and simplest kinds, and when we see the possibility of it in these instances, we may easily discover its universal extent.

An honest farmer will tell you that he studies the preservation and happiness of his children, and loves them without any design of good to himself. But, say some of our philosophers, the happiness of their children gives parents pleasure, and their misery gives them pain, and therefore to obtain the former and avoid the latter, they study from self-love the good of their children. Suppose several merchants joined in partnership of their whole effects; one of them is employed abroad in managing the stock of the company; his prosperity occasions gain to all and his losses give them pain from their share in the loss. Is this then the same kind of affection with that of parents to their children? Is there the same tender personal regard? I fancy no parent will say so. In this case of merchants there is a plain conjunction of interest, but whence the conjunction of interest between the parent and child? Do the child's sensations give pleasure or pain to the parent? Is the parent hungry, thirsty, sick when his children are so? No, but his naturally implanted desire of their good and aversion to their misery, makes him be affected with joy or sorrow from their pleasures or pains. This desire then is antecedent to the conjunction of interest, and the cause of it, not the effect. It must then be disinterested.

No, says another sophist, children are parts of ourselves, and in loving them we but love ourselves in them. A very good answer! Let us carry it as far as it will go. How are they parts of ourselves? Not as a leg or an arm; we are not conscious of their sensations. But their bodies were formed from parts of ours. So is a fly or a maggot which may breed in any discharged blood or humor: very dear insects surely! There must be something else then which makes children parts of ourselves, and what is this but that affection which nature determines us to have toward them? This love makes them parts of ourselves, and therefore does not flow from their being so before. This is indeed a good metaphor, and wherever we find a determination among several rational agents to mutual love, let each individual be looked upon as a part of a great whole or system, and concern himself in the public good of it.

But a later author observes[164] that natural affection in parents is weak, till the children begin to give evidences of knowledge and affections. Mothers say they feel it strong from the very first, and yet I could wish for the destruction of his hypothesis, that what he alleges was true, as I fancy it is in some measure, though we may find in some parents an affection toward idiots. The observing of understanding and affections in children, which can make them appear moral agents, can increase love toward them without prospect of interest, for I hope this increase of love is not from prospect of advantage from the knowledge or affections of children for whom parents are still toiling, and never intend to be refunded their expenses or recompensed for their labor but in cases of extreme necessity. If then the observing a moral capacity can be the occasion of increasing love without self-interest, even from the frame of our nature; pray may not this be a foundation of weaker degrees of love where there is no preceding tie of parentage, and extend it to all mankind?

DAVID HUME
(1711–1776)

Self-interest must be used to regulate itself [165]

This avidity alone, of acquiring goods and possessions for ourselves and our nearest friends, is insatiable, perpetual, universal, and directly destructive of society. There scarce is any one, who is not actuated by it; and there is no one, who has not reason to fear from it, when it acts without any restraint, and gives way to its first and most natural movements. So that upon the whole, we are to esteem the difficulties in the establishment of society, to be greater or less, according to those we encounter in regulating and restraining this passion.

'Tis certain, that no affection of the human mind has both a sufficient force, and a proper direction to counter-balance the love of gain, and render men fit members of society, by making them abstain from the possessions of others. Benevolence to strangers is too weak for this purpose, and as to the other passions, they rather inflame this avidity when we observe, that the larger our possessions are, the more ability we have of gratifying all our appetites. There is no passion, therefore, capable of controlling the interested affection, but the very affection itself, by an alteration of its direction. Now this alteration must necessarily take place upon the least reflection;

since 'tis evident, that the passion is much better satisfy'd by its restraint, than by its liberty, and that by preserving society, we make much greater advances in the acquiring possessions, than by running into the solitary and forlorn condition, which must follow upon violence and an universal license. The question, therefore, concerning the wickedness or goodness of human nature, enters not in the least into that other question concerning the origin of society; nor is there any thing to be consider'd but the degrees of men's sagacity or folly. For whether the passion of self-interest be esteemed vicious or virtuous, 'tis all a case; since itself alone restrains it: So that if it be virtuous, men become social by their virtue; if vicious, their vice has the same effect.

Now as 'tis by establishing the rule for the stability of possession, that this passion restrains itself; if that rule be very abstruse, and of difficult invention; society must be esteem'd, in a manner, accidental, and the effect of many ages. But if it be found, that nothing can be more simple and obvious than that rule; that every parent, in order to preserve peace among his children, must establish it; and that these first rudiments of justice must every day be improv'd, as the society enlarges: If all this appear evident, as it certainly must, we may conclude, that 'tis utterly impossible for men to remain any considerable time in that savage condition, which precedes society; but that this very first state and situation may justly be esteem'd social.

Selfishness and scarce resources create the need for justice [166]

I have already observ'd, that justice takes its rise from human conventions; and that these are intended as a remedy to some inconveniences, which proceed from the concurrence of certain *qualities* of the human mind with the *situation* of external objects. The qualities of the mind are *selfishness* and *limited generosity*: And the situation of external objects is their *easy change* join'd to their *scarcity* in comparison of the wants and desires or men. But however philosophers may have been bewilder'd in those speculations, poets have been guided more infallibly, by a certain taste or common instinct, which in most kinds of reasoning goes farther than any of that art and philosophy, with which we have been yet acquainted. They easily perceiv'd, if every man had a tender regard for another, or if nature supplied abundantly all our wants and desires, that the jealousy of interest, which justice supposes, could no longer have place; nor would there be any occasion for those distinctions and limits of property and possession, which at present are in use among mankind. Increase to a sufficient degree the benevolence of men, or the bounty of nature, and you render justice useless, by supplying its place with much nobler virtues, and more valuable blessings. The selfishness of men is animated by the few possessions we have, proportioned to our wants; and 'tis to restrain this selfishness, that men have been oblig'd to separate themselves from the community, and to distinguish betwixt their own goods and those of others.

Nor need we have recourse to the fictions of poets to learn this; but beside the reason of the thing, may discover the same truth by common experience and observation. 'Tis easy to remark, that a cordial affection renders all things common among friends; and that married people in particular mutually lose their property, and are unacquainted with the *mine* and *thine*, which are so necessary, and yet cause such disturbance in human society. The same effect arises from any alteration in the circumstances of mankind; as when there is such a plenty of any thing as satisfies all the desires of men: In which case the distinction of property is entirely lost, and every thing remains in common. This we may observe with regard to air and water, tho' the most valuable of all external objects; and may easily conclude, that if men were supplied with every thing in the same abundance, or if *every one* had the same affection and tender regard for *every one* as for himself; justice and injustice would be equally unknown among mankind.

Here then is a proposition, which, I think, may be regarded as certain, that 'tis from the selfishness and confin'd generosity of men, along with the scanty provision nature has made for his wants, that justice derives its origin.

Human beings naturally show concern for others' interests [167]

How, indeed, can we suppose it possible in anyone who wears a human heart that, if there be subjected to his censure one character or system of conduct which is beneficial, and another which is pernicious to his species or community, he will not so much as give a cool preference to the former or ascribe to it the smallest merit or regard? Let us suppose a person ever so selfish, let private interest have engrossed ever so much his attention, yet in instances where that is not concerned he must unavoidably feel some propensity to the good of mankind and make it an object of choice, if everything else be equal. Would any man who is walking alone tread as willingly on another's gouty toes, whom he has no quarrel with, as on the hard flint and pavement? There is here surely a difference in the case. We surely take into consideration the happiness and misery of others in weighing the several motives of action, and incline to the former where no private regards draw us to seek our own promotion or advantage by the injury of our fellow creatures. And if the principles of humanity are capable, in many instances, of influencing our actions, they must, at all times, have some authority over our sentiments and give us a general approbation of what is useful to society, and blame of what is dangerous or pernicious. The degrees of these sentiments may be the subject of controversy, but the reality of their existence, one should think, must be admitted in every theory or system.

Benevolence is not a species of self-interest [168]

There is a principle, supposed to prevail among many, which is utterly incompatible with all virtue or moral sentiment; and as it can proceed from nothing but the most depraved disposition, so in its turn it tends still further to encourage that depravity. This principle is that all *benevolence* is mere hypocrisy, friendship a cheat, public spirit a farce, fidelity a snare to procure trust and confidence; and that, while all of us, at bottom, pursue only our private interest, we wear these fair disguises in order to put others off their guard and expose them the more to our wiles and machinations. What heart one must be possessed of who professes such principles, and who feels no internal sentiment that belies so pernicious a theory, it is easy to imagine; and also, what degree of affection and benevolence he can bear to a species whom he represents under such odious colors and supposes so little susceptible of gratitude or any return of affection. Or, if we should not ascribe these principles wholly to a corrupted heart, we must at least account for them from the most careless and precipitate examination. Superficial reasoners, indeed, observing many false pretenses among mankind, and feeling, perhaps, no very strong restraint in their own disposition, might draw a general and a hasty conclusion that all is equally corrupted, and that men, different from all other animals, and indeed from all other species of existence, admit of no degrees of good or bad, but are, in every instance, the same creatures under different disguises and appearances.

There is another principle, somewhat resembling the former, which has been much insisted on by philosophers, and has been the foundation of many a system—that, whatever affection one may feel, or imagine he feels for others, no passion is, or can be, disinterested; that the most generous friendship, however sincere, is a modification of self-love; and that, even unknown to ourselves, we seek only our own gratification while we appear the most deeply engaged in schemes for the liberty and happiness of mankind. By a turn of imagination, by a refinement of reflection, by an enthusiasm of passion, we seem to take part in the interests of others and imagine ourselves divested of all selfish considerations. But, at bottom, the most generous patriot, and most niggardly miser, the bravest hero, and most abject coward have, in every action, an equal regard to their own happiness and welfare. . . .

The most obvious objection to the selfish hypothesis is that as it is contrary to common feeling and our most unprejudiced notions, there is required the highest stretch of philosophy to establish so extraordinary a paradox. To the most careless observer there appear to be such dispositions as benevolence and generosity, such affections as love, friendship, compassion, gratitude. These sentiments have their causes, effects, objects, and operations marked by common language and observation, and plainly distinguished from those of the selfish passions. And as this is the obvious appearance of things, it must be admitted till some hypothesis be discovered which, by penetrating deeper into human nature, may prove the former affections to be nothing but modifications of the latter. All attempts of this kind have hitherto proved fruitless, and seem to have proceeded entirely from that love of *simplicity* which has been the source of much false reasoning in philosophy. I shall not here enter into any detail on the present subject. Many able philosophers have shown the insufficiency of these systems; and I shall take for granted what, I believe, the smallest reflection will make evident to every impartial inquirer. . . .

The simplest and most obvious cause which can there be assigned for any phenomenon is probably the true one. When a philosopher, in the explication of his system, is obliged to have recourse to some very intricate and refined reflections, and to suppose them essential to the production of any passion or emotion, we have reason to be extremely on our guard against so fallacious a hypothesis. The affections are not susceptible of any impression from the refinements of reason or imagination; and it is always found that a vigorous exertion of the latter faculties, necessarily from the narrow capacity of the human mind, destroys all activity in the former. Our predominant motive or intention is, indeed, frequently concealed from ourselves when it is mingled and confounded with other motives which the mind, from vanity or self-conceit, is desirous of supposing more prevalent. But there is no instance that a concealment of this nature has ever arisen from the abstruseness and intricacy of the motive. A man that has lost a friend and patron may flatter himself that all his grief arises from generous sentiments, without any mixture of narrow or interested considerations; but a man that grieves for a valuable friend who needed his patronage and protection— how can we suppose that his passionate tenderness arises from some metaphysical regards to a self-interest which has no foundation or reality? We may as well imagine that minute wheels and springs, like those of a watch, give motion to a loaded wagon, as account for the origin of passion from such abstruse reflections.

Animals are found susceptible of kindness, both to their own species and to ours; nor is there, in this case, the least suspicion of disguise or artifice. Shall we account for all *their* sentiments, too, from refined deductions of self-interest? Or if we admit a disinterested benevolence in the inferior species, by what rule of analogy can we refuse it in the superior?

Love between the sexes begets a complacency and good will very distinct from the gratification of an appetite. Tenderness to their offspring, in all sensible beings, is commonly able alone to counterbalance the strongest motives of self-love, and has no manner of dependence on that affection. What interest can a fond mother have in view who loses her health by assiduous attendance on her sick child, and afterwards languishes and dies of grief when freed, by its death, from the slavery of that attendance?

Is gratitude no affection of the human breast, or is that a word merely without any meaning or reality? Have we no satisfaction in one man's company above another's, and no desire of the welfare of our friend, even though absence or death should prevent us from all participation in it? Or what is it commonly that gives us any participation in it, even while alive and present, but our affection and regard to him?

These and a thousand other instances are marks of a general benevolence in human nature, where no *real* interest binds us to the object. And how an *imaginary* interest, known and avowed for such, can be the origin of any passion or emotion seems difficult to explain. No satisfactory hypothesis of this kind has yet been discovered, nor is there the smallest probability that the future industry of men will ever be attended with more favorable success.

Virtue is in our interest [169]

Having explained the moral *approbation* attending merit or virtue, there remains nothing but briefly to consider our interested *obligation* to it, and to inquire whether every man who has any regard to his own happiness and welfare will not best find his account in the practice of every moral duty. If this can be clearly ascertained from the foregoing theory, we shall have the satisfaction to reflect that we have advanced principles which not only, it is hoped, will stand the test of reasoning and inquiry, but may contribute to the amendment of men's lives and their improvement in morality and social virtue. And though the philosophical truth of any proposition by no means depends on its tendency to promote the interests of society, yet a man has but a bad grace who delivers a theory, however true, which he must confess leads to a practice dangerous and pernicious. . . .

But what philosophical truths can be more advantageous to society than those here delivered, which represent virtue in all her genuine and most engaging charms and make us approach her with ease, familiarity, and affection? The dismal dress falls off, with which many divines and some philosophers have covered her, and nothing appears but gentleness, humanity, beneficence, affability, nay, even at proper intervals, play, frolic, and gaiety. She talks not of useless austerities and rigors, suffering, and self-denial. She declares that her sole purpose is to make her votaries, and all mankind, during every instant of their existence, if possible, cheerful and happy; nor does she ever willingly part with any pleasure but in hopes of ample compensation in some other period of their lives. The sole trouble which she demands is that of just calculation and a steady preference of the greater happiness. And if any austere pretenders approach her, enemies to joy and pleasure, she either rejects them as hypocrites and deceivers, or, if she admit them in her train they are ranked, however, among the least favored of her votaries.

And, indeed, to drop all figurative expression, what hopes can we ever have of engaging mankind to a practice which we confess full of austerity and rigor? Or what theory of morals can ever serve any useful purpose unless it can show, by a particular detail, that all the duties which it recommends are also the true interest of each individual? The peculiar advantage of the foregoing system seems to be that it furnishes proper mediums for that purpose.

That the virtues which are immediately useful or *agreeable* to the person possessed of them are desirable in a view to self-interest, it would surely be superfluous to prove.

Moralists, indeed, may spare themselves all the pains which they often take in recommending these duties. To what purpose collect arguments, to evince that temperance is advantageous and the excesses of pleasure hurtful? When it appears that these excesses are only denominated such because they are hurtful, and that if the unlimited use of strong liquors, for instance, no more impaired health or the faculties of mind and body, than the use of air or water, it would not be a whit more vicious or blamable.

It seems equally superfluous to prove that the *companionable* virtues of good manners and wit, decency and genteelness are more desirable than the contrary qualities. Vanity alone, without any other consideration, is a sufficient motive to make us wish for the possession of these accomplishments. No man was ever willingly deficient in this particular. All our failures here proceed from bad education, want of capacity, or a perverse and unpliable disposition. Would you have your company coveted, admired, followed rather than hated, despised, avoided? Can anyone seriously deliberate in the case? As no enjoyment is sincere without some reference to company and society, so no society can be agreeable, or even tolerable, where a man feels his presence unwelcome and discovers all around him symptoms of disgust and aversion.

But why, in the greater society or confederacy of mankind, should not the case be the same as in particular clubs and companies? Why is it more doubtful that the enlarged virtues of humanity, generosity, beneficence are desirable, with a view to happiness and self-interest, than the limited endowments of ingenuity and politeness? Are we apprehensive lest those social affections interfere in a greater and more immediate degree than any other pursuits with private utility, and cannot be gratified without some important sacrifice of honor and advantage? If so, we are but ill instructed in the nature of the human passions, and are more influenced by verbal distinctions than by real differences.

Whatever contradiction may vulgarly be supposed between the selfish and *social* sentiments or dispositions, they are really no more opposite than selfish and ambitious, selfish and revengeful, selfish and vain. It is requisite that there be an original propensity of some kind, in order to be a basis to self-love, by giving a relish to the objects of its pursuit; and none more fit for this purpose than benevolence or humanity. The goods of fortune are spent in one gratification or another: the miser who accumulates his annual income and lends it out at interest has really spent it in the gratification of his avarice. And it would be difficult to show why a man is more a loser by a generous action than by any other method of expense, since the utmost which he can attain by the most elaborate selfishness is the indulgence of some affection.

Now if life without passion must be altogether insipid and tiresome, let a man suppose that he has full power of modeling his own disposition, and let him deliberate what appetite or desire he would choose for the foundation of his happiness and enjoyment. Every affection, he would observe, when gratified by success, gives a satisfaction proportioned to its force and violence; but besides this advantage, common to all, the immediate feeling of benevolence and friendship, humanity and kindness is sweet, smooth, tender, and agreeable, independent of all fortune and accidents. These virtues are, besides, attended with a pleasing consciousness or remembrance and keep us in humor with ourselves as well as others, while we retain the agreeable reflection of having done our part toward mankind and society. And though all men show a jealousy of our success in the pursuits of avarice and ambition, yet are we almost sure of their good will and good wishes so long as we persevere in the paths of virtue and employ ourselves in the execution of generous plans and purposes. What other passion is there where we shall find so many advantages united: an agreeable sentiment, a pleasing consciousness, a good reputation? But of these truths we may observe, men are of themselves pretty much convinced nor are they deficient in their duty to society because they would not wish to be generous, friendly, and humane, but because they do not feel themselves such.

Treating vice with the greatest candor and making it all possible concessions, we must acknowledge that there is not, in any instance, the smallest pretext for giving it the preference above virtue with a view to self-interest, except, perhaps, in the case of justice, where a man, taking things in a certain light, may often seem to be a loser by his integrity. And though it is allowed that, without a regard to property, no society could subsist, yet, according to the imperfect way in which human affairs are conducted, a sensible knave, in particular incidents, may think that an act of iniquity or infidelity will make a considerable addition to his fortune without causing any considerable breach in the social union and confederacy. That *honesty is the best policy* may be a good general rule, but is liable to many exceptions. And he, it may perhaps be thought, conducts himself with most wisdom who observes the general rule and takes advantage of all the exceptions.

I must confess that if a man think that this reasoning much requires an answer, it will be a little difficult to find any which will to him appear satisfactory and convincing. If his heart rebel not against such pernicious maxims, if he feel no reluctance to the thoughts of villainy or baseness, he has indeed lost a considerable motive to virtue; and we may expect that his practice will be answerable to his speculation. But in all ingenuous natures the antipathy to treachery and roguery is too strong to be counterbalanced by any views of profit or pecuniary advantage. Inward peace of mind, consciousness of integrity, a satisfactory review of our own conduct—these are circumstances very requisite to happiness and will be cherished and cultivated by every honest man who feels the importance of them.

Such a one has, besides, the frequent satisfaction of seeing knaves, with all their pretended cunning and abilities, betrayed by their own maxims; and while they purpose to cheat with moderation and secrecy, a tempting incident occurs—nature is frail—and they give in to the snare, whence they can never extricate themselves without a total loss of reputation and the forfeiture of all future trust and confidence with mankind.

But were they ever so secret and successful, the honest man, if he has any tincture of philosophy, or even common observation and reflection, will discover that they themselves are, in the end, the greatest dupes, and have sacrificed the invaluable enjoyment of a character, with themselves at least, for the acquisition of worthless toys and gewgaws. How little is requisite to supply the *necessities* of nature? And in a view to *pleasure*, what comparison between the unbought satisfaction of conversation, society, study, even health and the common beauties of nature, but above all, the peaceful reflection on one's own conduct? What comparison, I say, between these and the feverish, empty amusements of luxury and expense? These natural leisures, indeed, are really without price, both because they are below all price in their attainment and above it in their enjoyment.

Adam Smith, born in Kirkcaldy, Scotland, was a student of Francis Hutcheson and a close friend of David Hume. Though he is best known today for his work in political economy, he spent much of his academic career as a professor of moral philosophy in the University of Edinburgh. Unlike his economic writings, his ethical theory emphasizes sympathy and self-command over bald self-interest.

ADAM SMITH
(1723–1790)

Sympathy makes possible disinterested concern for others [170]

How selfish soever man may be supposed, there are evidently some principles in his nature, which interest him in the fortune of others, and render their happiness necessary to him, though he derives nothing from it except the pleasure of seeing it. Of this kind is pity or compassion, the emotion which we feel for the misery of others, when we either see it, or are made to conceive it in a very lively manner. That we often derive sorrow from the sorrow of others, is a matter of fact too obvious to require any instances to prove it; for this sentiment, like all the other original passions of human nature, is by no means confined to the virtuous and humane, though they perhaps may feel it with the most exquisite sensibility. The greatest ruffian, the most hardened violator of the laws of society, is not altogether without it.

As we have no immediate experience of what other men feel, we can form no idea of the manner in which they are affected, but by conceiving what we ourselves should feel in the like situation. Though our brother is upon the rack, as long as we ourselves are at our ease, our senses will never inform us of what he suffers. They never did, and never can, carry us beyond our own person, and it is by the imagination only that we can form any conception of what are his sensations. Neither can that faculty help us to this any other way, than by representing to us what would be our own, if we were in his case. It is the impressions of our own senses only, not those of his, which our imaginations copy. By the imagination we place ourselves in his situation, we conceive ourselves enduring all the same torments, we enter as it were into his body, and become in some measure the same person with him, and thence form some idea of his sensations, and even feel something which, though weaker in degree, is not altogether unlike them. His agonies, when they are thus brought home to ourselves, when we have thus adopted and made them our own, begin at last to affect us, and we then tremble and shudder at the thought of what he feels. For as to be in pain or distress of any kind excites the most excessive sorrow, so to conceive or to imagine that we are in it, excites some degree of the same emotion, in proportion to the vivacity or dullness of the conception. . . .

Neither is it those circumstances only, which create pain or sorrow, that call forth our fellow-feeling. Whatever is the passion which arises from any object in the person principally concerned, an analogous emotion springs up, at the thought of his situation, in the breast of every attentive spectator. Our joy for the deliverance of those heroes of tragedy or romance who interest us, is as sincere as our grief for their distress, and our fellow-feeling with their misery is not more real than that with their happiness. We enter into their gratitude towards those faithful friends who did not desert them in their difficulties; and we heartily go along with their resentment against those perfidious traitors who injured, abandoned, or deceived them. In every passion of which the mind of man is susceptible, the emotions of the bystander always correspond to what, by bringing the case home to himself, he imagines should be the sentiments of the sufferer.

Sympathy, however, cannot, in any sense, be regarded as a selfish principle. When I sympathize with your sorrow or your indignation, it may be pretended, indeed, that my emotion is founded in self-love, because it arises from bringing your case home to myself, from putting myself in your situation, and thence conceiving what I should feel in the like circumstances. But though sympathy is very properly said to arise from an imaginary change of situations with the person principally concerned, yet this imaginary change is not supposed to happen to me in my own person and character, but in that of the person with whom I sympathize. When I condole with you for the loss of your only son, in order to enter into your grief I do not consider what I, a person of such a character and profession, should suffer, if I had a son, and if that son was unfortunately to die: but I consider what I should suffer if I was really you, and I not only change circumstances with you, but I change persons and characters. My grief, therefore, is entirely upon your account, and not in the least upon my own. It is not, therefore, in the least selfish. How can that be regarded as a selfish passion, which does not arise even from the imagination of any thing that has befallen, or that relates to myself, in my own proper person and character, but which is entirely occupied about what relates to you? A man may sympathize with a woman in child-bed; though it is impossible that he should conceive himself as suffering her pains in his own proper person and character. That whole account of human nature, however, which deduces all sentiments and affections from self-love, which has made much noise in the world, but which, so far as I know, has never yet been fully and distinctly explained, seems to me to have arisen from some confused misapprehension of the system of sympathy.

We balance self and others by taking the attitude of an impartial spectator [171]

But though the approbation of his own conscience can scarce, upon some extraordinary occasions, content the weakness of man; though the testimony of the supposed impartial spectator, of the great inmate of the breast, cannot always alone support him; yet the influence and authority of this principle is, upon all occasions, very great; and it is only by consulting this judge within, that we can ever see what relates to ourselves in its proper shape and dimensions; or that we can ever make any proper comparison between our own interests and those of other people.

As to the eye of the body, objects appear great or small, not so much according to their real dimensions, as according to the nearness or distance of their situation; so do they likewise to what may be called the natural eye of the mind: and we remedy the defects of both these organs pretty much in the same manner. In my present situation an immense landscape of lawns, and woods, and distant mountains, seems to do no more than cover the little window which I write by, and to be out of all proportion less than the chamber in which I am sitting. I can form a just comparison between those great objects and the little objects around me, in no other way, than by transporting myself, at least in fancy, to a different station, from whence I can survey both at nearly equal distances, and thereby form some judgment of their real proportions. Habit and experience have taught me to do this so easily and so readily, that I am scarce sensible that I do it; and a man must be, in some measure, acquainted with the philosophy of vision, before he can be thoroughly convinced, how little those distant objects would appear to the eye, if the imagination, from a knowledge of their real magnitudes, did not swell and dilate them.

In the same manner, to the selfish and original passions of human nature, the loss or gain of a very small interest of our own, appears to be of vastly more importance, excites a much more passionate joy or sorrow, a much more ardent desire or aversion, than the greatest concern of another with whom we have no particular connection. His interests, as long as they are surveyed from this station, can never be put into the balance with our own, can never restrain us from doing whatever may tend to promote our own, how ruinous soever to him. Before we can make any proper comparison of those opposite interests, we must change our position. We must view them, neither from our own place nor yet from his, neither with our own eyes nor yet with his, but from the place and with the eyes of a third person, who has no particular connection with either, and who judges with impartiality between us. Here, too, habit and experience have taught us to do this so easily and so readily, that we are scarce sensible that we do it; and it requires, in this case too, some degree of reflection, and even of philosophy, to convince us, how little interest we should take in the greatest concerns of our neighbor, how little we should be affected by whatever relates to him, if the sense of propriety and justice did not correct the otherwise natural inequality of our sentiments.

Let us suppose that the great empire of China, with all its myriads of inhabitants, was suddenly swallowed up by an earthquake, and let us consider how a man of humanity in Europe, who had no sort of connection with that part of the world, would be affected upon receiving intelligence of this dreadful calamity. He would, I imagine, first of all, express very strongly his sorrow for the misfortune of that unhappy people, he would make many melancholy reflections upon the precariousness of human life, and the vanity of all the labors of man, which could thus be annihilated in a moment. He would too, perhaps, if he was a man of speculation, enter into many reasonings concerning the effects which this disaster might produce upon the commerce of Europe, and the trade and business of the world in general. And when all this fine philosophy was over, when all these humane sentiments had been once fairly expressed, he would pursue his business or his pleasure, take his repose or his diversion, with the same ease and tranquillity, as if no such accident had happened. The most frivolous disaster which could befall himself would occasion a more real disturbance. If he was to lose his little finger tomorrow, he would not sleep tonight; but, provided he never saw them, he will snore with the most profound security over the ruin of a hundred millions of his brethren, and the destruction of that immense multitude seems plainly an object less interesting to him, than this paltry misfortune of his own. To prevent, therefore, this paltry misfortune to himself, would a man of humanity be willing to sacrifice the lives of a hundred millions of his brethren, provided he had never seen them? Human nature startles with horror at the thought, and the world, in its greatest depravity and corruption, never produced such a villain as could be capable of entertaining it. But what makes this difference? When our passive feelings are almost always so sordid and so selfish, how comes it that our active principles should often be so generous and so noble? When we are always so much more deeply affected by whatever concerns ourselves, than by whatever concerns other men; what is it which prompts the generous, upon all occasions, and the mean upon many, to sacrifice their own interests to the greater interests of others? It is not the soft power of humanity, it is not that feeble spark of benevolence which Nature has lighted up in the human heart, that is thus capable of counteracting the strongest impulses of self-love. It is a stronger power, a more forcible motive, which exerts itself upon such occasions. It is reason, principle, conscience, the inhabitant of the breast, the man within the great judge and arbiter of our conduct. It is he who, whenever we are about to act so as to affect the happiness of others, calls to us, with a voice capable of astonishing the most presumptuous of our passions, that we are but one of the multitude, in no respect better than any other in it; and that when we prefer ourselves so shamefully and so blindly to others, we become the proper objects of resentment, abhorrence, and execration. It is from him only that we learn the real littleness of ourselves, and of whatever relates to ourselves, and the natural misrepresentations of self-love can be corrected only by the eye of this impartial spectator. It is he who shows us the propriety of generosity and the deformity of injustice; the propriety of resigning the greatest interests of our own, for the yet greater interests of others, and the deformity of doing the smallest injury to another, in order to obtain the greatest benefit to ourselves. It is not the love of our neighbor, it is not the love of mankind, which upon many occasions prompts us to the practice of those divine virtues. It is a stronger love, a more powerful affection, which generally takes place upon such occasions; the love of what is honorable and noble, of the grandeur, and dignity, and superiority of our own characters.

When the happiness or misery of others depends in any respect upon our conduct, we dare not, as self-love might suggest to us, prefer the interest of one to that of many. The man within immediately calls to us, that we value ourselves too much and other people too little, and that, by doing so, we render ourselves the proper object of the contempt and indignation of our brethren. Neither is this sentiment confined to men of extraordinary magnanimity and virtue. It is deeply impressed upon every tolerably good soldier, who feels that he would become the scorn of his companions, if he could be supposed capable of shrinking from danger, or of hesitating, either to expose or to throw away his life, when the good of the service required it.

One individual must never prefer himself so much even to any other individual, as to hurt or injure that other, in order to benefit himself, though the benefit to the one should be much greater than the hurt or injury to the other. The poor man must neither defraud nor steal from the rich, though the acquisition might be much more beneficial to the one than the loss could be hurtful to the other. The man within immediately calls to him, in this case too, that he is no better than his neighbor, and that by this unjust preference he renders himself the proper object of the contempt and indignation of mankind; as well as of the punishment which that contempt and indignation must naturally dispose them to inflict, for having thus violated one of those sacred rules, upon the tolerable observation of which depend the whole security and peace of human society. There is no commonly honest man who does not more dread the inward disgrace of such an action, the indelible stain which it would for ever stamp upon his own mind, than the greatest external calamity which, without any fault of his own, could possibly befall him; and who does not inwardly feel the truth of that great stoical maxim, that for one man to deprive another unjustly of any thing, or unjustly to promote his own advantage by the loss or disadvantage of another, is more contrary to nature, than death, than poverty, than pain, than all the misfortunes which can affect him, either in his body, or in his external circumstances.

When the happiness or misery of others, indeed, in no respect depends upon our conduct, when our interests are altogether separated and detached from theirs, so that there is neither connection nor competition between them, we do not always think it so necessary to restrain, either our natural and, perhaps, improper anxiety about our own affairs, or our natural and, perhaps, equally improper indifference about those of other men. The most vulgar education teaches us to act, upon all important occasions, with some sort of impartiality between ourselves and others, and even the ordinary commerce of the world is capable of adjusting our active principles to some degree of propriety. But it is the most artificial and refined education only, it has been said, which can correct the inequalities of our passive feelings; and we must for this purpose, it has been pretended, have recourse to the severest, as well as to the profoundest philosophy.

Disregard for others leads to remorse and self-loathing [172]

The violator of the more sacred laws of justice can never reflect on the sentiments which mankind must entertain with regard to him, without feeling all the agonies of shame, and horror, and consternation. When his passion is gratified, and he begins coolly to reflect on his past conduct, he can enter into none of the motives which influenced it. They appear now as detestable to him as they did always to other people. By sympathizing with the hatred and abhorrence which other men must entertain for him, he becomes in some measure the object of his own hatred and abhorrence. The situation of the person, who suffered by his injustice, now calls upon his pity. He is grieved at the thought of it; regrets the unhappy effects of his own conduct, and feels at the same time that they have rendered him the proper object of the resentment and indignation of mankind, and of what is the natural consequence of resentment, vengeance, and punishment. The thought of this perpetually haunts him, and fills him with terror and amazement. He dares no longer look society in the face, but imagines himself as it were rejected, and thrown out from the affections of all mankind. He cannot hope for the consolation of sympathy in this his greatest and most dreadful distress. The remembrance of his crimes has shut out all fellow-feeling with him from the hearts of his fellow-creatures. The sentiments which they entertain with regard to him, are the very thing which he is most afraid of. Every thing seems hostile, and he would be glad to fly to some inhospitable desert, where he might never more behold the face of a human creature, nor read in the countenance of mankind the condemnation of his crimes. But solitude is still more dreadful than society. His own thoughts can present him with nothing but what is black, unfortunate, and disastrous, the melancholy forebodings of incomprehensible misery and ruin. The horror of solitude drives him back into society, and he comes again into the presence of mankind, astonished to appear before them, loaded with shame and distracted with fear, in order to supplicate some little protection from the countenance of those very judges, who he knows have already all unanimously condemned him. Such is the nature of that sentiment, which is properly called remorse; of all the sentiments which can enter the human breast the most dreadful. It is made up of shame from the sense of the impropriety of past conduct; of grief for the effects of it; of pity for those who suffer by it; and of the dread and terror of punishment from the consciousness of the justly provoked resentment of all rational creatures.

The twin virtues of sympathy and self-command [173]

Upon these two different efforts, upon that of the spectator to enter into sentiments of the person principally concerned, and upon that of the person principally concerned, to bring down his emotions to what the spectator can go along with, are founded two different sets of virtues. The soft, the gentle, the amiable virtues, the virtues of candid condescension and indulgent humanity, are founded upon the one: the great, the awful and respectable, the virtues of self-denial, of self-government, of that command of the passions which subjects all the movements of our nature to what our own dignity and honor, and the propriety of our own conduct require, take their origin from the other.

How amiable does he appear to be, whose sympathetic heart seems to re-echo all the sentiments of those with whom he converses, who grieves for their calamities, who resents their injuries, and who rejoices at their good fortune! When we bring home to ourselves the situation of his companions, we enter into their gratitude, and feel what consolation they must derive from the tender sympathy of so affectionate a friend. And for a contrary reason, how disagreeable does he appear to be, whose hard and obdurate heart feels for himself only, but is altogether insensible to the happiness or misery of others! We enter, in this case too, into the pain which his presence must give to every mortal with whom he converses, to those especially with whom we are most apt to sympathize, the unfortunate and the injured.

On the other hand, what noble propriety and grace do we feel in the conduct of those who, in their own case, exert that recollection and self-command which constitute the dignity of every passion, and which bring it down to what others can enter into! We are disgusted with that clamorous grief, which, without any delicacy, calls upon our compassion with sighs and tears and importunate lamentations. But we reverence that reserved, that silent and majestic sorrow, which discovers itself only in the swelling of the eyes, in the quivering of the lips and cheeks, and in the distant, but affecting, coldness of the whole behavior. It imposes the like silence upon us. We regard it with respectful attention, and watch with anxious concern over our whole behavior, lest by any impropriety we should disturb that concerted tranquillity, which it requires so great an effort to support. . . .

And hence it is, that to feel much for others and little for ourselves, that to restrain our selfish, and to indulge our benevolent affections, constitutes the perfection of human nature; and can alone produce among mankind that harmony of sentiments and passions in which consists their whole grace and propriety. As to love our neighbor as we love ourselves is the great law of Christianity, so it is the great precept of nature to love ourselves only as we love our neighbor, or what comes to the same thing, as our neighbor is capable of loving us. . . .

Our sensibility to the feelings of others, so far from being inconsistent with the manhood of self-command, is the very principle upon which that manhood is founded. The very same principle or instinct which, in the misfortune of our neighbor, prompts us to compassionate his sorrow; in our own misfortune, prompts us to restrain the abject and miserable lamentations of our own sorrow. The same principle or instinct which, in his prosperity and success, prompts us to congratulate his joy; in our own prosperity and success, prompts us to restrain the levity and intemperance of our own joy. In both cases, the propriety of our own sentiments and feelings seems to be exactly in proportion to the vivacity and force with which we enter into and conceive his sentiments and feelings.

The man of the most perfect virtue, the man whom we naturally love and revere the most, is he who joins, to the most perfect command of his own original and selfish feelings, the most exquisite sensibility both to the original and sympathetic feelings of others. The man who, to all the soft, the amiable, and the gentle virtues, joins all the great, the awful, and the respectable, must surely be the natural and proper object of our highest love and admiration. . . .

The degree of the self-approbation with which every man, upon such occasions, surveys his own conduct, is higher or lower, exactly in proportion to the degree of self-command which is necessary in order to obtain that self-approbation. Where little self-command is necessary, little self-approbation is due. The man who has only scratched his finger, cannot much applaud himself, though he should immediately appear to have forgot this paltry misfortune. The man who has lost his leg by a cannon shot, and who, the moment after, speaks and acts with his usual coolness and tranquillity, as he exerts a much higher degree of self-command, so he naturally feels a much higher degree of self-approbation. With most men, upon such an accident, their own natural view of their own misfortune would force itself upon them with such a vivacity and strength of coloring, as would entirely efface all thought of every other view. They would feel nothing, they could attend to nothing, but their own pain and their own fear; and not only the judgment of the ideal man within the breast, but that of the real spectators who might happen to be present, would be entirely overlooked and disregarded.

The reward which Nature bestows upon good behavior under misfortune, is thus exactly proportioned to the degree of that good behavior. The only compensation she could possibly make for the bitterness of pain and distress is thus too, in equal degrees of good behavior, exactly proportioned to the degree of that pain and distress. In proportion to the degree of the self-command which is necessary in order to conquer our natural sensibility, the pleasure and pride of the conquest are so much the greater; and this pleasure and pride are so great that no man can be altogether unhappy who completely enjoys them. . . .

The market operates on the principle of self-interest [174]

In civilized society [man] stands at all times in need of the cooperation and assistance of great multitudes, while his whole life is scarce sufficient to gain the friendship of a few persons. In almost every other race of animals each individual, when it is grown up to maturity, is entirely independent, and in its natural state has occasion for the assistance of no other living creature. But man has almost constant occasion for the help of his brethren, and it is in vain for him to expect it from their benevolence only. He will be more likely to prevail if he can interest their self-love in his favor, and show them that it is for their own advantage to do for him what he requires of them. Whoever offers to another a bargain of any kind, proposes to do this. Give me that which I want, and you shall have this which you want, is the meaning of every such offer; and it is in this manner that we obtain from one another the far greater part of those good offices which we stand in need of. It is not from the benevolence of the butcher, the brewer, or the baker, that we expect our dinner, but from their regard to their own interest. We address ourselves, not to their humanity but to their self-love, and never talk to them of our own necessities but of their advantages. Nobody but a beggar chooses to depend chiefly upon the benevolence of his fellow-citizens. Even a beggar does not depend upon it entirely. The charity of well-disposed people, indeed, supplies him with the whole fund of his subsistence. But though this principle ultimately provides him with all the necessaries of life which he has occasion for, it neither does nor can provide him with them as he has occasion for them. The greater part of his occasional wants are supplied in the same manner as those of other people, by treaty, by barter, and by purchase. With the money which one man gives him he purchases food. The old clothes which another bestows upon him he exchanges for other old clothes which suit him better, or for lodging, or for food, or for money, with which he can buy either food, clothes, or lodging, as he has occasion.

When individuals pursue their self-interest, they are led by an "invisible hand" to promote the common good [175]

As every individual, therefore, endeavors as much as he can both to employ his capital in the support of domestic industry, and so to direct that industry that its produce may be of the greatest value; every individual necessarily labors to render the annual revenue of the society as great as he can. He generally, indeed, neither intends to promote the public interest, nor knows how much he is promoting it. By preferring the support of domestic to that of foreign industry, he intends only his own security; and by directing that industry in such a manner as its produce may be of the greatest value, he intends only his own gain, and he is in this, as in many other cases, led by an invisible hand to promote an end which was no part of his intention. Nor is it always the worse for the society that it was no part of it. By pursuing his own interest he frequently promotes that of the society more effectually than when he really intends to promote it. I have never known much good done by those who affected to trade for the public good. It is an affectation, indeed, not very common among merchants, and very few words need be employed in dissuading them from it.

Immanuel Kant was born in Königsberg, East Prussia and educated at the university bearing that city's name. Though he recognizes the ubiquity of self-regard, Kant does not consider self-interest a proper basis for morality, even in cases where one's moral duty is to oneself.

IMMANUEL KANT
(1724–1804)

Happiness, though an indefinite concept, is the goal of all rational beings [176]

There is one end . . . which we may presuppose as actual in all rational beings so far as imperatives apply to them, that is, so far as they are dependent beings. There is one purpose which they not only *can* have but which we can presuppose that they all *do* have by a necessity of nature. This purpose is happiness. The hypothetical imperative which represents the practical necessity of an action as means to the promotion of happiness is an assertorical imperative. We may not expound it as necessary to a merely uncertain and merely possible purpose, but as necessary to a purpose which we can *a priori* and with assurance assume for everyone because it belongs to his essence. Skill in the choice of means to one's own highest well-being can be called prudence in the narrowest sense. Thus the imperative which refers to the choice of means to one's own happiness (i.e., the precept of prudence) is still only hypothetical, and the action is not commanded absolutely but commanded only as a means to another end in view. . . .

But it is a misfortune that the concept of happiness is so indefinite that, although each person wishes to attain it, he can never definitely and self-consistently state what it is that he really wishes and wills. The reason for this is that all elements which

belong to the concept of happiness are empirical (i.e., they must be taken from experience), while for the Idea of happiness an absolute whole, a maximum, of well-being
is needed in my present and in every future condition. Now it is impossible for even a
most clear-sighted and most capable but finite being to form here a definite concept
of that which he really wills. If he wills riches, how much anxiety, envy, and intrigues
might he not thereby draw upon his shoulders! If he wills much knowledge and
vision, perhaps it might become only an eye that much sharper to show him as more
dreadful the evils which are now hidden from him and which are yet unavoidable; or it
might be to burden his desires — which already sufficiently engage him — with even
more needs! If he wills long life, who guarantees that it will not be long misery! If he
wills at least health, how often has not the discomfort of his body restrained him
from excesses into which perfect health would have led him? In short, he is not capable, on any principle and with complete certainty, of ascertaining what would make
him truly happy; omniscience would be needed for this. He cannot, therefore, act
according to definite principles so as to be happy, but only according to empirical
counsels (e.g., those of diet, economy, courtesy, restraint, etc.) which are shown by
experience best to promote well-being on the average. Hence the imperatives of prudence cannot, in the strict sense, command (i.e., present actions objectively as practically necessary); thus they are to be taken as counsels (consilia) rather than as commands
(praecepta) of reason, and the task of determining infallibly and universally what action
will promote the happiness of a rational being is completely unsolvable. There can be
no imperative which would, in the strict sense, command us to do what makes for
happiness, because happiness is an ideal not of reason but of imagination, depending
only on empirical grounds which one would expect in vain to determine an action
through which the totality of consequences — which in fact is infinite — could be
achieved. Assuming that the means to happiness could be infallibly stated, this imperative of prudence would be an analytically practical proposition for it differs from the
imperative of skill only in that its purpose is given, while in the imperative of skill it is
merely a possible purpose. Since both, however, command the means to that which
one presupposes as a willed purpose, the imperative which commands the willing of
the means to him who wills the end is in both cases analytical. There is, consequently,
no difficulty in seeing the possibility of such an imperative.

Reason is ill-equipped to secure Happiness [177]

In the natural constitution of an organized being (i.e., one suitably adapted to life),
we assume as an axiom that no organ will be found for any purpose which is not the
fittest and best adapted to that purpose. Now if its preservation, its welfare, in a word
its happiness, were the real end of nature in a being having reason and will, then
nature would have hit upon a very poor arrangement in appointing the reason of the

creature to be the executor of this purpose. For all the actions which the creature has to perform with this intention of nature, and the entire rule of his conduct, would be dictated much more exactly by instinct, and the end would be far more certainly attained by instinct than it ever could be by reason. And if, over and above this, reason should have been granted to the favored creature, it would have served only to let him contemplate the happy constitution of his nature, to admire it, to rejoice in it, and to be grateful for it to its beneficent cause. But reason would not have been given in order that the being should subject his faculty of desire to that weak and delusive guidance and to meddle with the purpose of nature. In a word, nature would have taken care that reason did not break forth into practical use nor have the presumption, with its weak insight, to think out for itself the plan of happiness and the means of attaining it. Nature would have taken over the choice not only of ends but also of the means, and with wise foresight she would have entrusted both to instinct alone.

And, in fact, we find that the more a cultivated reason deliberately devotes itself to the enjoyment of life and happiness, the more the man falls short of true contentment. . . .

Since reason is not competent to guide the will safely with regard to its objects and the satisfaction of all our needs (which it in part multiplies), to this end an innate instinct would have led with far more certainty. But reason is given to us as a practical faculty (i.e., one which is meant to have an influence on the will). As nature has elsewhere distributed capacities suitable to the functions they are to perform, reason's proper function must be to produce a will good in itself and not one good merely as a means, since for the former, reason is absolutely essential. This will need not be the sole and complete good, yet it must be the condition of all others, even of the desire for happiness. In this case it is entirely compatible with the wisdom of nature that the cultivation of reason, which is required for the former unconditional purpose, at least in this life restricts in many ways—indeed, can reduce to nothing—the achievement of the latter unconditional purpose, happiness. For one perceives that nature here does not proceed unsuitably to its purpose, because reason, which recognizes its highest practical vocation in the establishment of a good will, is capable of a contentment of its own kind (i.e., one that springs from the attainment of a purpose determined by reason), even though this injures the ends of inclination.

Moral action must be motivated by duty, not personal advantage [178]

Duty is the necessity to do an action from respect for law. I can certainly have an inclination to an object as an effect of the proposed action, but I can never have respect for it precisely because it is a mere effect and not an activity of a will. Similarly, I can have no respect for any inclination whatsoever, whether my own or that of another; in the former case I can at most approve of it and in the latter I can even love it (i.e., see it as favorable to my own advantage). But that which is connected with my will merely as ground and not as consequence, that which does not serve my inclination but overpowers it or at least excludes it from being considered in making a choice—in a word, law itself—can be an object of respect and thus a command. Now as an act from duty wholly excludes the influence of inclination and therewith every object of the will, nothing remains which can determine the will objectively except law and subjectively except pure respect for this practical law. This subjective element is the maxim that I should follow such a law even if it thwarts all my inclinations.

I here omit all actions which are recognized as opposed to duty, even though they may be useful in one respect or another, for with these the question does not arise as to whether they may be done *from* duty, since they conflict with it. I also pass over actions which are really in accord with duty and to which one has no direct inclination, rather doing them because impelled to do so by another inclination. For it is easily decided whether an action in accord with duty is done from duty or for some selfish purpose. It is far more difficult to note this difference when the action is in accord with duty and, in addition, the subject has a direct inclination to do it. For example, it is in accord with duty that a dealer should not overcharge an inexperienced customer, and wherever there is much trade the prudent merchant does not do so, but has a fixed price for everyone so that a child may buy from him as cheaply as any other. Thus the customer is honestly served, but this is far from sufficient to warrant the belief that the merchant has behaved in this way from duty and principles of honesty. His own advantage required this behavior, but it cannot be assumed that over and above that he had a direct inclination to his customers and that, out of love, as it were, he gave none an advantage in price over another. The action was done neither from duty nor from direct inclination but only for a selfish purpose.

On the other hand, it is a duty to preserve one's life, and moreover everyone has a direct inclination to do so. But for that reason, the often anxious care which most men take of it has no intrinsic worth, and the maxim of doing so has no moral import. They preserve their lives according to duty, but not from duty. But if adversities and hopeless sorrow completely take away the relish for life; if an unfortunate man, strong in soul, is indignant rather than despondent or dejected over his fate and wishes for death, and yet preserves his life without loving it and from neither inclination nor fear but from duty—then his maxim has moral merit.

To be kind where one can is a duty, and there are, moreover, many persons so sympathetically constituted that without any motive of vanity or selfishness they find an inner satisfaction in spreading joy and rejoice in the contentment of others which they have made possible. But I say that, however dutiful and however amiable it may be, that kind of action has no true moral worth. It is on a level with [actions done from] other inclinations, such as the inclination to honor, which, if fortunately directed to what in fact accords with duty and is generally useful and thus honorable, deserve praise and encouragement, but no esteem. For the maxim lacks the moral import of an action done not from inclination but from duty. But assume that the mind of that friend to mankind was clouded by a sorrow of his own which extinguished all sympathy with the lot of others, and though he still had the power to benefit others in distress their need left him untouched because he was preoccupied with his own. Now suppose him to tear himself, unsolicited by inclination, out of his dead insensibility and to do this action only from duty and without any inclination—then for the first time his action has genuine moral worth. Furthermore, if nature has put little sympathy into the heart of a man, and if he, though an honest man, is by temperament cold and indifferent to the sufferings of others perhaps because he is provided with special gifts of patience and fortitude and expects and even requires that others should have them too—and such a man would certainly not be the meanest product of nature— would not he find in himself a source from which to give himself a far higher worth than he could have got by having a good-natured temperament? This is unquestionably true even though nature did not make him philanthropic, for it is just here that the worth of character is brought out, which is morally the incomparably highest of all: he is beneficent not from inclination, but from duty.

To secure one's own happiness is at least indirectly a duty, for discontent with one condition under pressure from many cares and amid unsatisfied wants could easily become a great temptation to transgress against duties. But, without any view to duty, all men have the strongest and deepest inclination to happiness, because in this Idea all inclinations are summed up. But the precept of happiness is often so formulated that it definitely thwarts some inclinations, and men can make no definite and certain concept of the sum of satisfaction of all inclinations, which goes under the name of happiness. It is not to be wondered at, therefore, that a single inclination, definite as to what it promises and as to the time at which it can be satisfied, can outweigh a fluctuating idea and that, for example, a man with the gout can choose to enjoy what he likes and to suffer what he may, because according to his calculations at least on this occasion he has not sacrificed the enjoyment of the present moment to a perhaps groundless expectation of a happiness supposed to lie in health. But even in this case if the universal inclination to happiness did not determine his will, and if health were not at least for him a necessary factor in these calculations, there would still remain, as in all other cases, a law that he ought to promote his happiness not from inclination but from duty. Only from this law could his conduct have true moral worth.

We can never determine whether an action is wholly devoid of self-love [179]

[I]f we attend to our experience of the way men act, we meet frequent and, as we must confess, justified complaints that we cannot cite a single sure example of the disposition to act from pure duty. There are also justified complaints that, though much may be done that accords with what duty commands, it is nevertheless always doubtful whether it is done from duty and thus whether it has moral worth. There have always been philosophers who for this reason have absolutely denied the reality of this disposition in human actions, attributing everything to more or less refined self-love. They have done so without questioning the correctness of the concept of morality. Rather they spoke with sincere regret of the frailty and corruption of human nature, which is noble enough to take as its precept an Idea so worthy of respect but which at the same time is too weak to follow it, employing reason, which should give laws for human nature, only to provide for the interest of the inclinations either singly or, at best, in their greatest possible harmony with one another.

It is, in fact, absolutely impossible by experience to discern with complete certainty a single case in the maxim of an action, however much it might conform to duty, rested solely on moral grounds and on the conception of one's duty. It sometimes happens that in the most searching self-examination we can find nothing except the moral ground of duty which could have been powerful enough to move us to this or that good action and to such great sacrifice. But from this we cannot by any means conclude with certainty that a secret impulse of self-love, falsely appearing as the Idea of duty, was not actually the true determining cause of the will. For we like to flatter ourselves with a pretended nobler motive, while in fact even the strictest examination can never lead us entirely behind the secret incentives, for when moral worth is in question it is not a matter of actions which one sees but of their inner principles which one does not see.

Moreover, one cannot better serve the wishes of those who ridicule all morality as a mere phantom of human imagination overreaching itself through self-conceit than by conceding that the concepts of duty must be derived only from experience (for they are ready, from indolence, to believe that this is true of all other concepts too). For, by this concession, a sure triumph is prepared for them. Out of love for humanity I am willing to admit that most of our actions are in accord with duty; but if we look more closely at our thoughts and aspirations, we come everywhere upon the dear self, which is always turning up, and it is this instead of the stern command of duty (which would often require self-denial) which supports our plans. One need not be an enemy of virtue, but only a cool observer who does not confuse even the liveliest aspiration for the good with its actuality, to be sometimes doubtful whether true virtue can really be found anywhere in the world.

Duties toward the self should be based in self-esteem [180]

The duties we owe ourselves do not depend on the relation of the action to the ends of happiness. If they did, they would depend on our inclinations and so be governed by rules of prudence. Such rules are not moral, since they indicate only the necessity of the means for the satisfaction of inclinations, and cannot therefore bind us. The basis of such obligation is not to be found in the advantages we reap from doing our duty towards ourselves, but in the worth of manhood. This principle does not allow us an unlimited freedom in respect of our own persons. It insists that we must reverence humanity in our own person, because apart from this man becomes an object of contempt, worthless in the eyes of his fellows and worthless in himself. Such faultiness is absolute. Our duties towards ourselves constitute the supreme condition and the principle of all morality; for moral worth is the worth of the person as such; our capacities have a value only in regard to the circumstances in which we find ourselves. Socrates lived in a state of wretchedness; his circumstances were worthless; but though his circumstances were so ill-conditioned, yet he himself was of the highest value. Even though we sacrifice all life's amenities we can make up for their loss and sustain approval by maintaining the worth of our humanity. We may have lost everything else, and yet still retain our inherent worth. Only if our worth as human beings is intact can we perform our other duties; for it is the foundation stone of all other duties. A man who has destroyed and cast away his personality, has no intrinsic worth, and can no longer perform any manner of duty. . . .

Not self-favor but self-esteem should be the principle of our duties towards ourselves. This means that our actions must be in keeping with the worth of man. The legal maxim, *Neminem laede*, can be said to apply in this connection in the form *Noli naturam humanam in te ipso laedere*. There are in us two grounds of action; inclinations, which belong to our animal nature, and humanity, to which the inclinations must be subjected. Our duties to ourselves are negative; they restrict our freedom in respect of our inclinations, which aim at our own welfare. Just as law restricts our freedom in our relations with other men, so do our duties to ourselves restrict our freedom in dealing with ourselves. All such duties are grounded in a certain love of honor consisting in self-esteem; man must not appear unworthy in his own eyes; his actions must be in keeping with humanity itself if he is to appear in his own eyes worthy of inner respect. To value approbation is the essential ingredient of our duties towards ourselves.

Self-love as distinguished from arrogance and self-esteem [181]

The love which takes delight in others is the judgment of delight in their perfection; the love which takes delight in ourselves, or self-love, is an inclination to be well-content with ourselves in judging our own perfection. *Philautia*, or moral self-love, is not arrogance or moral self-sufficiency. *Philautia* and arrogance differ in that the former is merely an inclination to be satisfied with one's *perfections*, whereas the latter is an unwarranted claim to merit; whilst the one pretends to be possessed of more moral perfections than it has, the other claims nothing and is merely satisfied with itself and does not take itself to task; the one is proud of its moral perfections, the other is not, simply believing itself blameless and innocent. Arrogance is a harmful fault. *Philautia* tests itself by the moral law not by taking it as a guide, but through examples, and so finds cause for self-satisfaction. The examples of moral men are criteria taken from experience; but the moral law is a criterion of the reason. If we make use of the first of these criteria the result is either *philautia* or arrogance. We have arrogance if we take a narrow and indulgent view of the moral law, or if the moral judge within us is not impartial. The less strict our view of the moral law and the less strictly the judge within us judges us, the more arrogant we are apt to be.

Self-love differs from self-esteem. Esteem refers to intrinsic worth; love to the bearing which worth has on welfare. We esteem that which has intrinsic worth, and we love that which has worth through its bearing on something else. Thus intellect has intrinsic worth irrespective of the purposes to which it is applied. He who does his duty, who does not degrade his person, is estimable; he who is sociable is lovable. We can judge ourselves to be worthy either of esteem or of love. The man who believes himself kindhearted, who thinks that he would gladly help other men if he were only rich (and if he is, in fact, rich, if he were still richer—as rich as so and so, for what he has he needs badly himself, as all miserly people believe), such a man judges himself to be lovable. On the other hand, the man who believes that he is fulfilling the essential ends of humanity, thinks himself worthy of esteem. If a man believes himself kindhearted and promotes the welfare of all mankind by empty wishes, he is a prey to *philautia*. That a man should wish himself well is natural; but it is not natural that he should have a good opinion of himself. Men fall into *philautia* or arrogance according to their temperaments. Gellert's philosophy is full of talk of love and kindness and friendship—the hobbyhorses of all moralists; such philosophy conduces to self-love. But man is required to be worthy, not so much of love, as of respect and of esteem. A conscientious and righteous man who is impartial and will accept no bribe, is not an object of love, and because he is conscientious in the matter of what he accepts, he will have few opportunities to act with magnanimity and love, and he will consequently not be thought lovable by his fellows. But he finds happiness in being considered by his fellows worthy of esteem; virtue is his true, intrinsic worth. A man might therefore be an object of esteem without being an object of love, because he refuses to curry favor. We can also love a bad man without in the least respecting him. Whatever increases self-love ought to be rejected from moral philosophy, and only that ought to be commended which makes one worthy of respect, e.g., doing one's duty to oneself, righteousness and conscientiousness; these things may not make us objects of love, but we can hold our head high, though not defiantly, and look men straight in the eye, for we have worth. This is not arrogance, for we do not strain the standard of the moral law. By that standard we feel humble; by the standard of comparison with other men we can regard ourselves as worthy of respect. Moral *philautia*, which gives a man a high opinion of himself in respect of his moral perfections, is detestable; it springs up when we preen ourselves upon the goodness of our disposition, and think to promote the welfare of the world by empty wishes and romantic ideas. We love the Hottentot and would fain do good to him, but give no thought to our neighbor because he is too near us. *Philautia* is unpractical, and consists of wishes which merely shrivel the heart. Self-lovers are generally milksops, not solid and practical; the arrogant are at least practical.

In man's moral court of justice there exists a type of sophistication to which self-love gives rise. Our inner advocate becomes a pettifogger, expounding the law sophistically to our advantage. More than this, he grows deceitful and cheats about the facts. All his sophistries serve but to undermine his credit with us, so that we look upon him as a twister. Only a weak man fails to appreciate this. Our pettifogger engages in all manner of legal quibbles; he makes use of the letter of the law for his own purposes; when dealing with facts he pays no heed to disposition, but only to external circumstances; he deals in probabilities. This theory of moral probability is a means of self-deception whereby a man persuades himself that he has been acting on principle and rightly. There is nothing worse, nothing more abominable than the artifice that invents a false law to enable us, under the shelter of the true law, to do evil. A man who has transgressed against the moral law, but still recognizes it in its purity, can be improved because he still has a pure law before his eyes; but a man who has invented for himself a favorable and false law has a principle in his wickedness, and in his case we can hope for no improvement.

A man may compare himself with others and esteem only himself. This is moral egoism. We ought not to measure our worth by comparing ourselves with others but with the standard of the moral law. To compare ourselves with others is to use a fortuitous standard, which may lead to a very different estimate of our worth. We may conclude that we are of lesser value than others. This makes us hate them and produces envy and jealousy. Parents sow the seeds of these in their children when they do not bring them up by the principles of morality, but constantly point to other children as examples. Envy and jealousy are thus engendered in them; because if these others did not exist, they themselves would not be regarded as inferior.

To love oneself alone in comparison with others is moral solipsism, which belongs properly to the sphere of duties towards others and not of duties to ourselves.

IV | NINETEENTH CENTURY

*J*eremy Bentham (1748–1832), the first philosopher we consider from the nineteenth century, grounds his analysis of self-interest on a psychological profile of human beings, from which he then derives various ethical and political conclusions. Human beings, he argues, are subject to two "sovereign masters," namely, pleasure and pain; all that we do is ultimately motivated by the desire to either attain the former or avoid the latter. Since "interests" are simply correlates of motives—that is, for any motive A, there will be a corresponding interest, B, which A seeks to realize—the same principle applies to interests: "A man is said *to have an interest in any subject*, in so far as that *subject* is considered as more or less likely to be to him a source of pleasure or exemption."[182]

Bentham believes that human beings may find pleasure, and so take an interest, in the well-being of others, but he supposes self-regarding interests to predominate over all the rest. As evidence of this he cites the continued existence of the species, arguing that if it were *not* the case that each human being were principally interested in his own welfare, the human race would long ago have perished. Bentham presents a little thought experiment to prove his point. Imagine two individuals, A and B, each of whom is solely responsible for the other's happiness, and neither of whom attends to his own. "If, as has with less truth been said of the blind leading the blind," he assures us, "both would, in such a state of things, be continually falling into the ditch."[183]

Bentham concludes on the basis of his psychological analysis of self-interest that utility forms the ultimate standard of morals. "It is for [pleasure and pain] alone to point out what we ought to do, as well as to determine what we shall do." However, each individual must seek not merely his private utility, but the *aggregate* utility of all sentient beings. Bentham's reasoning is that if utility is a good, it is better if there is more of it. It has been submitted that Bentham does not adequately explain, in light of his own psychological theory, what reason an individual has to pursue the interests of anyone but himself. Some interesting appeal to Bentham's conception of sympathy to solve this problem, yet though sympathy clearly has a role to play in the Benthamite psychology, Bentham makes it abundantly clear that self-interest is the only motive which can be counted upon at all times.

We have seen that some philosophers regard the ubiquity of self-interested motivation with dismay, but not so Bentham. What matters from the moral standpoint is the maximization of aggregate utility; if this outcome can be accomplished via self-seeking, so the much the better for self-seeking. Indeed, Bentham concludes in one of his later works, *Deontology*, that the aim of morality is precisely to bring about a coincidence of duty and self-interest. In Bentham's estimate, there is nothing inherently wrong with self-interested motivation, nor is there is anything particularly hallowed about self-sacrifice. Quite the reverse, if the aim of morality is to maximize aggregate happiness, the less call for sacrifice, the better.[184]

The *Deontology* almost makes it sound as if Bentham subscribes to the natural harmony of interests, but his legal and political writings reveal otherwise. Sound legislation, he insists, will be based upon the reality of human nature, and the reality is that the majority of people act mainly on the principle of narrow self-interest. Theorists who serenade us with talk of "purity of motives" (by which they mean "the utter absence of every particle of self-regard") are spewing nonsense, and their declarations of unself-interestedness are about as convincing—and insulting—as a declaration of chastity by a whore. Good laws will bring the self-interest of different individuals into a sort of "artificial" harmony, but we must make no mistake about the fact that the rapprochement is artificial.

Bentham concludes his political discussions by considering the possibility of legislating self-interest. That is, he asks whether the government should play a role in dictating to individuals how to best exercise "prudence." Bentham concludes that the government must be given no such role. If the agent himself lacks the self-knowledge necessary to best promote his own happiness, it is manifestly absurd to assume that the government will somehow know better. Where the government *can* play a role is in the legislating of the rules of "probity" or positive duties to others. Indeed, the public interest is generally best served when the government punishes those who violate the just claims of others. As for beneficence, or the negative duties owed to others, here the government must once again step aside. If someone is sympathetically disposed, he will naturally include concern for others among his interests; if not, the law cannot force him to be otherwise.

John Stuart Mill (1806–1873) was educated in the Benthamite tradition, and was deeply influenced by Bentham's conception of self-interest, acknowledging both the motivational force of self-concern and its hedonistic foundation. Mill embraced as well both the utilitarian standard of morals and the general happiness principle. As any apt student is wont to do, however, Mill challenged his teacher on certain points.

Mill was dissatisfied, for instance, with the disproportionate motivational strength which Bentham assigned to self-interest over sympathy. Though Bentham rightly distinguished self-regarding from social interests, Mill remarks, he was wrong to assume that, ultimately, self-regard must always prevail over sympathy. Human beings are able to develop independent social interests and feelings—for instance, benevolence and patriotism—which are capable, at least in principle, of overriding self-interest. Which of these interests an individual will prefer is not dictated by brute human nature, but by the sort of character he possesses. As Coleridge noted, it is the man who makes the motive, not the motive, the man.

Mill is critical as well of Bentham's account of the *content* of self-interest. Though he agrees that interests are a function of pleasure, he rejects Bentham's view that pleasures differ only in intensity and duration. On Mill's account, there are *qualitative* differences between pleasures, too. The pleasures of the mind, for instance, are qualitatively greater than those which arise through the satisfaction of animal urges. This suggests that mental pleasures are more productive of an individual's true interests than bodily ones. Mill cannot, of course, mean by this that on any given instance a person who has experienced both higher and lower pleasures will always choose the higher; even the most cerebral among us will need to satisfy his physical appetites— for food, sex, sleep, and so forth—from time to time. What he is referring to, rather, is lifestyle. The lifestyle led by a "Socrates" is overall more productive of pleasure than that led by a "pig." The mere fact that a person is reaping pleasure, therefore, does not of itself indicate whether his best interests are being served.

Although Mill takes certain pleasures to be objectively superior, he does not regard them as necessarily best for those who are unaccustomed to them. He invokes the idea of lifestyle once again to explain, suggesting that the nature of one's lifestyle dictates the nature of one's pleasures and interests. For example, it would be useless to attempt to persuade a wife-beating child-abuser that he would derive more pleasure from treating his family with kindness. "He would be happier if he were the kind of person who *could* so live; but he is not, and it is probably too late for him to become, that kind of person." From the standpoint of human nature, then, we can say that certain pleasures, such as those of the mind, are superior to others, but it does not follow that the superior pleasures will always best serve the interests of each individual. This idea has political implications for Mill, as we shall see.

Following Bentham, Mill draws from his psychological account of self-interest various ethical conclusions. He explicitly formulates and names his "Principle of Utility" (or "Greatest Happiness Principle"), and sets this at the foundation of his moral theory. According to this principle, actions are right just insofar as they tend to promote happiness (pleasure). Mill, like Bentham, has in mind the happiness not simply of the agent, but of everyone. Unlike Bentham, however, he thinks that individuals can often be motivated to uphold the greatest happiness by non-self-interested motives. The ultimate sanction of general utility, he argues, is not self-concern, but the "social feelings of mankind," which make us desire unity with our fellows. Justice, too, is a sentiment which, though partly arising from concern for self-defense, derives from sympathetic identification with others.

Though Mill takes the promotion of happiness to be the greatest good, he is adamant that society not interfere with an individual's private choices in the name of better promoting his self-interest. The interest which others take in an agent's private good, he declares, is "trifling" compared with that of himself, and, in any case, others are not usually in a cognitive position to assess his best interests. We must each assume primary responsibility for our own welfare, and we may regard this as the foremost duty to the self; unlike with our social duties, we are accountable for this duty to no one but ourselves. Mill encapsulates his defense of non-interference in the pursuit of private happiness with his famous "Liberty Principle": "the sole end for which mankind are warranted, individually or collectively, in interfering with the liberty of action of any of their number, is self-protection. His own good, either physical or moral, is not a sufficient warrant."

Mill is the only thinker in our collection to consider the relation between self-interest and sex-roles, and we may conclude our discussion by briefly reflecting on this. Mill was highly critical of the role allotted to women in Victorian society, arguing that it established a fundamental rift between men's and women's interests, and ensured the predominance of the former. A woman's self-interest tends to be of no intrinsic concern to her husband, he submits, since men are given unlimited power over their wives, and tend to consider them as simply one of their effects. This power "seeks out and evokes the latent germs of selfishness in the remotest corners of [man's] nature" and consequently "immolate[s]" women's interests. The male child is raised to believe that women are his lifelong subordinates—no matter how he behaves, or how base his character becomes. This quickly turns him into an uncaring narcissist. "Is it imagined," Mill ridicules, "that all this does not pervert the whole manner of existence of the man, both as an individual and as a social being?"

Henry Sidgwick (1838–1900), the last of the major nineteenth-century Utilitarians, shares neither Bentham's neutral attitude toward self-love nor Mill's optimism about the effectiveness of sanctions in overriding it. Though Sidgwick affirms that the "maxim of prudence" is self-evident and axiomatic, he takes prudence to be something of a necessary evil, remarking that, "A dubious guidance to an ignoble end appears to be all that the calculus of Egoistic Hedonism has to offer." Nor is Sidgwick confident that the egoist will brought to the universal utilitarian perspective merely by means of the social and internal sanctions that Mill outlines in *Utilitarianism*. Sanctions are unreliable and sometimes have the opposite of their intended effect. The egoist has to be given some sort of *proof* of utilitarianism — yet, as we shall see, Sidgwick is doubtful whether such a proof can be given, at least in cases where certain crucial premises are not already conceded.

Sidgwick's philosophical interest in what he calls the "maxim of rational self-love or prudence" stems from his belief that as a self-evidently true axiom, it will necessarily rest at the foundation of any rational system of conduct. This axiom asserts that "one ought to aim at one's own good," and it reinforces the common-sense belief that it is reasonable to pursue personal happiness. Sidgwick himself evidently embraces this dictum of common sense: "I do not hold the reasonableness of aiming at happiness generally with any stronger conviction than I do that of aiming at one's own."

Yet, though Sidgwick agrees with the thought it expresses, he finds unsatisfactory the manner in which the maxim of prudence is commonly stated. Granting that we may define "good" as "what one ought to aim at," the description of rational self-love as the proposition "that one ought to aim at one's own good" immediately reduces to tautology. To avoid this danger, Sidgwick introduces the idea of pursuing "one's good on the whole" — which is to say, of displaying "impartial concern for all parts of our conscious life." The mere fact that the consciousness of one moment is prior to that of another imparts to it no special status or authority, he argues. This is not to say that in certain cases, present goods are not to be preferred to future ones, or vice versa, but only that "Hereafter *as such* is to be regarded as neither less nor more than Now."

This principle yields Sidgwick's definition of self-interest, which states that an individual's "future good on the whole is what he would now desire and seek on the whole if all the consequences of all the different lines of conduct open to him were accurately foreseen and adequately realized in imagination at the present point of time." Following Bentham in identifying the agent's good in hedonic terms, Sidgwick notes that the consequences of action should be evaluated in terms of their ability to produce pleasure or avoid pain.

Sidgwick conceives of the rational egoist as the individual who attends carefully to his future good on the whole, establishing for himself as great a balance of pleasure over pain as possible. Yet, he recognizes there is no guarantee that the egoist will indeed serve his best interests merely for trying. As Butler had argued, one often foils one's own interests by focusing on them too closely. Sidgwick concurs: "a certain subordination of self-regard seems to be necessary in order to obtain full enjoyment." For instance, many people naturally enjoy behaving benevolently, but they would soon cease to enjoy it were they to attend to their enjoyment rather than to the acting benevolently itself. Sidgwick calls this the "fundamental paradox of hedonistic egoism."

Perhaps the most important element of Sidgwick's analysis of self-interest is its relationship to his account of "rational benevolence," another of the basic axioms of human conduct. Just as an individual's interest is constituted by a series of temporally ordered goods, so the "Universal Good" is constituted by the good of all sentient individuals; and just as the individual is unjustified in preferring one good over another simply in virtue of its temporal locale, so "the good of any one individual is of no more importance, from the point of view (if I may say so) of the Universe, than the good of any other." Not everyone will grant this, Sidgwick confesses. The egoist is bound to acknowledge the Maxim of Rational Benevolence only if he first grants the premise that there exists a universal good. If he insists on the subjectivity of the good, however, he may well claim that his happiness is merely relatively good for him, and similarly that the good of others is merely relatively good for them. If this is all he concedes, he cannot be lead to the idea that objectively speaking, no one individual's good counts for more than another's. It should not surprise us to find individuals defending the relativity of good, Sidgwick thinks; common sense itself recognizes that the distinction between individuals is "real and fundamental," and that each individual is concerned with his own happiness in a special way.

Why then does anyone become a universal utilitarian? The third and final maxim of conduct—that of Justice—clearly does not necessitate the conversion. All this maxim requires is that we recognize the reasonableness of the proposition that it cannot be right for A to treat B in a manner in which, under similar circumstances, it would not be right for B to treat A.[185] This leaves open the question of what sort of treatment should be given in the first instance, however. Some utilitarians have become universally-minded on account of the various legal, social, and internal sanctions that afford them greater pleasure for attending to the universal good than for ignoring it. But Sidgwick surveys a wide number of cases in which the normal sanctions are ineffective.

Inasmuch as both proofs and sanctions fail, what remains to convince the rational egoist to perform his duties toward others? Sidgwick's solution is to conclude that there *is* no solution. It is both rational for an individual to pursue the universal good and rational for him to hold his own happiness as an end which he will not sacrifice to any other. There is no assurance that the good of different individuals will necessarily coincide, or, therefore, that sacrifice will not sometimes be required. If there were a benevolent deity, *it* might assure the ultimate harmony of interests, but we cannot adopt any such theological postulate merely in order to reconcile duty and self-interest. We must accept the reality that practical reason will sometimes make contradictory demands upon us, and in those cases where practical reason is "divided against itself," conflicts will have to be decided by "the comparative preponderance of one or other of two groups of non-rational impulses."

Moving away from Utilitarianism, we come to William James (1842–1910), one of the founders of the American philosophical school known as pragmatism. James was perhaps foremost a psychologist, and it is largely from the psychological standpoint that he presents his views on self-love. His analysis centers on two issues: the nature of the self and the character of the emotion we experience in loving it.

James is critical of what he conceives of as the traditional conception of selfhood. Most philosophers have meant by "self" simply "pure Ego"—to which they have referred variously as our "stream of consciousness," "I," or "soul-substance." Without himself wishing to identify the pure Ego beyond describing it as the "principle of individual existence," James acknowledges the "direct feeling of regard" it evokes. Nonetheless, he denies that this principle, whatever it may be, could serve as the object of self-love properly understood.

Before one can experience self-love, he argues, one must develop the sort of self that can *be* loved, and such is not the pure Ego. The pure Ego or "thinker" is simply an "abstract" reflective source, "empty of content," that could exist inside me and yet "I should still be cold, and fail to exhibit anything worthy of the name of selfishness." Further, it is invoked in altruistic concerns as well as in self-regarding ones: both equally require the operation of a principle of consciousness. The pure Ego is a pre-condition of experiencing and loving anything at all, but it is no more the object of self-love than it is of love for others.

Self-love originates only with the development of what James calls the "empirical self"—an "objective designation" for those objects which excite the "primitive and instinctive impulses of our nature" and which are valued for their own sakes. In responding to such objects, we may be said to "take an interest" in them, and this is all that loving the empirical self consists in.

James illustrates by discussing what he calls "material self-love." Material or bodily self-love consists of emotions and actions relating to our material self, which is constituted by our body and all the things that provide it pleasure and comfort. When we exhibit this form of self-love, we are simply expressing our interest in these things. For instance, when we are led by self-love to grab a seat from someone else, what we really love is the seat which we grab. "The more utterly 'selfish' I am in this primitive way, the more blindly absorbed my thought will be in the objects and impulses of my lusts, and the more devoid of any inward looking glance."

The material self is just one aspect of the empirical self, which also contains "social" and "spiritual" aspects. Though each aspect of the empirical self relates to different objects, each expresses self-love in the same way, namely, by focusing on certain intrinsically interesting objects. James finds nothing objectionable in self-love so construed—indeed, invoking evolution theory, he finds it required by survival itself.

If we each did not take a special instinctive interest in our own bodies, minds and affairs, he observes, we would not last very long.

This is not to say that Nature has so limited human nature that it finds nothing intrinsically interesting except those objects which contribute directly to its own sustenance. Just as the objects we need to survive naturally excite our passions and evoke our intrinsic concern, so, too, do other people and their good and interests. The sympathetic and the egoistic interests are fully "co-ordinate" in this sense. They arise in precisely the same way—on the "same psychological level"—and differ only in their objects.

James finds support for his "objective" theory of self-love in the writing of the 19th-century German psychologist, Adolf Horwicz. In a lengthy psychological treatise[186] published during 1872-1878, Horwicz had rejected the idea that the Ego must first, so to speak, "imprint" itself on an object before that object could be loved. On the contrary, we come to love objects in virtue of themselves, not in virtue their prior relationship to us. Why, then, do our own possessions hold such a special place for us? As Horwicz explains, it is simply because we "live closer" to our own possessions; "we know them better, 'realize' them more intimately, feel them more deeply. We learn to appreciate what is ours in all its details and shadings, whilst the goods of others appear to us in coarse outlines and rude averages." It is the vividness with which our own things confront us, not the mere fact that they are our own, that generates our special attachment to them.

Endorsing Horwicz's conclusions, and having now finished discussing the self-love associated with instinct and emotion, James concludes by turning to that associated with the intellect. Is it possible for the intellect to assess something objectively, without being prejudiced by that thing's connection to the empirical self? James affirms that it is possible, but difficult. To judge oneself impartially, one must abstract away from one's own narrow affairs while at the same time vividly conceiving of the concern of others. Self-love will always pose a challenge to attaining such objectivity, but at stake is nothing less than the possibility of justice.

The last philosopher of the nineteenth century we consider is Friedrich Nietzsche (1844–1900), whose views on self-interest are among the most challenging in Western thought. Rather than viewing altruism as an ideal up to which the average self-interested individual never quite lives, Nietzsche rejects the morality of altruism as a symptom of declining life.

The mark of ascending life, in his view, is instinctive self-assertion. Strong and healthy human beings brim with vitality, and project this into their environment. They do not fall in with the "herd" and allow their own good to become a mere function of the good of the whole. Indeed, they define themselves and their values in opposition to the herd, establishing a "pathos of distance."

On Nietzsche's psychology, all human beings—even the weak—are self-assertive, and thus egoistic, in some sense; the important question is *how* their egoism is manifested. Strong individuals evince a healthy egoism, of the sort just described. The weak, in contrast, engage in "mass-egoism": that is, they establish a group ethic which seeks to subordinate ascending life to its own sickly advantage. Such is the nature of Christianity, in Nietzsche's view. It calls upon the strong not to follow their animal instincts and assert themselves, but to submit their will to the weak. It devalues life and health in name of that bugbear, equality. If the sick are accorded equal value as the healthy, however, natural selection is unmercifully reversed and the entire species is doomed.

Though Nietzsche sometimes speaks of egoism as an instinct to covet and over-power, there is another side to his understanding of this drive, and it may be summed up in the phrase "self-reverence." Part of what altruistic morality undermines, in his view, is the individual's capacity for self-respect, and relatedly, for self-trust. In several passages, Nietzsche opposes altruism not out of contempt for benevolence but, rather, for altruism's tendency to devalue the individual in his own eyes, instructing him that his own good is less important than that of others. Nietzsche distinguishes the self-respect that rejects these lessons from the "blind drive" of self-love. True ego-ism is not simply the drive to preserve one's being at any cost, but to ennoble and revere oneself.

Nietzsche closes the nineteenth century with a plea for recognition of the sover-eignty of the individual, and for the individual's right to pursue his own happiness as an end in itself, without feeling obligated to sacrifice it to some allegedly higher divine or social good. Despite the great popularity of utilitarianism in the twentieth century, this theme remains a strong undercurrent in the contemporary debate.

Jeremy Bentham was born in London, earned both liberal arts and law degrees by age nineteen, and, finding himself profoundly dissatisfied with England's civil and penal law, devoted his life to legal reform. A member of the Utilitarian school, Bentham's philosophy centers around the idea of promoting the general interest, as understood in terms of maximizing aggregate pleasure.

JEREMY BENTHAM
(1748–1832)

"Interest" defined [187]

I. Nature has placed mankind under the governance of two sovereign masters, *pain* and *pleasure*. It is for them alone to point out what we ought to do, as well as to determine what we shall do. On the one hand the standard of right and wrong, on the other the chain of causes and effects, are fastened to their throne. They govern us in all we do, in all we say, in all we think: every effort we can make to throw off our subjection, will serve but to demonstrate and confirm it. In words a man may pretend to abjure their empire: but in reality he will remain subject to it all the while. The *principle of utility* recognizes this subjection, and assumes it for the foundation of that system, the object of which is to rear the fabric of felicity by the hands of reason and of law. Systems which attempt to question it, deal in sounds instead of sense, in caprice instead of reason, in darkness instead of light. But enough of metaphor and declamation: it is not by such means that moral science is to be improved.

II. The principle of utility is the foundation of the present work: it will be proper therefore at the outset to give an explicit and determinate account of what is meant by it. By the principle of utility is meant that principle which approves or disapproves of every action whatsoever, according to the tendency which it appears to have to augment or diminish the happiness of the party whose interest is in question: or, what is the same thing, in other words, to promote or to oppose that happiness. I say of every action whatsoever; and therefore not only of every action of a private individual, but of every measure of government.

III. By utility is meant that property in any object, whereby it tends to produce benefit, advantage, pleasure, good, or happiness (all this in the present case comes to the same thing), or (what comes again to the same thing) to prevent the happening of mischief, pain, evil, or unhappiness to the party whose interest is considered: if that party be the community in general, then the happiness of the community: if a particular individual then the happiness of that individual.

IV. The interest of the community is one of the most general expressions that can occur in the phraseology of morals: no wonder that the meaning of it is often lost. When it has a meaning, it is this. The community is a fictitious *body*, composed of the individual persons who are considered as constituting as it were its *members*. The interest of the community then is, what?—the sum of the interests of the several members who compose it.

V. It is in vain to talk of the interest of the community, without understanding what is the interest of the individual. A thing is said to promote the interest, or to be *for* the interest, of an individual, when it tends to add to the sum total of his pleasures: or what comes to the same thing, to diminish the sum total of his pains.

VI. An action then may be said to be conformable to the principle of utility, or, for shortness sake, to utility (meaning with respect to the community at large), when the tendency it has to augment the happiness of the community is greater than any it has to diminish it.

The myth of motivational purity [188]

By this phrase ["purity of motives"] what is meant to be insinuated is, either that in the part the man takes he has no regard whatsoever for his own personal interest, or any other narrow interest, or that if he has any, it gives way at all times to his regard for the national or some other more extensive interest. But preferably the meaning is, such being the more direct and obvious import of the words, the utter absence of every particle of self-regard. Of this immaculate purity, each man in the most peremptory manner asserts the existence in his own instance: deny it, or hesitate to admit it, you offer him an affront—an affront, the stain of which he perhaps not infrequently invites you to permit him to wash away with your blood. Of this same purity he calls upon you, though perhaps in a tone not quite so loud, to admit, on the part of his colleagues and supporters. Nor yet, unless under the smart of some particular provocation, or in the ardor of some particularly advantageous thrust, is he

backward in the acknowledgment of the same purity in the breasts of honorable gen-
tlemen on the other side of the house. By this means while the praise of good temper
and candor is obtained, the price for the purchase of the corresponding acknowledgment on the other side, is thus paid in advance.

No government is so corrupt but that it is in the habit of receiving acknowledgments of this sort from its opponents. Nor are these acknowledgments inconsistent
with the rules of policy. For if the position were—all is impurity on that side, all is
purity on our side—people might be found to doubt of it, especially in those
instances in which the very same men have been seen sometimes on the one side sometimes on the other: and in that case the result might be, in some eyes, a rational supposition of its non-existence on either side.

At the expense of truth (need it be said?) is all this laudation and self-worship,
every atom of it. But the more irrefragably true is the contrary position, the more
strenuous is the urgency of the demand for it. Thus it is, that urged by the necessity
which on all sides they are under of making men in general continue in the belief of
the non-existence of that which they are seeing and feeling the effects of at every
moment, public men join in the inculcating of the errors correspondent and opposite
to the most important truths: in causing men to believe that, under a form of government so thoroughly corrupt, that all who belong to it are in a state of corruption—
none are: to believe in that fabled purity which is not ever true even where temptation
is at its minimum, much less in a situation in which it is at its maximum.

This being the language of ruler-craft, what is the language of simple truth? That
in spite of everything which is *said*, the general predominance of self-regard over every
other sort of regard, is demonstrated by everything that is *done:* that in the ordinary
tenor of life, in the breasts of human beings of ordinary mold, self is everything, to
which all other persons, added to all other things put together, are as nothing: that
this general habit of self-preference is so far from being a just subject of denial, or
even a reasonable cause of regret, that the existence of it is an indispensable condition
not only to the well-being but to the very being of the human species, and should
therefore be a cause of satisfaction: that admitting, as perhaps it may be admitted,
that in a highly matured state of society, in here and there a highly cultivated and
expanded mind, under the stimulus of some extraordinary excitement, a sacrifice of
self-regarding interest to social interest, upon a national scale, has not been without
example—public virtue in this shape cannot reasonably be regarded as being so frequently exemplified as insanity: and that as in the case of insanity so in this,—it is in
what has place in the conduct on the part of the thousands, and not in what has place
in the conduct of one in every thousand, that all rational and useful political arrangements will be grounded.

Of a state of things thus incontrovertible, no sooner is the existence to a certain
degree extensively acknowledged, than all pretense to this species of purity will be

regarded as would an assertion of chastity in the mouth of a prostitute at the very moment of solicitation: regarded as an insult to the understandings of all those to whom it is addressed — and will as such be resented.

The relation between self- an other-regard [189]

At the outset an objection presents itself, and that an objection applying to every thing that follows or can follow. It shall be allowed to present itself in its full force.

According to you, the principle which in the case of every action establishes as the ground and measure of its propriety its conduciveness or repugnance to the greatest happiness of the greatest number is the sure and only true principle.

But on the other hand, according to you, it is by a regard for his own happiness, and by that alone, that on every occasion a man's conduct will actually be guided.

In like manner also, according to you, each man, being of ripe years and an ordinarily sound constitution of mind, is at all times a better [judge than others] [190] on the question what pleasures there are the enjoyment of which, and what pains there are the exemption from which will, at any rate at the moment in question, be most conducive to his well-being.

This being the case, of what use according to you can this work of yours, or any other work that can be written on the subject ever come to be?

Be he who he may, according to you, it is by his own particular interest, his own self-regarding interest, that on every occasion, be it what it may, a man's conduct will be governed. This being the case, to what use speak to him of his extra-regarding interest, of the interest constituted by the pleasures or exemptions [from] [191] pains of others?

Again, in the field of self-regarding interest, as to the competition and conflict between the present and the contingent future, each man being, according to you, the sole competent judge as to what is most conducive to his aggregate and ultimate interest, to what use speak to him on the subject of the preference to be given on any occasion to the one in comparison of the other? [192]

In respect to the competition as referred to between self-regarding and extra-regarding interest, true it is that between the two interests thus denominated a strong and almost continual competition does really exist.

But on the other hand what is no less true is that into the composition of a man's self-regarding interest enters, on every occasion, a quantity of extra-regarding interest, and that in a variety of shapes. In other words, on most not to say on all occasions a man has an interest — a self-regarding interest — in promoting and accommodating his conduct to the interest, the self-regarding interest, of others: and in so far as a self-regarding interest of this description has place, it acts in alliance with his extra-regarding interest and as a check upon the force of that self-regarding interest which operates in other shapes.

What then is the business of the Deontologist? In every instance to bring out of their obscurity, out of the neglect in which they have hitherto in so large a proportion been buried, the points of coincidence to the extent of which extra-regarding interest is connected and has by the hands of nature been identified with self-regarding interest: and this in such sort and with such effect that by the alliance thus formed, by this conjunct kind of interest, the force of self-regarding interest in those shapes in which it is purely self-regarding is commonly already in use, and by apt means may be rendered more and more in use, to be outweighed and overpowered. In this way it will, it is believed, be found that for this species of artist there is no want of work. Nature has provided no inconsiderable quantity of useful work which as yet remains unattempted, and thus it will be his own fault if his office be a sinecure.

1. In the first place comes the interest corresponding to, and produced by, the affection of sympathy or benevolence. This it is true is an extra-regarding interest, but it is not the less a self-regarding one. Egenus is in distress. This distress is observed by Liberalis. By the force of sympathy, the pain felt by Egenus becomes, by means of the manifestation made of it, productive of correspondent pain in the bosom of Liberalis. To relieve himself from this pain and to obtain, at the same time, by means of the same act, a portion of the opposite and correspondent pleasure, he applies relief to this distress. If for the purpose of applying to Egenus this relief or exemption from pain, the correspondent relief heightened by the correspondent pleasure, Liberalis puts himself to any expense, in this case as in other cases of expenditure, a competition has place between the interest served by the expenditure and the interest (in this case the pecuniary interest) disserved by it. But by the supposition the relief is applied: therefore the interest served by the expenditure, the interest of sympathy, has been the preponderant one.

2. In the next place comes the interest correspondent to and produced by the love of reputation: in other words, the interest created by the power of the popular or moral sanction. Proportioned in general to the regard which, by his deportment, a man appears to have for the well-being of other men, is the regard which by the like tokens they are disposed to manifest for him. Here again is another extra-regarding interest, but it is not the less a self-regarding one.[193]

3. In the third and last place comes the interest corresponding to and produced by, the desire of amity: the desire of becoming, or continuing to be, with relation to this or that particular individual or small assortment of determinate individuals, an object of sympathetic affection, or a recipient of any such good thing as by that affection a man is prompted to bestow upon a person who is the object of it.

Of these three interests, the two former are capable of operating and are wont to operate upon all sorts of men, upon all sorts of occasions, and in all sorts of situations.

Of the third, the operation in the instance of each man is confined to particular and comparatively casual situations. It may be termed the interest of the popular or moral sanction in miniature. Between the two, although they are capable of operating in opposition and competition with relation to each other, there is evidently no precise boundary line. In proportion as the field of a man's particular connection enlarges itself, it approaches to a coincidence with that of the public at large.

By his own interest, and even by his own self-regarding interest, i.e., by that which in that character presents itself to his view, will, on every occasion, the conduct of every man be determined. But by what branch of his own interest? It has just been seen that in every man's self-regarding interest there are two branches: one, indeed, in a state of competition with and opposition to the body of extra-regarding interest, but another in alliance with and acting in support of it.

In proportion to the degree in which extra-regarding interest, i.e., that part of his self-regarding which acts in alliance with extra-regarding interest, predominates in his breast, will he be inclined to preserve his conduct in a state of subserviency to the well-being of those to whose lot it happens to be within the range of his activity.

But it is only in so far as it is present to his mind, that by the action of any interest whatsoever a man's conduct is determined; and by a variety of circumstances, the elements of that branch of a man's self-regarding interests which are in alliance with interests of other men, and thence with his extra-regarding interests, are kept from being so manifest and in general from acting so efficiently as those of which the purely self-regarding branch of his self-regarding interest is composed.

To bring to view these comparatively latent ties—this, in so far as concerns the competition between purely self-regarding and social or say extra-regarding interest; this, in so far as concerns the competition between probity and the self-regarding branch of prudence—this is what belongs to the field of deontology, in this part of that field the labor of the human kind seems capable of being expended not altogether without fruit.

Self-interest, beneficence, and legislation [194]

It may here be asked, how it is that upon the principle of private ethics, legislation and religion out of the question, a man's happiness depends upon such parts of his conduct as affect, immediately at least, the happiness of no one but himself: this is as much as to ask, What motives (independent of such as legislation and religion may chance to furnish) can one man have to consult the happiness of another? By what motives, or (which comes to the same thing) by what obligations, can he be bound to obey the dictates of *probity* and *beneficence*? In answer to this, it cannot but be admitted that the only interests which a man at all times and upon all occasions is sure to find adequate motives for consulting, are his own. Notwithstanding this, there are no occasions in which a man has not some motives for consulting the happiness of other men. In the first place, he has, on all occasions, the purely social motive of sympathy or benevolence: in the next place he has, on most occasions, the semisocial motives of love of amity and love of reputation. The motive of sympathy will act upon him with more or less effect, according to the bias of his sensibility: the two other motives, according to a variety of circumstances, principally according to the strength of his intellectual powers, the firmness and steadiness of his mind, the quantum of his moral sensibility, and the characters of the people he has to deal with. . . .

For the sake of obtaining the clearer idea of the limits between the art of legislation and private ethics, it may now be time to call to mind the distinctions above established with regard to ethics in general. The degree in which private ethics stands in need of the assistance of legislation is different in the three branches of duty above distinguished. Of the rules of moral duty, those which seem to stand least in need of the assistance of legislation, are the rules of *prudence*. It can only be through some defect on the part of the understanding, if a man be ever deficient in point of duty to himself. If he does wrong there is nothing else that it can be owing to but either some *inadvertence* or some *missupposal*, with regard to the circumstances on which his happiness depends. It is a standing topic of complaint, that a man knows too little of himself. Be it so: but is it so certain that the legislator must know more?[195/196] It is plain, that of individuals the legislator can know nothing: concerning those points of conduct which depend upon the particular circumstances of each individual, it is plain therefore, that he can determine nothing to advantage. It is only with respect to those broad lines of conduct in which all persons, or very large and permanent descriptions of persons, may be in a way to engage, that he can have any pretense for interfering; and even here the propriety of his interference will, in most instances, lie very open to dispute. . . .

The rules of *probity* are those, which in point of expediency stand most in need of assistance on the part of the legislator, and in which, in point of fact, his interference has been most extensive. There are few cases in which it *would* be expedient to punish a man for hurting *himself*: but there are few cases, if any, in which it would *not* be expedient to punish a man for injuring his neighbor. . . .

As to the rules of beneficence, these, as far as concerns matters of detail, must necessarily be abandoned in great measure to the jurisdiction of private ethics. In many cases the beneficial quality of the act depends essentially upon the disposition of the agent; that is, upon the motives by which he appears to have been prompted to perform it: upon their belonging to the head of sympathy, love of amity, or love of reputation; and not to any head of self-regarding motives, brought into play by the force of political constraint: in a word, upon their being such as denominate his conduct *free* and *voluntary*, according to one of the many senses given to those ambiguous expressions. The limits of the law on this head seem, however, to be capable of being extended a good deal farther than they seem ever to have been extended hitherto. In particular, in cases where the person is in danger, why should it not be made the duty of every man to save another from mischief when it can be done without prejudicing himself, as well as to abstain from bringing it on him?. . . [197]

To conclude this section, let us recapitulate and bring to a point the difference between private ethics, considered as an art or science on the one hand, and that branch of jurisprudence which contains the art or science of legislation, on the other. Private ethics teaches how each man may dispose himself to pursue the course most conducive to his own happiness, by means of such motives as offer of themselves: the art of legislation (which may be considered as one branch of the science of jurisprudence) teaches how a multitude of the men, composing a community, may be disposed to pursue that course which upon the whole is the most conducive to the happiness of the whole community, by means of motives to be applied by the legislator.

John Stuart Mill was born in London and educated in the Utilitarian tradition by his father, James, who was a close associate of Bentham. The younger Mill embraces several of Bentham's ideas about self-interest, but, among other innovations, he gives sympathy a stronger motivational role and discovers conflict between men's and women's interests.

JOHN STUART MILL
(1806–1873)

The limits of societal interference with the individual's pursuit of his self-interest [198]

The object of this Essay is to assert one very simple principle, as entitled to govern absolutely the dealings of society with the individual in the way of compulsion and control, whether the means used be physical force in the form of legal penalties, or the moral coercion of public opinion. That principle is, that the sole end for which mankind are warranted, individually or collectively, in interfering with the liberty of action of any of their number, is self-protection. That the only purpose for which power can be rightfully exercised over any member of a civilized community, against his will, is to prevent harm to others. His own good, either physical or moral, is not a sufficient warrant. He cannot rightfully be compelled to do or forbear because it will be better for him to do so, because it will make him happier, because, in the opinions of others, to do so would be wise, or even right. These are good reasons for remonstrating with him, or reasoning with him, or persuading him, or entreating him, but not for compelling him, or visiting him with any evil in case he do otherwise. To justify that, the conduct from which it is desired to deter him, must be calculated to produce evil to some one else. The only part of the conduct of any one, for which he is amenable to society, is that which concerns others. In the part which merely concerns himself, his independence is, of right, absolute. Over himself, over his own body and mind, the individual is sovereign.

What, then, is the rightful limit to the sovereignty of the individual over himself? Where does the authority of society begin? How much of human life should be assigned to individuality, and how much to society?

Each will receive its proper share, if each has that which more particularly concerns it. To individuality should belong the part of life in which it is chiefly the individual that is interested; to society, the part which chiefly interests society.

Though society is not founded on a contract, and though no good purpose is answered by inventing a contract in order to deduce social obligations from it, every one who receives the protection of society owes a return for the benefit, and the fact of living in society renders it indispensable that each should be bound to observe a certain line of conduct towards the rest. This conduct consists first, in not injuring the interests of one another; or rather certain interests, which, either by express legal provision or by tacit understanding, ought to be considered as rights; and secondly, in each person's bearing his share (to be fixed on some equitable principle) of the labors and sacrifices incurred for defending the society or its members from injury and molestation. These conditions society is justified in enforcing at all costs to those who endeavor to withhold fulfillment. Nor is this all that society may do. The acts of an individual may be hurtful to others, or wanting in due consideration for their welfare, without going the length of violating any of their constituted rights. The offender may then be justly punished by opinion, though not by law. As soon as any part of a person's conduct affects prejudicially the interests of others, society has jurisdiction over it, and the question whether the general welfare will or will not be promoted by interfering with it, becomes open to discussion. But there is no room for entertaining any such question when a person's conduct affects the interests of no persons besides himself, or needs not affect them unless they like (all the persons concerned being of full age, and the ordinary amount of understanding). In all such cases there should be perfect freedom, legal and social, to do the action and stand the consequences.

It would be a great misunderstanding of this doctrine to suppose that it is one of selfish indifference, which pretends that human beings have no business with each other's conduct in life, and that they should not concern themselves about the well-doing or well-being of one another, unless their own interest is involved. Instead of any diminution there is need of a great increase of disinterested exertion to promote the good of others. But disinterested benevolence can find other instruments to persuade people to their good, than whips and scourges, either of the literal or the metaphorical sort. I am the last person to undervalue the self-regarding virtues; they are only second in importance, if even second, to the social. It is equally the business of education to cultivate both. But even education works by conviction and persuasion as well as by compulsion, and it is by the former only that, when the period of education is past, the self-regarding virtues should be inculcated. Human beings owe to each other help to distinguish the better from the worse, and encouragement to choose the former and avoid the latter. They should be forever stimulating each other to increased exercise of their higher faculties, and increased direction of their feelings and aims towards wise instead of foolish, elevating instead of degrading objects and contemplations. But neither one person, nor any number of persons, is warranted in saying to another human creature of ripe years, that he shall not do with his life for his own benefit what he chooses to do with it. He is the person most interested in his own well-being: the interest which any other person, except in cases of strong personal attachment, can have in it is trifling, compared with that which he himself has; the interest which society has in him individually (except as to his conduct to others) is fractional, and altogether indirect: while, with respect to his own feelings and circumstances, the most ordinary man or woman has means of knowledge immeasurably surpassing those that can be possessed by any one else. The interference of society to overrule his judgment and purposes in what only regards himself, must be grounded on general presumptions; which may be altogether wrong, and even if right, are as likely as not to be misapplied to individual cases, by persons no better acquainted with the circumstances of such cases than those are who look at them merely from without. In this department, therefore, of human affairs, Individuality has its proper field of action. In the conduct of human beings towards one another, it is necessary that general rules should for the most part be observed, in order that people may know what they have to expect; but in each person's own concerns, his individual spontaneity is entitled to free exercise. Considerations to aid his judgment, exhortations to strengthen his will, may be offered to him even obtruded on him by others; but he himself is the final judge. All errors which he is likely to commit against advice and warning, are far outweighed by the evil of allowing others to constrain him to what they deem his good.

I do not mean that the feelings with which a person is regarded by others, ought not to be in any way affected by his self-regarding qualities or deficiencies. This is neither possible nor desirable. If he is eminent in any of the qualities which conduce to his own good, he is, so far, a proper object of admiration. He is so much the nearer to the ideal perfection of human nature. If he is grossly deficient in those qualities, a sentiment the opposite of admiration will follow. There is a degree of folly, and a degree of what may be called (though the phrase is not unobjectionable) lowness or depravation of taste, which, though it cannot justify doing harm to the person who manifests it, renders him necessarily and properly a subject of distaste, or, in extreme cases, even of contempt: a person could not have the opposite qualities in due strength without entertaining these feelings. Though doing no wrong to any one, a person may so act as to compel us to judge him, and feel to him, as a fool, or as a being of an inferior order: and since this judgment and feeling are a fact which he would prefer to avoid it is doing him a service to warn him of it beforehand, as of any other disagreeable consequence to which he exposes himself. It would be well, indeed, if this good office were much more freely rendered than the common notions of politeness at present permit, and if one person could honestly point out to another that he thinks him in fault, without being considered unmannerly or presuming. We have a right, also, in various ways, to act upon our unfavorable opinion of any one, not to the oppression of his individuality, but in the exercise of ours. We are not bound, for example, to seek his society; we have a right to avoid it (though not to parade the avoidance), for we have a right to choose the society most acceptable to us. We have a right, and it may be our duty, to caution others against him, if we think his example or conversation likely to have a pernicious effect on those with whom he associates. We may give others a preference over him in optional good offices, except those which tend to his improvement. In these various modes a person may suffer very severe penalties at the hands of others, for faults which directly concern only himself; but he suffers these penalties only in so far as they are the natural, and, as it were, the spontaneous consequences of the faults themselves, not because they are purposely inflicted on him for the sake of punishment. A person who shows rashness, obstinacy, self-conceit—who cannot live within moderate means—who cannot restrain himself from hurtful indulgences—who pursues animal pleasures at the expense of those of feeling and intellect—must expect to be lowered in the opinion of others, and to have a less share of their favorable sentiments; but of this he has no right to complain, unless he has merited their favor by special excellence in his social relations, and has thus established a title to their good offices, which is not affected by his demerits towards himself.

What I contend for is, that the inconveniences which are strictly inseparable from the unfavorable judgment of others, are the only ones to which a person should ever be subjected for that portion of his conduct and character which concerns his own good but which does not affect the interests of others in their relations with him. Acts injurious to others require a totally different treatment. Encroachment on their rights; infliction on them of any loss or damage not justified by his own rights, falsehood or duplicity in dealing with them; unfair or ungenerous use of advantages over them; even selfish abstinence from defending them against injury—these are fit objects of moral reprobation, and, in grave cases, of moral retribution and punishment. And not only these acts, but the dispositions which lead to them, are properly immoral, and fit subjects of disapprobation which may rise to abhorrence. Cruelty of disposition; malice and ill-nature; that most anti-social and odious of all passions, envy; dissimulation and insincerity; irascibility on insufficient cause, and resentment disproportioned to the provocation; the love of domineering over others; the desire to engross more than one's share of advantages (the *pleonexia* of the Greeks); the pride which derives gratification from the abasement of others; the egotism which thinks self and its concerns more important than everything else, and decides all doubtful questions in its own favor;—these are moral vices, and constitute a bad and odious moral character: unlike the self-regarding faults previously mentioned, which are not properly immoralities, and to whatever pitch they may be carried, do not constitute wickedness. They may be proofs of any amount of folly, or want of personal dignity and self-respect: but they are only a subject of moral reprobation when they involve a breach of duty to others, for whose sake the individual is bound to have care for himself. What are called duties to ourselves are not socially obligatory, unless circumstances render them at the same time duties to others. The term duty to oneself, when it means anything more than prudence, means self-respect or self-development; and for none of these is any one accountable to his fellow creatures, because for none of them is it for the good of mankind that he be held accountable to them.

But the strongest of all the arguments against the interference of the public with purely personal conduct, is that when it does interfere, the odds are that it interferes wrongly, and in the wrong place. On questions of social morality, of duty to others, the opinion of the public, that is, of an overruling majority, though often wrong, is likely to be still oftener right; because on such questions they are only required to judge of their own interests; of the manner in which some mode of conduct, if allowed to be practiced, would affect themselves. But the opinion of a similar majority, imposed as a law on the minority, on questions of self-regarding conduct, is quite as likely to be wrong as right; for in these cases public opinion means, at the best, some people's opinion of what is good or bad for other people; while very often it does not even mean that; the public, with the most perfect indifference, passing over the pleasure or convenience of those whose conduct they censure, and considering only their own preference. There are many who consider as an injury to themselves any conduct which they have a distaste for, and resent it as an outrage to their feelings; as a religious bigot, when charged with disregarding the religious feelings of others, has been known to retort that they disregard his feelings, by persisting in their abominable worship or creed. But there is no parity between the feeling of a person for his own opinion, and the feeling of another who is offended at his holding it; no more than between the desire of a thief to take a purse, and the desire of the right owner to keep it. And a person's taste is as much his own peculiar concern as his opinion or his purse. It is easy for any one to imagine an ideal public, which leaves the freedom and choice of individuals in all uncertain matters undisturbed, and only requires them to abstain from modes of conduct which universal experience has condemned. But where has there been seen a public which set any such limit to its censorship? Or when does the public trouble itself about universal experience? In its interferences with personal conduct it is seldom thinking of anything but the enormity of acting or feeling differently from itself; and this standard of judgment, thinly disguised, is held up to mankind as the dictate of religion and philosophy, by nine-tenths of all moralists and speculative writers. These teach that things are right because they are right; because we feel them to be so. They tell us to search in our own minds and hearts for laws of conduct binding on ourselves and on all others. What can the poor public do but apply these instructions, and make their own personal feelings of good and evil, if they are tolerably unanimous in them, obligatory on all the world?

How character and power affect self-interest [199]

When we talk of the interest of a body of men, or even of an individual man, as a principle determining their actions, the question what would be considered their interest by an unprejudiced observer, is one of the least important parts of the whole matter. As Coleridge observes, the man makes the motive, not the motive the man.[200] What it is the man's interest to do or refrain from, depends less on any outward circumstances, than upon what sort of man he is. If you wish to know what is practically a man's interest, you must know the cast of his habitual feelings and thoughts. Everybody has two kinds of interests, interests which he cares for, and interests which he does not care for. Everybody has selfish and unselfish interests, and a selfish man has cultivated the habit of caring for the former, and not caring for the latter. Every one has present and distant interests and the improvident man is he who cares for the present interests and does not care for the distant. It matters little that on any correct calculation the latter may be the more considerable, if the habits of his mind lead him to fix his thoughts and wishes solely on the former. It would be vain to attempt to persuade a man who beats his wife and ill-treats his children, that he would be happier if he lived in love and kindness with them. He would be happier if he were the kind of person who *could* so live; but he is not, and it is probably too late for him to become, that kind of person. Being what he is, the gratification of his love of domineering, and the indulgence of his ferocious temper, are to his perceptions a greater good to himself, than he would be capable of deriving from the pleasure and affection of those dependent on him. He has no pleasure in their pleasure, and does not care for their affection. His neighbor, who does, is probably a happier man than he; but could he be persuaded of this, the persuasion would, most likely only still further exasperate his malignity or his irritability. On the average, a person who cares for other people, for his country, or for mankind, is a happier man than one who does not; but of what use is it to preach this doctrine to a man who cares for nothing but his own ease, or his own pocket? He cannot care for other people if he would. It is like preaching to the worm who crawls on the ground, how much better it would be for him if he were an eagle.

Now it is an universally observed fact, that the two evil dispositions in question, the disposition to prefer a man's selfish interests to those which he shares with other people, and his immediate and direct interests to those which are indirect and remote, are characteristics most especially called forth and fostered by the possession of power. The moment a man, or a class of men, find themselves with power in their hands, the man's individual interest, or the class's separate interest, acquires an entirely new degree of importance in their eyes. Finding themselves worshipped by others, they become worshippers of themselves, and think themselves entitled to be counted at a hundred times the value of other people; while the facility they acquire of doing as they like without regard to consequences, insensibly weakens the habits which make men look forward even to such consequences as affect themselves. This is the meaning of the universal tradition, grounded on universal experience, of men's being corrupted by power. Every one knows how absurd it would be to infer from what a man is or does when in a private station, that he will be and do exactly the like when a despot on a throne; where the bad parts of his human nature, instead of being restrained and kept in subordination by every circumstance of his life and by every person surrounding him, are courted by all persons, and ministered to by all circumstances. It would be quite as absurd to entertain a similar expectation in regard to a class of men; the Demos, or any other. Let them be ever so modest and amenable to reason while there is a power over them stronger than they, we ought to expect a total change in this respect when they themselves become the strongest power.

Governments must be made for human beings as they are, or as they are capable of speedily becoming: and in any state of cultivation which mankind, or any class among them, have yet attained, or are likely soon to attain, the interests by which they will be led, when they are thinking only of self-interest, will be almost exclusively those which are obvious at first sight, and which operate on their present condition. It is only a disinterested regard for others, and especially for what comes after them, for the idea of posterity, of their country, or of mankind, whether grounded on sympathy or on a conscientious feeling, which ever directs the minds and purposes of classes or bodies of men towards distant or unobvious interests. And it cannot be maintained that any form of government would be rational, which required as a condition that these exalted principles of action should be the guiding and master motives in the conduct of average human beings. A certain amount of conscience, and of disinterested public spirit, may fairly be calculated on in the citizens of any community ripe for representative government. But it would be ridiculous to expect such a degree of it, combined with such intellectual discernment, as would be proof against any plausible fallacy tending to make that which was for their class interest appear the dictate of justice and of the general good.

The self-interest of women [201]

When we consider how vast is the number of men, in any great country, who are little higher than brutes, and that this never prevents them from being able, through the law of marriage, to obtain a victim, the breadth and depth of human misery caused in this shape alone by the abuse of the institution swells to something appalling. Yet these are only the extreme cases. They are the lowest abysses, but there is a sad succession of depth after depth before reaching them. In domestic as in political tyranny, the case of absolute monsters chiefly illustrates the institution by showing that there is scarcely any horror which may not occur under it if the despot pleases, and thus setting in a strong light what must be the terrible frequency of things only a little less atrocious. Absolute fiends are as rare as angels, perhaps rarer: ferocious savages, with occasional touches of humanity, are however very frequent: and in the wide interval which separates these from any worthy representatives of the human species, how many are the forms and gradations of animalism and selfishness, often under an outward varnish of civilization and even cultivation, living at peace with the law, maintaining a creditable appearance to all who are not under their power, yet sufficient often to make the lives of all who are so, a torment and a burden to them! It would be tiresome to repeat the commonplaces about the unfitness of men in general for power, which, after the political discussions of centuries, every one knows by heart, were it not that hardly any one thinks of applying these maxims to the case in which above all others they are applicable, that of power, not placed in the hands of a man here and there, but offered to every adult male, down to the basest and most ferocious. It is not because a man is not known to have broken any of the Ten Commandments, or because he maintains a respectable character in his dealings with those whom he cannot compel to have intercourse with him, or because he does not fly out into violent bursts of ill-temper against those who are not obliged to bear with him, that it is possible to surmise of what sort his conduct will be in the unrestraint of home. Even the commonest men reserve the violent, the sulky, the undisguisedly selfish side of their character for those who have no power to withstand it. The relation of superiors to dependents is the nursery of these vices of character, which, wherever else they exist, are an overflowing from that source. A man who is morose or violent to his equals, is sure to be one who has lived among inferiors, whom he could frighten or worry into submission. If the family in its best forms is, as it is often said to be, a school of sympathy, tenderness, and loving forgetfulness of self, it is still oftener, as respects its chief, a school of willfulness, overbearingness, unbounded self-indulgence, and a double-dyed and idealized selfishness, of which sacrifice itself is only a particular form: the care for the wife and children being only care for them as parts of the man's own interests and belongings, and their individual happiness being immolated in every shape to his smallest preferences. What better is to be looked for under the existing form of the institution? We know that the bad propensities of human nature are only kept within bounds when they are allowed no scope for their indulgence. We know that from impulse and habit, when not from deliberate purpose, almost every one to whom others yield, goes on encroaching upon them, until a point is reached at which they are compelled to resist. Such being the common tendency of human nature; the almost unlimited power which present social institutions give to the man over at least one human being—the one with whom he resides, and whom he has always present—this power seeks out and evokes the latent germs of selfishness in the remotest corners of his nature—fans its faintest sparks and smoldering embers—offers to him a license for the indulgence of those points of his original character which in all other relations he would have found it necessary to repress and conceal, and the repression of which would in time have become a second nature. I know that there is another side to the question. I grant that the wife, if she cannot effectually resist, can at least retaliate; she, too, can make the man's life extremely uncomfortable, and by that power is able to carry many points which she ought, and many which she ought not, to prevail in. But this instrument of self-protection—which may be called the power of the scold, or the shrewish sanction—has the fatal defect, that it avails most against the least tyrannical superiors, and in favor of the least deserving dependents. It is the weapon of irritable and self-willed women; of those who would make the worst use of power if they themselves had it, and who generally turn this power to a bad use. The amiable cannot use such an instrument, the high-minded disdain it. And on the other hand, the husbands against whom it is used most effectively are the gentler and more inoffensive: those who cannot be induced, even by provocation, to resort to any very harsh exercise of authority. The wife's power of being disagreeable generally only establishes a counter-tyranny, and makes victims in their turn chiefly of those husbands who are least inclined to be tyrants.

The law of servitude in marriage is a monstrous contradiction to all the principles of the modern world, and to all the experience through which those principles have been slowly and painfully worked out. It is the sole case, now that Negro slavery has been abolished, in which a human being in the plenitude of every faculty is delivered up to the tender mercies of another human being, in the hope forsooth that this other will use the power solely for the good of the person subjected to it. Marriage is the only actual bondage known to our law. There remain no legal slaves, except the mistress of every house.

It is not, therefore, on this part of the subject, that the question is likely to be asked, *Cui bono?* We may be told that the evil would outweigh the good, but the reality of the good admits of no dispute. In regard, however, to the larger question, the removal of women's disabilities—their recognition as the equals of men in all that belongs to citizenship—the opening to them of all honorable employments, and of the training and education which qualifies for those employments—there are many persons for whom it is not enough that the inequality has no just or legitimate defense; they require to be told what express advantage would be obtained by abolishing it.

To which let me first answer, the advantage of having the most universal and pervading of all human relations regulated by justice instead of injustice. The vast amount of this gain to human nature, it is hardly possible, by any explanation or illustration, to place in a stronger light than it is placed by the bare statement, to any one who attaches a moral meaning to words. All the selfish propensities, the self-worship, the unjust self-preference, which exist among mankind, have their source and root in, and derive their principal nourishment from, the present constitution of the relation between men and women. Think what it is to a boy, to grow up to manhood in the belief that without any merit or any exertion of his own, though he may be the most frivolous and empty or the most ignorant and stolid of mankind, by the mere fact of being born a male he is by right the superior of all and every one of an entire half of the human race: including probably some whose real superiority to himself he has daily or hourly occasion to feel; but even if in his whole conduct he habitually follows a woman's guidance, still, if he is a fool, he thinks that of course she is not, and cannot be, equal in ability and judgment to himself; and if he is not a fool, he does worse. He sees that she is superior to him, and believes that, notwithstanding her superiority, he is entitled to command and she is bound to obey. What must be the effect on his character, of this lesson? And men of the cultivated classes are often not aware how deeply it sinks into the immense majority of male minds. For, among right-feeling and well-bred people, the inequality is kept as much as possible out of sight; above all, out of sight of the children. As much obedience is required from boys to their mother as to their father: they are not permitted to domineer over their sisters, nor are they accustomed to see these postponed to them, but the contrary; the compensations of the chivalrous feeling being made prominent, while the servitude which requires them is kept in the background. Well brought-up youths in the higher classes thus often escape the bad influences of the situation in their early years, and only experience them when, arrived at manhood, they fall under the dominion of facts as they really exist. Such people are little aware, when a boy is differently brought up, how early the notion of his inherent superiority to a girl arises in his mind; how it grows with his growth and strengthens with his strength; how it is inoculated by one schoolboy upon another; how early the youth thinks himself superior to his mother, owing her perhaps forbearance, but no real respect; and how sublime and sultan-like a sense of superiority he feels, above all, over the woman whom he honors by admitting her to a partnership of his life. Is it imagined that all this does not pervert the whole manner of existence of the man, both as an individual and as a social being?

*H*enry Sidgwick was born in Yorkshire and is the last of the great nineteenth-century English Utilitarians. His most important treatise, The Methods of Ethics (1874), expressed doubt about the possibility of reconciling rational self-interest with the morality of universal hedonism.

HENRY SIGWICK
(1838–1900)

Self-interest as an individual's "ultimate good on the whole" [202]

What then can we state as the general meaning of the term "good"? Shall we say— with Hobbes, and many since Hobbes—that "whatsoever is the object of any man's Desire, that it is which he for his part calleth Good, and the object of his aversion Evil"? To simplify the discussion, we will consider only what a man desires for itself—not as a means to an ulterior result,—and for himself—not benevolently for others: his own Good [203] and ultimate Good. We have first to meet the obvious objection that a man often desires what he knows is on the whole bad for him: the pleasure of drinking champagne which is sure to disagree with him, the gratification of revenge when he knows that his true interest lies in reconciliation. The answer is that in such cases the desired result is accompanied or followed by other effects which when they come excite aversion stronger than the desire for the desired effect: but that these bad effects, though fore-*seen* are not fore-*felt*: the representation of them does not adequately modify the predominant direction of desire as a present fact. But, granting this, and fixing attention solely on the result desired, apart from its concomitants and consequences—it would still seem that what is desired at any time is, as such, merely apparent Good, which may not be found good when fruition comes, or at any rate not so good as it appeared. It may turn out a "Dead Sea apple," mere dust and ashes in the eating: more often, fruition will partly correspond to expectation, but may still fall short of it in a marked degree. And sometimes—even while yielding to the desire— we are aware of the illusoriness of this expectation of "good" which the desire carries with it. I conclude, therefore, that if we are to conceive of the elements of ultimate Good as capable of quantitative comparison—as we do when we speak of preferring a "greater" good to a "lesser,"—we cannot identify the object of desire with "good" simply, or "true good," but only with "apparent good."

But further: a prudent man is accustomed to suppress, with more or less success, desires for what he regards as out of his power to attain by voluntary action—as fine weather, perfect health, great wealth, or fame, etc.; but any success he may have in diminishing the actual intensity of such desires has no effect in leading him to judge the objects desired less "good."

It would seem then, that if we interpret the notion "good" in relation to "desire," we must identify it not with the actually *desired* but rather with the *desirable*: meaning by "desirable" not necessarily "what ought to be desired" but what would be desired with strength proportioned to the degree of desirability, if it were judged attainable by vol- untary action, supposing the desirer to possess a perfect forecast, emotional as well as intellectual, of the state of attainment or fruition.

It still remains possible that the choice of any particular good, thus defined as an object of pursuit, may be on the whole bad, on account of its concomitants and con- sequences; even though the particular result when attained is not found other than it was imagined in the condition of previous desire. If, therefore, in seeking a definition of "ultimate Good" we mean "good on the whole," we have—following the line of thought of the preceding paragraph—to express its relation to Desire differently. In the first place we have to limit our view to desire which becomes practical in volition; as I may still regard as desirable results which I judge it on the whole imprudent to aim at. But, even with this limitation, the relation of my "good on the whole" to my desire is very complicated. For it is not even sufficient to say that my Good on the whole is what I should actually desire and seek if all the consequences of seeking it could be foreknown and adequately realized by me in imagination at the time of mak- ing my choice. No doubt an equal regard for all the moments of our conscious expe- rience—so far, at least, as the mere difference of their position in time is concerned—is an essential characteristic of rational conduct. But the mere fact, that a man does not afterwards feel for the consequences of an action aversion strong enough to cause him to regret it, cannot be accepted as a complete proof that he has acted for his "good on the whole." Indeed, we commonly reckon it among the worst consequences of some kinds of conduct that they alter men's tendencies to desire, and make them desire their lesser good more than their greater: and we think it all the worse for a man—even in this world—if he is never roused out of such a condition and lives till death the life of a contented pig, when he might have been something better. To avoid this objection, it would have to be said that a man's future good on the whole is what he would now desire and seek on the whole if all the consequences of all the different lines of conduct open to him were accurately foreseen and adequately realized in imagination at the present point of time.

This hypothetical composition of impulsive forces involves so elaborate and complex a conception, that it is somewhat paradoxical to say that this is what we commonly *mean* when we talk of a man's "good on the whole." Still, I cannot deny that this hypothetical object of a resultant desire supplies an intelligible and admissible interpretation of the terms "good" (substantive) and "desirable," as giving philosophical precision to the vaguer meaning with which they are used in ordinary discourse: and it would seem that a calm comprehensive desire for "good" conceived somewhat in this way, though more vaguely, is normally produced by intellectual comparison and experience in a reflective mind. The notion of "Good" thus attained has an ideal element: it is something that *is* not always actually desired and aimed at, by human beings but the ideal element is entirely interpretable in terms of *fact*, actual or hypothetical, and does not introduce any judgment of value, fundamentally distinct from judgments relating to existence;—still less any "dictate of Reason." [205]

It seems to me, however, more in accordance with common sense to recognize—as Butler does—that the calm desire for my "good on the whole" is *authoritative*; and therefore carries with it implicitly a rational dictate to aim at this end, if in any case a conflicting desire urges the will in an opposite direction. Still we may keep the notion of "dictate" or "imperative" merely implicit and latent,—as it seems to be in ordinary judgments as to "my good" and its opposite—by interpreting "ultimate good on the whole for me" to mean what I should practically desire if my desires were in harmony with reason, assuming my own existence alone to be considered. On this view, "ultimate good on the whole," unqualified by reference to a particular subject, must be taken to mean what as a rational being I should desire and seek to realize, assuming myself to have an equal concern for *all* existence. When conduct is judged to be "good" or "desirable" in itself, independently of its consequences, it is, I conceive, this latter point of view that is taken.

On the relationship between egoistic and universalistic hedonism [205]

It remains for us to consider the relation of the two species of Hedonism which we have distinguished as Universalistic and Egoistic. In chap. ii. of this Book we have discussed the rational process (called by a stretch of language "proof") by which one who holds it reasonable to aim at his own greatest happiness may be determined to take Universal Happiness instead, as his ultimate standard of right conduct. We have seen, however that the application of this process requires that the Egoist should affirm, implicitly or explicitly, that his own greatest happiness is not merely the rational ultimate end for himself but a part of Universal Good: and he may avoid the proof of Utilitarianism by declining to affirm this. It would be contrary to Common Sense to deny that the distinction between any one individual and any other is real and fundamental, and that consequently "I" am concerned with the quality of my existence as an individual in a sense, fundamentally important, in which I am not concerned with the quality of the existence of other individuals: and this being so, I do not see how it can be proved that this distinction is not to be taken as fundamental in determining the ultimate end of rational action for an individual. And it may be observed that most Utilitarians, however anxious they have been to convince men of the reasonableness of aiming at happiness generally, have not commonly sought to attain this result by any logical transition from the Egoistic to the Universalistic principle. They have relied almost entirely on the Sanctions of Utilitarian rules; that is, on the pleasures gained or pains avoided by the individual conforming to them. Indeed, if an Egoist remains impervious to what we have called Proof, the only way of rationally inducing him to aim at the happiness of all, is to show him that his own greatest happiness can be best attained by so doing. And further, even if a man admits the self-evidence of the principle of Rational Benevolence, he may still hold that his own happiness is an end which it is irrational for him to sacrifice to any other; and that therefore a harmony between the maxim of Prudence and the maxim of Rational Benevolence must be somehow demonstrated, if morality is to be made completely rational. This latter view, indeed (as I have before said), appears to me, on the whole, the view of Common Sense: and it is that which I myself hold. It thus becomes needful to examine how far and in what way the required demonstration can be effected.

Now, in so far as Utilitarian morality coincides with that of Common Sense—as we have seen that it does in the main—this investigation has been partly performed in chap. v. of Book ii. It there appeared that while in any tolerable state of society the performance of duties towards others and the exercise of social virtues seem *generally* likely to coincide with the attainment of the greatest possible happiness in the long run for the virtuous agent, still the *universality* and *completeness* of this coincidence are at least incapable of empirical proof: and that, indeed, the more carefully we analyze and estimate the different sanctions—Legal, Social, and Conscientious considered as operating under the actual conditions of human life, the more difficult it seems to believe that they can be always adequate to produce this coincidence. The natural effect of this argument upon a convinced Utilitarian is merely to make him anxious to alter the actual conditions of human life: and it would certainly be a most valuable contribution to the actual happiness of mankind, if we could so improve the adjustment of the machine of Law in any society, and so stimulate and direct the common awards of praise and blame, and so develop and train the moral sense of the members of the community, as to render it clearly prudent for every individual to promote as much as possible the general good. However, we are not now considering what a consistent Utilitarian will try to effect for the future, but what a consistent Egoist is to do in the present. And it must be admitted that, as things are, whatever difference exists between Utilitarian morality and that of Common Sense is of such a kind as to render the coincidence with Egoism still more improbable in the case of the former. For we have seen that Utilitarianism is more rigid than Common Sense in exacting the sacrifice of the agent's private interests where they are incompatible with the greatest happiness of the greatest number: and of course in so far as the Utilitarian's principles bring him into conflict with any of the commonly accepted rules of morality, the whole force of the Social Sanction operates to deter him from what he conceives to be his duty.

There are, however, writers of the Utilitarian school[206] who seem to maintain or imply, that by due contemplation of the paramount importance of Sympathy as an element of human happiness we shall be led to see the coincidence of the good of each with the good of all. In opposing this view, I am as far as possible from any wish to depreciate the value of sympathy as a source of happiness even to human beings as at present constituted. . . .

But allowing[207] all this, it yet seems to me as certain as any conclusion arrived at by hedonistic comparison can be, that the utmost development of sympathy, intensive and extensive, which is now possible to any but a very few exceptional persons, would not cause a perfect coincidence between Utilitarian duty and self-interest. Here it seems to me that what was said in Book ii. chap. v. §4, to show the insufficiency of the Conscientious Sanction, applies equally, *mutatis mutandis*, to Sympathy. Suppose a man finds that a regard for the general good—Utilitarian Duty—demands from him a sacrifice, or extreme risk, of life. There are perhaps one or two human beings so dear to him that the remainder of a life saved by sacrificing their happiness to his own would be worthless to him from an egoistic point of view. But it is doubtful whether many men, "sitting down in a cool hour" to make the estimate, would affirm even this: and of course that particular portion of the general happiness, for which one is called upon to sacrifice one's own, may easily be the happiness of persons not especially dear to one. But again, from this normal limitation of our keenest and strongest sympathy to a very small circle of human beings, it results that the very development of sympathy may operate to increase the weight thrown into the scale against Utilitarian duty. There are very few persons, however strongly and widely sympathetic, who are so constituted as to feel for the pleasures and pains of mankind generally a degree of sympathy at all commensurate with their concern for wife or children, or lover, or intimate friend: and if any training of the affections is at present possible which would materially alter this proportion in the general distribution of our sympathy, it scarcely seems that such a training is to be recommended as on the whole felicific.[208] And thus when

Utilitarian Duty calls on us to sacrifice not only our own pleasures but the happiness of those we love to the general good, the very sanction on which Utilitarianism most relies must act powerfully in opposition to its precepts. . . .

It seems, then, that we must conclude, from the arguments given in Book ii. chap. v., supplemented by the discussion in the preceding section, that the inseparable connection between Utilitarian Duty and the greatest happiness of the individual who conforms to it cannot be satisfactorily demonstrated on empirical grounds. Hence another section of the Utilitarian school has preferred to throw the weight of Duty on the Religious Sanction: and this procedure has been partly adopted by some of those who have chiefly dwelt on sympathy as a motive. From this point of view the Utilitarian Code is conceived as the Law of God, who is to be regarded as having commanded men to promote the general happiness, and as having announced an intention of rewarding those who obey His commands and punishing the disobedient. It is clear that if we feel convinced that an Omnipotent Being has, in whatever way, signified such commands and announcements, a rational egoist can want no further inducement to frame his life on Utilitarian principles. It only remains to consider how this conviction is attained. This is commonly thought to be either by supernatural Revelation, or by the natural exercise of Reason, or in both ways. As regards the former it is to be observed that—with a few exceptions—the moralists who hold that God has disclosed His law either to special individuals in past ages who have left a written record of what was revealed to them, or to a permanent succession of persons appointed in a particular manner, or to religious persons generally in some supernatural way, do not consider that it is the Utilitarian Code that has thus been revealed, but rather the rules of Common-Sense morality with some special modifications and additions. Still, as Mill has urged, in so far as Utilitarianism is more rigorous than Common Sense in exacting the sacrifice of the individual's happiness to that of mankind generally, it is strictly in accordance with the most characteristic teaching of Christianity. It seems, however, unnecessary to discuss the precise relation of different Revelational Codes to Utilitarianism, as it would be going beyond our province to investigate the grounds on which a Divine origin has been attributed to them.

In so far, however, as a knowledge of God's law is believed to be attainable by the Reason, Ethics and Theology seem to be so closely connected that we cannot sharply separate their provinces. For, as we saw,[209] it has been widely maintained, that the relation of moral rules to a Divine Lawgiver is implicitly cognized in the act of thought by which we discern these rules to be binding. . . .

Still, though Common Sense does not regard moral rules as being *merely* the mandates of an Omnipotent Being who will reward and punish men according as they obey or violate them; it certainly holds that this is a true though partial view of them, and perhaps that it may be intuitively apprehended. If then reflection leads us to conclude that the particular moral principles of Common Sense are to be systematized as subordinate to that pre-eminently certain and irrefragable intuition which stands as the first principle of Utilitarianism then, of course, it will be the Utilitarian Code to which we shall believe the Divine Sanctions to be attached.

Or, again, we may argue thus. If—as all theologians agree—we are to conceive God as acting for some end, we must conceive that end to be Universal Good, and, if Utilitarians are right, Universal Happiness: and we cannot suppose that in a world morally governed it can be prudent for any man to act in conscious opposition to what we believe to be the Divine Design. Hence if in any case after calculating the consequences of two alternatives of conduct we choose that which seems likely to be less conducive to Happiness generally, we shall be acting in a manner for which we cannot but expect to suffer.

To this it has been objected, that observation of the actual world shows us that the happiness of sentient beings is so imperfectly attained in it, and with so large an inter-mixture of pain and misery, that we cannot really conceive Universal Happiness to be God's end, unless we admit that He is not Omnipotent. And no doubt the assertion that God is omnipotent will require to be understood with some limitation; but per-haps with no greater limitation than has always been implicitly admitted by thought-ful theologians. For these seem always to have allowed that some things are impossible to God: as, for example, to change the past. And perhaps if our knowledge of the Universe were complete, we might discern the *quantum* of happiness ultimately attained in it to be as great as could be attained without the accomplishment of what we should then see to be just as inconceivable and absurd as changing the past. This, however, is a view which it belongs rather to the theologian to develop. I should rather urge that there does not seem to be any other of the ordinary interpretations of Good according to which it would appear to be more completely realized in the actual uni-verse. For the wonderful perfections of work that we admire in the physical world are yet everywhere mingled with imperfection, and subject to destruction and decay: and similarly in the world of human conduct Virtue is at least as much balanced by Vice as Happiness is by misery. So that, if the ethical reasoning that led us to interpret Ulti-mate Good as Happiness is sound, there seems no argument from Natural Theology to set against it.

If, then, we may assume the existence of such a Being, as God, by the *consensus* of theologians, is conceived to be, it seems that Utilitarians may legitimately infer the existence of Divine sanctions to the code of social duty as constructed on a Utilitari-an basis; and such sanctions would, of course, suffice to make it always every one's interest to promote universal happiness to the best of his knowledge. It is, however, desirable, before we conclude, to examine carefully the validity of this assumption, in so far as it is supported on ethical grounds alone. For by the result of such an exami-nation will be determined, as we now see, the very important question whether ethical science can be constructed on an independent basis, or whether it is forced to borrow a fundamental and indispensable premise from Theology or some similar source.[210] In order fairly to perform this examination, let us reflect upon the clearest and most certain of our moral intuitions. I find that I undoubtedly seem to perceive, as clearly and certainly as I see any axiom in Arithmetic or Geometry, that it is "right" and "reasonable" for me to treat others as I should think that I myself ought to be treated under similar conditions, and to do what I believe to be ultimately conducive to universal Good or Happiness. But I cannot find inseparably connected with this conviction, and similarly attainable by mere reflective intuition, any cognition that there actually is a Supreme Being who will adequately[211] reward me for obeying these rules of duty, or punish me for violating them.[212] Or,—omitting the strictly theological element of the proposition,—I may say that I do not find in my moral consciousness any intuition, claiming to be clear and certain, that the performance of duty will be adequately rewarded and its violation punished. I feel indeed a desire, apparently inseparable from the moral sentiments that this result may be realized not only in my own case but universally; but the mere existence of the desire would not go far to establish the probability of its fulfillment, considering the large proportion of human desires that experience shows to be doomed to disappointment. I also judge that in a certain sense this result *ought* to be realized: in this judgment, however, "ought" is not used in a strictly ethical meaning; it only expresses the vital need that our Practical Reason feels of proving or postulating this connection of Virtue and self-interest, if it is to be made consistent with itself. For the negation of the connection must force us to admit an ultimate and fundamental contradiction in our apparent intuitions of what is Reasonable in conduct; and from this admission it would seem to follow that the apparently intuitive operation of the Practical Reason, manifested in these contradictory judgments, is after all illusory.

I do not mean that if we gave up the hope of attaining a practical solution of this fundamental contradiction, through any legitimately obtained conclusion or postulate as to the moral order of the world, it would become reasonable for us to abandon morality altogether: but it would seem necessary to abandon the idea of rationalizing it completely. We should doubtless still, not only from self-interest, but also through sympathy and sentiments protective of social well-being, imparted by education and sustained by communication with other men, feel a desire for the general observance of rules conducive to general happiness; and practical reason would still impel us decisively to the performance of duty in the more ordinary cases in which what is recognized as duty is in harmony with self-interest properly understood. But in the rarer cases of a recognized conflict between self-interest and duty, practical reason, being divided against itself, would cease to be a motive on either side; the conflict would have to be decided by the comparative preponderance of one or other of two groups of non-rational impulses.

William James was born in New York City and spent a long and distinguished career at Harvard as professor of both medicine and philosophy. In 1890 he published his two-volume Principles of Psychology, which addressed itself to the nature of self-love with the help of insights gleaned from the writings of the now obscure nineteenth-century German psychologist, Adolf Horwicz.

WILLIAM JAMES
(1842–1910)

What self is loved in 'self-love'? [213]

We must now try to interpret the facts of self-love and self-seeking a little more delicately from within.

A man in whom self-seeking of any sort is largely developed is said to be selfish.[214] He is on the other hand called unselfish if he shows consideration for the interests of other selves than his own. Now what is the intimate *nature* of the selfish emotion in him? And what is the primary *object* of its regard? We have described him pursuing and fostering as his self first one set of things and then another; we have seen the same set of facts gain or lose interest in his eyes, leave him indifferent, or fill him either with triumph or despair according as he made pretensions to appropriate them, treated them as if they were potentially or actually parts of himself, or not. We know how little it matters to us whether *some* man, a man taken at large and in the abstract, prove a failure or succeed in life,—he may be hanged for aught we care—but we know the utter momentousness and terribleness of the alternative when the man is the one whose name we ourselves bear. I must not be a failure, is the very loudest of the voices that clamor in each of our breasts: let fail who may, I at least must succeed. Now the first conclusion which these facts suggest is that each of us is animated by a *direct feeling of regard for his own pure principle of individual existence,* whatever that may be, taken merely as such. It appears as if all our concrete manifestations of selfishness might be the conclusions of as many syllogisms, each with this principle as the subject of its major premise, thus: Whatever is me is precious; this is me; therefore this is precious; whatever is mine must not fail; this is mine; therefore this must not fail, etc. It appears, I say, as if this principle inoculated all it touched with its own intimate quality of worth; as if, previous to the touching, everything might be matter of indifference, and nothing interesting in its own right; as if my regard for my own body even were an interest not simply in this body; but in this body only so far as it is mine.

But what is this abstract numerical principle of identity, this "Number One" within me, for which, according to proverbial philosophy, I am supposed to keep so constant a "lookout"? Is it the inner nucleus of my spiritual self, that collection of obscurely felt "adjustments," *plus* perhaps that still more obscurely perceived subjectivity as such, of which we recently spoke ? Or is it perhaps the concrete stream of my thought in its entirety, or some one section of the same? Or may it be the indivisible soul-substance, in which, according to the orthodox tradition, my faculties inhere? Or, finally, can it be the mere pronoun I? Surely it is none of these things, that self for which I feel such hot regard. Though all of them together were put within me, I should still be cold, and fail to exhibit anything worthy of the name of selfishness or of devotion to "Number One." To have a self that I can *care for,* nature must first present me with some *object* interesting enough to make me instinctively wish to appropriate it for its *own* sake, and out of it to manufacture one of those material, social, or spiritual selves, which we have already passed in review. We shall find that all the facts of rivalry and substitution that have so struck us, all the shiftings and expansions and contractions of the sphere of what shall be considered me and mine, are but results of the fact that certain *things* appeal to primitive and instinctive impulses of our nature, and that we follow their destinies with an excitement that owes nothing to a reflective source. These objects our consciousness treats as the primordial constituents of its Me. Whatever other objects, whether by association with the fate of these, or in any other way, come to be followed with the same sort of interest, form our remoter and more secondary self. *The words* ME, *then, and* SELF, *so far as they arouse feeling and connote emotional worth, are* OBJECTIVE *designations, meaning* ALL THE THINGS *which have the power to produce in a stream of consciousness excitement of a certain peculiar sort.* Let us try to justify this proposition in detail.

The most palpable selfishness of a man is his bodily selfishness; and his most palpable self is the body to which that selfishness relates. Now I say that he identifies himself with this body because he loves *it,* and that he does not love it because he finds it to be identified with himself. Reverting to natural history-psychology will help us to see the truth of this. In the chapter on Instincts we shall learn that every creature has a certain selective interest in certain portions of the world, and that this interest is as often connate as acquired. Our *interest in things* means the attention and emotion which the thought of them will excite, and the actions which their presence will evoke. Thus every species is particularly interested in its own prey or food, its own enemies, its, own sexual mates, and its own young. These things fascinate by their intrinsic power to do so; they are cared for for their own sakes.

Well, it stands not in the least otherwise with our bodies. They too are percepts in our objective field—they are simply the most interesting percepts there. What happens to them excites in us emotions and tendencies to action more energetic and habitual than any which are excited by other portions of the "field." What my comrades call my bodily selfishness or self-love, is nothing but the sum of all the outer acts which this interest in my body spontaneously draws, from me. My "selfishness" is here but a descriptive name for grouping together the outward symptoms which I show. When I am led by self-love to keep my seat whilst ladies stand, or to grab something first and cut out my neighbor, what I really love is the comfortable seat, is the thing itself which I grab. I love them primarily, as the mother loves her babe, or a generous man an heroic deed. Wherever, as here, self-seeking is the outcome of simple instinctive propensity, it is but a name for certain reflex acts. Something rivets my attention fatally, and fatally provokes the "selfish" response. Could an automaton be so skillfully constructed as to ape these acts, it would be called selfish as properly as I. It is true that I am no automaton, but a thinker. But my thoughts, like my acts, are here concerned only with the outward things. They need neither know nor care for any pure principle within. In fact the more utterly "selfish" I am in this primitive way, the more blindly absorbed my thought will be in the objects and impulses of my lusts, and the more devoid of any inward looking glance. A baby, whose consciousness of the pure Ego, of himself as a thinker, is not usually supposed developed, is, in this way, as some German has said, "*der vollendeteste Egoist.*" His corporeal person, and what ministers to its needs, are the only self he can possibly be said to love. His so-called self-love is but a name for his insensibility to all but this one set of things. It may be that he needs a pure principle of subjectivity, a soul or pure Ego (he certainly needs a stream of thought) to make him sensible at all to anything, to make him discriminate and love *überhaupt*,—how that may be, we shall see ere long; but this pure Ego, which would then be the *condition* of his loving, need no more be the *object* of his love than it need be the object of his thought. If his interests lay altogether in other bodies than his own, if all his instincts were altruistic and all his acts suicidal, still he would need a principle of *consciousness* just as he does now. Such a principle cannot then be the principle of his bodily *selfishness* any more than it is the principle of any other tendency he may show.

So much for the bodily self-love. But my *social* self-love, my interest in the images other men have framed of me, is also an interest in a set of objects external to my thought. These thoughts in other men's minds are out of my mind and "ejective" to me. They come and go, and grow and dwindle, and I am puffed up with pride, or blush with shame, at the result, just as at my success or failure in the pursuit of a material thing. So that here again, just as in the former case, the pure principle seems out of the game as an *object* of regard, and present only as the general form or condition under which the regard and the thinking go on in me at all.

But, it will immediately be objected, this is giving a mutilated account of the facts. These images of me in the minds of other men are, it is true, things outside of me, whose changes I perceive just as I perceive any other outward change. But the pride and shame which I feel are not concerned merely with *those* changes. I feel as if something else had changed too, when I perceive my image in your mind to have changed for the worse, something in me to which that image belongs, and which a moment ago I felt inside of me, big and strong and lusty, but now weak, contracted, and collapsed. Is not this latter change the change I feel the shame about? Is not the condition of this thing inside of me the proper object of my egoistic concern, of my self-regard? And is it not, after all, my pure Ego, my bare numerical principle of distinction from other men, and no empirical part of me at all?

No, it is no such pure principle, it is simply my total empirical selfhood again, my historic Me, a collection of objective facts, to which the depreciated image in your mind "belongs." In what capacity is it that I claim and demand a respectful greeting from you instead of this expression of disdain? It is not as being a bare I that I claim it; it is as being an I who has always been treated with respect, who belongs to a certain family and "set," who has certain powers, possessions, and public functions, sensibilities, duties, and purposes, and merits and deserts. All this is what your disdain negates and contradicts; this is "the thing inside of me" whose changed treatment I feel the shame about; this is what was lusty, and now, in consequence of your conduct, is collapsed; and this certainly is an empirical objective thing. Indeed, the thing that is felt modified and changed for the worse during my feeling of shame is often more concrete even than this,— it is simply my bodily person, in which your conduct immediately and without any reflection at all on my part works those muscular, glandular, and vascular changes which together make up the "expression" of shame. In this instinctive, reflex sort of shame, the body is just as much the entire vehicle of the self-feeling as, in the coarser cases which we first took up, it was the vehicle of the self-seeking. As, in simple "hoggishness," a succulent morsel gives rise, by the reflex mechanism, to behavior which the bystanders find "greedy," and consider to flow from a certain sort of "self-regard"; so here your disdain gives rise, by a mechanism quite as reflex and immediate, to another sort of behavior, which the bystanders call "shame-faced" and which they consider due to another kind of self-regard. But in both cases there may be no particular self *regarded* at all by the mind; and the name self-regard may be only a descriptive title imposed from without the reflex acts themselves, and the feelings that immediately result from their discharge.

After the bodily and social selves come the spiritual. But which of my spiritual selves do I really care for? my Soul-substance? my "transcendental Ego, or Thinker"? my pronoun I? my subjectivity as such? my nucleus of cephalic adjustments? or my more phenomenal and perishable powers, my loves and hates, willingnesses and sensibilities, and the like? Surely the latter. But they, relatively to the central principle, whatever it may be, are external and objective. They come and go, and it remains— "so shakes the magnet, and so stands the pole." It may indeed have to be there for them to be loved, but being there is not identical with being loved itself.

To sum up, then, *we see no reason to suppose that self-love is primarily, or secondarily, or ever, love for one's mere principle of conscious identity*. It is always love for something which, as compared with that principle, is superficial, transient, liable to be taken up or dropped at will.

And zoological psychology again comes to the aid of our understanding and shows us that this must needs be so. In fact, in answering the question what things it is that a man loves in his self-love, we have implicitly answered the farther question, of why he loves them.

Unless his consciousness were something more than cognitive, unless it experienced a partiality for certain of the objects, which, in succession, occupy its ken, it could not long maintain itself in existence; for, by an inscrutable necessity, each human mind's appearance on this earth is conditioned upon the integrity of the body with which it belongs, upon the treatment which that body gets from others, and upon the spiritual dispositions which use it as their tool, and lead it either towards longevity or to destruction. *Its own body, then, first of all, its friends next, and finally its spiritual dispositions,* MUST *be the supremely interesting* OBJECTS *for each human mind.* Each mind, to begin with, must have a certain minimum of selfishness in the shape of instincts of bodily self-seeking in order to exist. This minimum must be there as a basis for all farther conscious acts, whether of self-negation or of a selfishness more subtle still. All minds must have come, by the way of the survival of the fittest, if by no directer path, to take an intense interest in the bodies to which they are yoked, altogether apart from any interest in the pure Ego which they also possess.

And similarly with the images of their person in the minds of others. I should not be extant now had I not become sensitive to looks of approval or disapproval on the faces among which my life is cast. Looks of contempt cast on other persons need affect me in no such peculiar way. Were my mental life dependent exclusively on some other person's welfare, either directly or in an indirect way, then natural selection would unquestionably have brought it about that I should be as sensitive to the social vicissitudes of that other person as I now am to my own. Instead of being egoistic I should be spontaneously altruistic, then. But in this case, only partially realized in actual human conditions, though the self I empirically love would have changed, my pure Ego or Thinker would have to remain just what it is now.

My spiritual powers, again, must interest me more than those of other people, and for the same reason. I should not be here at all unless I had cultivated them and kept them from decay. And the same law which made me once care for them makes me care for them still.

My own body and what ministers to its needs are thus the primitive object, instinctively determined, of my egoistic interests. Other objects may become interesting derivatively through association with any of these things, either as means or as habitual concomitants; *and so in a thousand ways the primitive sphere of the egoistic emotions may enlarge* and change its boundaries.

This sort of interest is really the *meaning of the word "my."* Whatever has it is *eo ipso* a part of me. My child, my friend dies, and where he goes I feel that part of myself now is and evermore shall be:

"For this losing is true dying;
This is lordly man's down-lying;
This his slow but sure reclining,
Star by star his world resigning."

The fact remains, however, that certain special sorts of things tend primordially to possess this interest, and form the *natural* me. But all these things are *objects*, properly so called, to the subject which does the thinking.[215] And this latter fact upsets at once the dictum of the old-fashioned sensationalist psychology, that altruistic passions and interests are contradictory to the nature of things, and that if they appear anywhere to exist, it must be as secondary products, resolvable at bottom into cases of selfishness taught by experience a hypocritical disguise. If the zoological and evolutionary point of view is the true one, there is no reason why any object whatever *might* not arouse passion and interest as primitively and instinctively as any other, whether connected or not with the interests of the me. The phenomenon of passion is in origin and essence the same, whatever be the target upon which it is discharged; and what the target actually happens to be is solely a question of fact. I might conceivably be as much fascinated, and as primitively so, by the care of my neighbor's body as by the care of my own. The only check to such exuberant altruistic interests is natural selection, which would weed out such as were very harmful to the individual or to his tribe. Many such interests, however, remain unweeded out——the interest in the opposite sex, for example, which seems in mankind stronger than is called for by its utilitarian need; and alongside of them remain interests, like that in alcoholic intoxication, or in musical sounds, which, for aught we can see, are without any utility whatever. The sympathetic instincts and the egoistic ones are thus co-ordinate. They arise, so far as we can tell, on the same psychologic level. The only difference between them is that the instincts called egoistic form much the larger mass.

The only author whom I know to have discussed the question whether the "pure

Ego," *per se*, can be an object of regard, is Herr Horwicz, in his extremely able and acute *Psychologische Analysen*. He too says that all self-regard is regard for certain objective things. He disposes so well of one kind of objection that I must conclude by quoting a part of his own words:

First, the objection:

"The fact is indubitable that one's own children always pass for the prettiest and brightest, the wine from one's own cellar for the best—at least for its price—one's own house and horses for the finest. With what tender admiration do we con over our own little deed of benevolence! our own frailties and misdemeanors, how ready we are to acquit ourselves for them, when we notice them at all, on the ground of 'extenuating circumstances'! How much more really comic are our own jokes than those of others, which, unlike ours, will not bear being repeated ten or twelve times over! How eloquent, striking, powerful, our own speeches are! How appropriate our own address! In short, how much more intelligent, soulful, better, is everything about us than in anyone else. The sad chapter of artists' and authors' conceit and vanity belongs here.

"The prevalence of this obvious preference which we feel for everything of our own is indeed striking. Does it not look as if our dear Ego must first lend its color and flavor to anything, in order to make it please us? . . . Is it not the simplest explanation for all these phenomena, so consistent among themselves, to suppose that the ego, the self, which forms the origin and center of our *thinking* life, is at the same time the original and central object of our life of feeling, and the ground both of whatever special ideas and of whatever special feelings ensue?"

Herr Horwicz goes on to refer to what we have already noticed, that various things which disgust us in others do not disgust us at all in ourselves.

"To most of us even the bodily warmth of another, for example the chair warm from another's sitting, is felt unpleasantly, whereas there is nothing disagreeable in the warmth of the chair in which we have been sitting ourselves."

After some further remarks, he replies to these facts and reasonings as follows:

"We may with confidence affirm that our own possessions in most cases please us better [not because they are ours], but simply because we know them better, 'realize' them more intimately, feel them more deeply. We learn to appreciate what is ours in all its details and shadings, whilst the goods of others appear to us in coarse outlines and rude averages. Here are some examples: A piece of music which one plays one's self is heard and understood better than when it is played by another. We get more exactly all the details, penetrate more deeply into the musical thought. We may meanwhile perceive perfectly well that the other person is the better performer, and yet nevertheless—at times get more enjoyment from our own playing because it brings the melody and harmony so much nearer home to us. This case may almost be taken as typical for the other cases of self-love. On close examination, we shall almost always find that a great part of our feeling about what is ours is due to the fact that we *live closer* to our own things, and so feel them more thoroughly and deeply. As a friend of mine was about to marry, he often bored me by the repeated and minute way in which he would discuss the details of his new household arrangements. I wondered that so intellectual a man should be so deeply interested in things of so external a nature. But as I entered, a few years later, the same condition myself, these matters acquired for me an entirely different interest, and it became my turn to turn them over and talk of them unceasingly. . . . The reason was simply this, that in the first instance I *understood* nothing of these things and their importance for domestic comfort, whilst in the latter case they came home to me with irresistible urgency, and vividly took possession of my fancy. So it is with many a one who mocks at decorations and titles, until he gains one himself. And this is also surely the reason why one's own portrait or reflection in the mirror is so peculiarly interesting a thing to contemplate . . . not on account of any absolute *"c'est moi,"* but just as with the music played by ourselves. What greets our eyes is what we know best, most deeply understand; because we ourselves have felt it and lived through it. We know what has ploughed these furrows, deepened these shadows, blanched this hair; and other faces may be handsomer, but none can speak to us or interest us like this." [216]

Moreover, this author goes on to show that our own things are *fuller* for us than those of others because of the memories they awaken and the practical hopes and expectations they arouse. This alone would emphasize them, apart from any value derived from their belonging to ourselves. We may conclude with him, then, that *an original central self-feeling can never explain the passionate warmth of our self-regarding emotions, which must, on the contrary, be addressed directly to special things less abstract and empty of content. To these things the name of "self" may be given, or to our conduct towards them the name of "selfishness," but neither in the self nor the selfishness does the pure Thinker play the "title-rôle."*

Only one more point connected with our self-regard need be mentioned. We have spoken of it so far as active instinct or emotion. It remains to speak of it as cold intellectual self-estimation. We may weigh our own Me in the balance of praise and blame as easily as we weigh other people,—though with difficulty quite as fairly. The *just* man is the one who can weigh himself impartially. Impartial weighing presupposes a rare faculty of abstraction from the vividness with which, as Herr Horwicz has pointed out, things known as intimately as our own possessions and performances appeal to our imagination; and an equally rare power of vividly representing the affairs of others. But, granting these rare powers, there is no reason why a man should not pass judgment on himself quite as objectively and well as on anyone else. No matter how he *feels* about himself, unduly elated or unduly depressed, he may still truly *know* his own worth by measuring it by the outward standard he applies to other men, and counteract the injustice of the feeling, he cannot wholly escape. This self-measuring process has nothing to do with the instinctive self-regard we have hitherto been dealing with. Being merely one application of intellectual comparison, it need no longer detain us here. Please note again, however, how the pure Ego appears merely as the vehicle in which the estimation is carried on, the objects estimated being all of them facts of an empirical sort, one's body, one's credit, one's fame, one's intellectual ability, one's goodness, or whatever the case may be.

Friedrich Nietzsche was born in Prussia and trained as a classicist. His reflections on self-interest—regarded as startling by some—identify altruism as a sickness and call for self-reverence born of nobility of soul.

FRIEDRICH NIETZSCHE
(1844–1900)

Altruism and the decline of life [217]

In moving the doctrine of selflessness and love into the foreground, Christianity was in no way establishing the interests of the species as of higher value than the interests of the individual. Its real *historical* effect, the fateful element in its effect, remains, on the contrary, in precisely the enhancement of egoism, of the egoism of the individual, to an extreme (—to the extreme of individual immortality). Through Christianity, the individual was made so important, so absolute, that he could no longer be sacrificed: but the species endures only through human sacrifice—All "souls" became equal before God: but this is precisely the most dangerous of all possible evaluations! If one regards individuals as equal, one calls the species into question, one encourages a way of life that leads to the ruin of the species: Christianity is the counterprinciple to the principle of *selection*. If the degenerate and sick ("the Christian") is to be accorded the same value as the healthy ("the pagan"), or even more value, as in Pascal's judgment concerning sickness and health, then unnaturalness becomes law—

This universal love of men is in practice the *preference* for the suffering, underprivileged, degenerate: it has in fact lowered and weakened the strength, the responsibility, the lofty duty to sacrifice men. All that remains, according to the Christian scheme of values, is to sacrifice oneself: but this residue of human sacrifice that Christianity concedes and even advises has, from the standpoint of general breeding, no meaning at all. The prosperity of the species is unaffected by the self-sacrifice of this or that individual (—whether it be in the monkish and ascetic manner or, with the aid of crosses, pyres, and scaffolds, as "martyrs" of error). The species requires that the ill-constituted, weak, degenerate, perish: but it was precisely to them that Christianity turned as a conserving force; it further enhanced that instinct in the weak, already so powerful, to take care of and preserve themselves and to sustain one another. What is "virtue" and "charity" in Christianity if not just this mutual preservation, this solidarity of the weak, this hampering of selection? What is Christian altruism if not the mass-egoism of the weak, which divines that if all care for one another each individual will be preserved as long as possible?—

If one does not feel such a disposition as an extreme immorality, as a crime against life, one belongs with the company of the sick and possesses its instincts oneself—

Genuine charity demands sacrifice for the good of the species—it is hard, it is full of self-overcoming, because it needs human sacrifice. And this pseudo humaneness called Christianity wants it established that no one should be sacrificed—

· · ·

The natural value of egoism.—The value of egoism depends on the physiological value of him who possesses it: it can be very valuable, it can be worthless and contemptible. Every individual may be regarded as representing the ascending or descending line of life. When one has decided which, one has thereby established a canon for the value of his egoism. If he represents the ascending line his value is in fact extraordinary and for the sake of the life-collective, which with him takes a step *forward*, the care expended on his preservation, on the creation of optimum conditions for him, may even be extreme. For the individual, the "single man," as people and philosophers have hitherto understood him, is an error: he does not constitute a separate entity, an atom, a "link in the chain," something merely inherited from the past—he constitutes the entire *single* line "man" up to and including himself. . . . If he represents the descending development, decay, chronic degeneration, sickening (—sickness is, broadly, speaking, already a phenomenon consequent upon decay, not the cause of it), then he can be accorded little value, and elementary fairness demands that he take away as little as possible from the well-constituted. He is no better than a parasite on them. . . .

A criticism of décadence morality.—An "altruistic" morality, a morality under which egoism *languishes*—is under all circumstances a bad sign. This applies to individuals, it applies especially to peoples. The best are lacking when egoism begins to be lacking. To choose what is harmful to *oneself*, to be *attracted* by "disinterested" motives, almost constitutes the formula for *décadence*. "Not to seek *one's own* advantage"—that is merely a moral figleaf for a quite different, namely physiological fact: "I no longer know how to *find* my advantage." . . . Disgregation of the instincts!—Man is finished when he becomes altruistic.—Instead of saying simply "I am no longer worth anything," the moral lie in the mouth of the *décadent* says: "Nothing is worth anything—*life* is not worth anything." . . .

Self-affirmation, not altruism, as the foundation of the good [218]

All respect then for the good spirits that may rule in these historians of morality! But it is, unhappily, certain that the *historical spirit* itself is lacking in them, that precisely all the good spirits of history itself have left them in the lurch! As is the hallowed custom with philosophers, the thinking of all of them is by nature unhistorical, there is no doubt about that. The way they have bungled their moral genealogy comes to light at the very beginning, where the task is to investigate the origin of the concept and judgment "good." "Originally"—so they decree—"one approved unegoistic actions and called them good from the point of view of those to whom they were done, that is to say, those to whom they were *useful*; later one *forgot* how this approval originated and, simply because unegoistic actions were always *habitually* praised as good, one also felt them to be good—as if they were something good in themselves." One sees straightaway that this primary derivation already contains all the typical traits of the idiosyncrasy of the English psychologists—we have "utility," "forgetting," "habit," and finally "error," all as the basis of an evaluation of which the higher man has hitherto been proud as though it were a kind of prerogative of man as such. This pride *has* to be humbled, this evaluation disvalued: has that end been achieved?

Now it is plain to me, first of all, that in this theory the source of the concept "good" has been sought and established in the wrong place: the judgment "good" did *not* originate with those to whom "goodness" was shown! Rather it was "the good" themselves, that is to say, the noble, powerful, high-stationed and high-minded, who felt and established themselves and their actions as good, that is, of the first rank, in contradistinction to all the low, low-minded, common and plebeian. It was out of this *pathos of distance* [219] that they first seized the right to create values and to coin names for values: what had they to do with utility! The viewpoint of utility is as remote and inappropriate as it possibly could be in face of such a burning eruption of the highest rank-ordering, rank-defining value judgments: for here feeling has attained the antithesis of that low degree of warmth which any calculating prudence, any calculus of utility, presupposes—and not for once only, not for an exceptional hour, but for good. The pathos of nobility and distance, as aforesaid, the protracted and domineering fundamental total feeling on the part of a higher ruling order in relation to a lower order, to a "below"—that is the origin of the antithesis "good" and "bad." (The lordly right of giving names extends so far that one should allow oneself to conceive the origin of language itself as an expression of power on the part of the rulers: they say "this is this and this," they seal every thing and event with a sound and, as it were, take possession of it.) It follows from this origin that the word "good" was definitely not linked from the first and by necessity to "unegoistic" actions, as the superstition of these genealogists of morality would have it. Rather it was only when aristocratic value judgments declined that the whole antithesis, "egoistic," "unegoistic" obtruded itself more and more on the human conscience—it is, to speak in my own language, the herd instinct that through this antithesis at last gets its word (and its words) in. And even then it was a long time before that instinct attained such dominion that moral evaluation was actually stuck and halted at this antithesis (as, for example, is the case in contemporary Europe: the prejudice that takes "moral," "unegoistic," "*désintéressé*" as concepts of equivalent value already rules today with the force of a "fixed idea" and brain-sickness).

Altruism versus the individual [220]

Egoism and its problem! The Christian gloominess in La Rochefoucauld which extracted egoism from everything and thought he had thereby *reduced* the value of things and of virtues! To counter that, I at first sought to prove that there could not be anything other than egoism—that in men whose ego is weak and thin the power of great love also grows weak—that the greatest lovers are so from the strength of their ego—that love is an expression of egoism, etc. In fact, the false valuation is aimed at the interests: (1) of those who are helped and aided, the herd; (2) it contains a pessimistic mistrustfulness of the basis of life; (3) it would like to deny the most splendid and best-constituted men; fear; (4) it wants to aid the subjected to their rights against their conquerors; (5) it brings with it a universal dishonesty, and precisely among the most valuable men.

• • •

To the teachers of selfishness.—A man's virtues are called good depending on their probable consequences not for him but for us and society: the praise of virtues has always been far from "selfless," far from "unegoistic." Otherwise one would have had to notice that virtues (like industriousness, obedience, chastity, filial piety, and justice) are usually harmful for those who possess them, being instincts that dominate them too violently and covetously and resist the efforts of reason to keep them in balance with their other instincts. When you have a virtue, a real, whole virtue (and not merely a mini-instinct for some virtue) you are its *victim*. But your neighbor praises your virtue precisely on that account. One praises the industrious even though they harm their eyesight or the spontaneity and freshness of their spirit. One honors and feels sorry for the youth who has worked himself into the ground because one thinks: "For society as a whole the loss of even the best individual is merely a small sacrifice. Too bad that such sacrifices are needed! But it would be far worse if the individual would think otherwise and considered his preservation and development more important than his work in the service of society." Thus one feels sorry for the youth not for his own sake but because a devoted *instrument*, ruthless against itself—a so-called "good man"—has been lost to society by his death.

Perhaps one gives some thought to the question whether it would have been more useful for society if he had been less ruthless against himself and had preserved himself longer. One admits that there would have been some advantage in that, but one considers the other advantage—that a sacrifice has been made and that the attitude of the sacrificial animal has once again been confirmed for all to see—greater and of more lasting significance.

Thus what is really praised when virtues are praised is, first, their instrumental nature and, secondly, the instinct in every virtue that refuses to be held in check by the over-all advantage for the individual himself—in sum, the unreason in virtue that leads the individual to allow himself to be transformed into a mere function of the whole. The praise of virtue is the praise of something that is privately harmful—the praise of instincts that deprive a human being of his noblest selfishness and the strength for the highest autonomy.[221]

To be sure, for educational purposes and to lead men to incorporate virtuous habits one emphasizes effects of virtue that make it appear as if virtue and private advantage were sisters; and some such relationship actually exists. Blindly raging industriousness, for example—this typical virtue of an instrument—is represented as the way to wealth and honor and as the poison that best cures boredom and the passions, but one keeps silent about its dangers, its extreme dangerousness. That is how education always proceeds: one tries to condition an individual by various attractions and advantages to adopt a way of thinking and behaving that, once it has become a habit, instinct, and passion, will dominate him to his own *ultimate disadvantage* but "for the general good."

How often I see that blindly raging industriousness does create wealth and reap honors while at the same time depriving the organs of their subtlety, which alone would make possible the enjoyment of wealth and honors; also that this chief antidote to boredom and the passions at the same time blunts the senses and leads the spirit to resist new attractions. (The most industrious of all ages—ours—does not know how to make anything of all its industriousness and money, except always still more money and still more industriousness; for it requires more genius to spend than to acquire.—Well, we shall have our "grandchildren"!)

If this education succeeds, then every virtue of an individual is a public utility and a private disadvantage, measured against the supreme private goal—probably some impoverishment of the spirit and the senses or even a premature decline. Consider from this point of view, one by one, the virtues of obedience, chastity, filial piety, and justice.

The praise of the selfless, the self-sacrificial, the virtuous—that is, of those who do not apply their whole strength and reason to their own preservation, development, elevation, promotion, and the expansion of their power, but rather live, in relation to themselves, modestly and thoughtlessly, perhaps even with indifference or irony—this praise certainly was not born from the spirit of selflessness. The "neighbor" praises selflessness *because it brings him advantages.* If the neighbor himself were "selfless" in his thinking, he would repudiate this diminution of strength, this mutilation for *his* benefit; he would work against the development of such inclinations, and above all he would manifest his selflessness by *not* calling it *good!*

This indicates the fundamental contradiction in the morality that is very prestigious nowadays: the *motives* of this morality stand opposed to its *principle.* What this morality considers its proof is refuted by its criterion of what is moral. In order not to contravene its own morality, the demand "You shall renounce yourself and sacrifice yourself" could be laid down only by those who thus renounced their own advantage and perhaps brought about their own destruction through the demanded sacrifice of individuals. But as soon as the neighbor (or society) recommends altruism *for the sake of its utility,* it applies the contradictory principle. "You shall seek your advantage even at the expense of everything else"—and thus one preaches, in the same breath, a "Thou shalt" and "Thou shalt not."

• • •

To get the whole of moralizing into focus as a phenomenon. Also as a riddle. The phenomena of morality have occupied me like riddles. Today I would know how to answer the question: What does it mean that the welfare of my neighbor ought to possess for me a higher value than my own? but that my neighbor himself ought to assess the value of his welfare differently than I, that is, that he should subordinate it to my welfare? What is the meaning of that "Thou shalt," which even philosophers regard as "given"?

The apparently crazy idea that a man should esteem the actions he performs for another more highly than those he performs for himself, and that this other should likewise, etc. (that one should call good only those actions that a man performs with an eye, not to himself, but to the welfare of another) has a meaning: namely, as the social instinct resting on the valuation that the single individual is of little account, but all individuals together are of very great account provided they constitute a community with a common feeling and a common conscience. Therefore a kind of training in looking in a certain definite direction, the will to a perspective that seeks to make it impossible to see oneself. . . .

Reflections on egoism [222]

Egoism.—Egoism is the law of perspective applied to feels: what is closest appears large and weighty, and as one moves farther away size and weight decrease.

• • •

The ego wants everything.—It seems that the sole purpose of human action is possession: this idea is, at least, contained in the various languages, which regard all past action as having put us in possession of something ("I *have* spoken, struggled, conquered": that is to say, I am now in possession of my speech, struggle, victory). How greedy man appears here! He does not want to extricate himself even from the past, but wants to continue to *have* it!

• • •

No egoism at all exists that remains within itself and does not encroach—consequently, that "allowable," "morally indifferent" egoism of which you speak does not exist at all.

"One furthers one's ego always at the expense of others"; "Life always lives at the expense of other life"—he who does not grasp this has not taken even the first step toward honesty with himself.

As every drive lacks intelligence, the viewpoint of "utility" cannot exist for it. Every drive, in as much as it is active, sacrifices force and other drives: finally it is checked; otherwise it would destroy everything through its excessiveness. Therefore: the "unegoistic," self-searching, imprudent, is nothing special—it is common to all the drives—they do not consider the advantage of the whole ego (because they do not consider at all!), they act contrary to our advantage, against the ego: and often *for* the ego—innocent in both cases!

Correction of the concept "egoism."—When one has grasped to what extent the concept "individual" is an error because every single creature constitutes the entire process in its entire course (not merely as "inherited," but the process itself —), then the single creature acquires a tremendously great significance. Instinct speaks quite correctly here. Where this instinct weakens—where the individual seeks a value for himself only in the service of others, one can be certain that exhaustion and degeneration are present. An altruistic disposition, genuine and without tartuffery, is an instinct for creating at least a secondary value for oneself in the service of other egoisms. Usually, however, altruism is only apparent; a detour to the preservation of one's own feeling of vitality and value.

Misunderstanding of egoism—on the part of common natures who know nothing whatever of the pleasure of conquest and the insatiability of great love, nor of the overflowing feeling of strength that desires to overpower, to compel to itself, to lay to its heart—the drive of the artist in relation to his material. Often it is merely the penchant for activity that is looking for a field of action.

    In ordinary "egoism" it is precisely the "non-ego," the profoundly average creature, the species man, who desires to preserve himself: if this is perceived by rarer, subtler, and less average men, it enrages them. For they judge: "we are nobler! Our preservation is more important than that of those cattle!"

• • •

In view of the modern popularity of praise of the "disinterested," we should bring to consciousness, perhaps not without some danger, what it is that elicits the people's interest, and what are the things about which the common man is deeply and profoundly concerned—including the educated, even the scholars, and unless all appearances deceive, perhaps even the philosophers. Then the fact emerges that the vast majority of the things that interest and attract choosier and more refined tastes and every higher nature seem to the average man totally "uninteresting"; and when he nevertheless notices a devotion to such matters he calls it "*désintéressé*" and wonders how it is possible to act "without interest." There have been philosophers who have known how to lend to this popular wonder a seductive and mystical-transcendental expression[223] (—perhaps because they did not know the higher nature from experience?)—instead of positing the naked truth, which is surely not hard to come by, that the "disinterested" action is an *exceedingly* interesting and interested action, assuming—

    "And love?"—What? Even an action done from love is supposed to be "unegoistic"? But you dolts! "And the praise of sacrifices?"—But anyone who has really made sacrifices knows that he wanted and got something in return—perhaps something of himself in return for something of himself—that he gave up here in order to have more there, perhaps in order to *be* more or at least to feel that he was "more." But this is a realm of questions and answers in which a choosier spirit does not like to dwell: even now truth finds it necessary to stifle her yawns when she is expected to give answers. In the end she is a woman: she should not be violated.

Self-love and self-reverence [224]

Do not let your devil enter into your neighbor!—Let us for the time being agree that benevolence and beneficence are constituents of the good man; only let us add: "presupposing that he is first benevolently and beneficently inclined *towards himself!*" For *without this*—if he flees from himself, hates himself, does harm to himself—he is certainly not a good man. For in this case all he is doing is rescuing himself from himself *in others*: let these others look to it that they suffer no ill effects from him, however well disposed he may want to appear!—But it is precisely this: to flee from the ego, and to hate it, and to live in others and for others—that has hitherto, with as much thoughtlessness as self-confidence, been called "unegoistic" and consequently "good."

• • •

For what does one have to atone most? For one's modesty; for having failed to listen to one's most personal requirements; for having mistaken oneself; for having underestimated oneself; for having lost a good ear for one's instincts: this lack of reverence for oneself revenges itself through every kind of deprivation: health, friendship, well-being, pride, cheerfulness, freedom, firmness, courage. One never afterward forgives oneself for this lack of genuine egoism: one takes it for an objection, for a doubt about a real ego.

I wish men would begin by *respecting* themselves: everything else follows from that. To be sure, as soon as one does this one is finished for others: for this is what they forgive last: "What? A man who respects himself?"—This is something different from the blind drive to *love* oneself: nothing is more common, in the love of the sexes as well as of that duality which is called "I," than contempt for what one loves:—fatalism in love.

• • •

It is not actions that prove him—actions are always open to many interpretations, always unfathomable—nor is it "works." Among artists and scholars today one finds enough of those who betray by their works how they are impelled by a profound desire for what is noble; but just this need *for* what is noble is fundamentally different from the needs of the noble soul itself and actually the eloquent and dangerous mark of its lack. It is not the works, it is the *faith* that is decisive here, that determines the order of rank—to take up again an ancient religious formula in a new and more profound sense: some fundamental certainty that a noble soul has about itself, something that cannot be sought, nor found, nor perhaps lost.
The noble soul has reverence for itself. [225]

TWENTIETH CENTURY

*J*ohn Dewey (1859–1952), the greatest of twentieth century pragmatists and the first philosopher of this section, tackles the problem of self-love from a broad functionalist perspective that begins with an analysis of the self. He rejects the conventional conception of the self as fixed at adulthood, and as plunked down in a society which serves only to constrain its further growth. He finds the self, rather, in a "continual process of construction," and society, as the setting for, not an inhibitor of, self-realization.

Not only is the fixed-self doctrine metaphysically suspect, according to Dewey, but it generates two false conceptions of self-interest. It either treats the self as a pre-existent "end" to which the individual subordinates everything else as mere "means"—thus reducing all human action to a form of selfishness—or it allows for the possibility of "disinterested" action, but assumes that since the self is not the end of such action, it must play no role whatsoever.

Dewey finds these alternatives unacceptable. They both divide the self from its activities, reducing the latter to a mere means to the interests of the former. But we cannot distinguish in this way between the self and its activity—"The act *is* the self. . . . "—or between self-interest and activity: "the act is the man's interest. His interest is not something aside from it and beyond it. . . . " Our actions define our selves and our interests, and together these form an integrated whole. No action can be regarded as wholly disinterested in the sense of not involving the self at all, since all action is in some sense "the self defined." Yet, neither must all action be viewed as occurring for the sake of the self simply because it is self-involving; we must distinguish acting *for* a self from acting *as* a self.

Failure to recognize this difference has led to the growth of a pernicious moral doctrine, in which the self is "denied, snubbed, sacrificed, mortified." Identifying the self with frivolous and narrow concerns and dissociating it from anything "generous and ideal," this doctrine deems self the source of evil, and advocates the altruistic pursuit of others' good. But this is a "strange plight," remarks Dewey: why should I give someone else's self preference to my own?

Dewey discusses several other problems with the altruistic doctrine and ultimately rejects it in favor of a conception of action that incorporates both the self and others, making the traditional egoism-altruism distinction unnecessary and untenable.

Showing his Aristotelian influence, Dewey starts from the premise that man is a social being, and that the development of selfhood can only be understood in social context. As we have seen, he denies the possibility of defining the self independently of its activities, or, therefore, of its concrete, practical setting. The so-called "metaphysical self—that is, out of space and time relations...is simply a nonentity." Yet, it is an inescapable feature of the concrete human situation that it is social. Since it is in this setting that we define the self into existence, Dewey boldly claims that, in fact, "there is no self until you ask what the self is called to do in relation to other people."

On this account, what goes by the name of ordinary selfishness is simply failure to appreciate one's comprehensive situation. It is a narrowing of one's focus to exclude relevant factors from one's choices—really just a form of "inadequacy." Proper self-realization avoids this narrowness and occurs as a "social process" that neglects neither ego nor alter.

Like Dewey, our next author, Ayn Rand (1905–1982), approaches the question of self-interest from a metaphysical standpoint. What is it about the nature of human life, she asks, that gives rise to the need for a moral code? Her answer: human beings are creatures of "volitional consciousness." They have no automatic course of behavior, so they must employ reason to survive, using a code of values to guide their actions. This code is morality.

The standard of moral value, Rand argues, is that which is proper to the life of a rational being: a proper moral code will foster life, an improper one will destroy it. Since each individual is an end in himself and exists for his own sake, the purpose of morality for each individual is the attainment of his own happiness—happiness being the psychological reward of achieving one's values.

Rand advocates ethical egoism because she thinks altruistic moralities fail to take seriously the intrinsic worth of the individual, rendering man—in a phrase she borrows from Nietzsche—a "sacrificial animal." But does egoism not lead the individual to sacrifice others to his *own* private interests? Not when he has defined his interests rationally, Rand insists. Only an egoism that conceives of self-interest in terms of irrational desires will lead to the conflict and sacrifice of individual interests. Rational egoism recognizes that just as the individual's life does not belong to others, so others' lives do not belong to him. It is not only compatible with, but *requires* respect for others' rights.

Rand finds additional problems with altruism. She suggests that it defines value in terms of a negation: "the good is the 'non-good' for me." It is anti-life in that it tells one how to sacrifice one's life, not how to live it. Further, as Dewey had observed, altruism is inconsistent: why should the promotion of others' happiness be morally good, but not that of oneself? Finally, altruism is demeaning, treating other people as helpless and dependent.

Altruists will often ask about the individual's responsibility to help others in times of emergency, and for Rand the evils of altruism are summed up in this question. Among other things, it shows that altruistic morality is focused on sacrificing, not living life. Further, it marginalizes morality by conceiving it in terms of situations one is not likely to encounter in daily living. Above all, this question implies a false conception of love. If a person goes to great lengths during an emergency to save a person he loves, Rand finds this, far from a sacrifice, a display of his commitment to his own values and interests. As for our obligation to strangers, Rand counsels respect and good will in the name of the potential value they represent.

In our final reading from Rand, she lays out the four considerations involved in a rational individual's conception of his interests, which she refers to as: reality, context, responsibility, and effort. It is only the person who pays proper attention to these concerns that will be able to define his values and interests rationally, and so be capable of the "non-contradictory joy" that is happiness.

The last author we consider, David Gauthier (b. 1932), attempts to reconcile self-interest and morality by using a contractarian argument. In doing so, he falls into the Hobbesian tradition of viewing morality as a mutually advantageous covenant for rational egoists. In his essay, Gauthier begins by distinguishing enlightened self-interest—or "prudence"—from morality, and then proposes to demonstrate that morality contributes to self-interest in a way that prudence alone cannot. As he expresses his thesis: "*Morality is a system of principles such that it is advantageous for everyone if everyone accepts and acts on it, yet acting on the system of principles requires that some persons perform disadvantageous acts.*"

Gauthier takes pains to distinguish this thesis from that of long-term prudence, which advocates morality on the grounds that the disadvantages it brings are short-term and unreal in that they are well-compensated for by the long-term advantages of the moral life. One cannot, in Gauthier's view, provide prudential reasons to be moral because morality imposes real and exacting costs, and from the standpoint of self-interest, these are never worth incurring.

To demonstrate his thesis, Gauthier uses a game-theoretic approach, which has us envision two opposed and hostile nations, A and B, who are attempting to negotiate a disarmament pact in order to avoid a full-scale war—a disaster for both. The pact is advantageous, however, only if both uphold it; if A complies and B does not, B will profit at A's expense, and vice versa. Of course, if B violates the pact without detection while A continues to adhere, it will attain the greatest advantage—all the benefits of the treaty, with none of the costs. The upshot it that, "public adherence to the pact is prudent and mutually advantageous, whereas private adherence is not prudent although mutually advantageous."

Gauthier applies these conclusions to morality, which he suggests has a nature similar to that of a pact. The outcome is the same: morality imposes real costs that are not offset by the moral behavior of others. Collectively, we all benefit from mutual adherence to moral rules, but individually, we each fare better by acting prudently, not morally. Prudence, then, cannot give us reason to be moral—a conclusion which Gauthier does not find surprising: why should one expect non-moral reasons for practicing morality? The moral man, like all men, is prudent, but he has the additional *moral* virtue of trustworthiness.

Gauthier applies these conclusions to morality, which he suggests has a nature similar to that of a pact. The outcome is the same: morality imposes real costs that are not offset by the moral behavior of others. Collectively, we all benefit from the mutual adherence to moral rules, but individually, we each fare better by acting prudently, not morally. Prudence, then, cannot give us reason to be moral—a conclusion which Gauthier does not find surprising: why should one expect non-moral reasons for practicing morality? The ethical individual, like his amoral counterpart, is prudent, but he has the additional "moral" virtue of trustworthiness.

Gauthier has been a pioneer in the development of this century's prevailing account of self-interest. This account—which, in fact, is the offspring of several thinkers and owes much to medieval and early modern sources as well—has told us that self-interest is a superficial, materialistic, and wholly non-moral concern; that despite its connection to rational agency, its content is determined by non-rational desires, including desires for the most immoral and harmful of things; that its pursuit places human beings in fundamental conflict with one another, and that the only resolution to such a conflict is some measure of sacrafice; and that a minimum of self-regard is a necessary evil, but that we should, as moral beings, devote ourselves to serving others.

Yet, there have been many thinkers—Dewey and Rand among them—who have challenged these claims and the conceptions of self and society upon which they depend. There are philosophers who regard true self-interest, far from a shallow and nonmoral concern, as constituted by wisdom and virtue; who see the content of self-interest as being determined not by happenstance desires, but by reason; who argue that there exists a harmony of human interests, and that conflict arises only to the extent we hold false conceptions of our own good; and who regard self-interest not as a necessary evil, but as the moral purpose of human life.

Such challenges to the traditional altruistic paradigm form part of an enterprise the philosopher John Cottingham has called "autodicy"—the justification of self to self. Autodicy redresses the self-other assymetry that has, with some exceptions, dominated Western moral thought since the advent of Christianity. It spurns talk of any divine or social altar at which we may justly immolate the individual, taking ehthically seriously the idea that each human being forms an end-in-himself. Contrary to the opponents of moral individualism, such a paradigm need neither curtail benevolence nor bolster wrongdoing. Autodicy requires merely that we eschew any ethic of self-abnegation, and that, reclaiming the wisdom of the ancients, we recognize once more that for the pursuit of our own happiness, we owe no moral apology.

John Dewey was born in Burlington, Vermont, and earned his doctorate at Johns Hopkins University. His ethical theory emphasized an ideal of self-realization, and Dewey used this concept to reveal inadequacies in traditional discussions of self-interest and altruism—most importantly, their failure to see the self not as a fixed end, but as perpetually evolving within a social dynamic.

JOHN DEWEY
(1859–1952)

Egoism and altruism—a false dichotomy [226]

I will take up today the topic of egoism and altruism. . . . The question which has recently taken form under the terminology of egoism and altruism, mainly under the influence—that is, so far as the terminology is concerned—of French positivism[227] and largely through George Eliot in English under the title of the relation of self-love and benevolence,[228] is the question whether all action is for the self, or whether such a thing as strictly disinterested action is possible. Or put in its extreme form as some writers would have it, whether any action is moral at all that occurs for the self, the assumption being often made, perhaps more often in popular discussion than in scientific, that morality and altruism are identical. Some moralists have laid down the principle that benevolence is the supreme ethical principle. The assertion has been made that the theory of self-realization denies the strictly altruistic or benevolent action—at least it always makes it a subordinate form of action for the self; the real end is to realize the self; it simply happens under certain circumstances that the best way to realize the self is through attention to the needs and interests of others. Hence the relevancy of this topic at this time.

At the last discussion it was shown that there is an ambiguity in the concept of self-realization, an ambiguity which is solved by a more adequate definition of the self. That same point of view can be applied to the analysis of the present question. Certainly from the standpoint of one conception of the self there is no alternative excepting either to say that all action is for the self and that altruism is simply a form of disguised selfishness in the sense that the self would not attain its own full development unless it did this particular kind of act that we call unselfish, or else to say that self-realization holds up to a certain point and then beyond that it must be supplemented by another theory of action for the welfare of others.

When Kant attempts to give a more concrete statement of morality than is found in his metaphysical writings, he gives that dualism. A man is to act for his own perfection and the happiness of others. He must not act for his own happiness. He must not act for the moral perfection of others, because he cannot. Every individual must moralize himself. It is a question of his own internal motive which nobody else can determine for him. If anybody else attempts it, it is simply an impertinence or interference. So we are in this strange plight that morally a man is bound to seek for something in others which in himself would be immoral. To get happiness for himself is immoral, but to get it for others is benevolent. Why happiness should be good for somebody else and bad for one's self is not clearly explained, and that is the basis of any theory which attempts to have two criteria of action, which says that action is a combination of rational self-love and rational benevolence, so that the truly virtuous man combines both a reasonable interest in his own well-being and a reasonable interest in the well-being of others. The difficulty is to find a unifying principle, to find a principle which tells where the limits of one cease and where the other begins.

Now . . . the discussion is futile excepting as one has some conception in advance of what is meant by the self. Is the self a presupposed, given existence, or does the self exist only as it operates? Is the self a continual synthetic construction? If the latter, the question between egoism and altruism is solved by getting a different purchase on the whole thing. We would have to say that a man always does act as himself, but that that is a different thing from saying that he acts for himself as an end. The objectionable character of the conception that a man always acts for himself has the same origin as the objectionable character of the doctrine of self-realization. It presupposes that a man is already there, and whatever he does, he does as the means to himself as an outside end. On that basis the relation between the act and the self is external. The self is the real end or aim whatever the pretended one may be, and the act that is done is a mere means to the welfare or the building up of that presupposed self. But if the self is identical organically with the act, then we can say that the act is [not] simply means to the welfare of the self. The act is the self. The man must do the act because it is himself and do it as himself—that is, throw himself thoroughly into it, put his whole being into the act. That is quite a different thing from saying that he acts for himself.

Or to state it [the objection] in terms of interest, one school says that a man's conduct is always motivated by his interest; that his interest will always control his action, and hence benevolence is really an enlightened selfishness. Once more, the objection to that is the false psychology that is back of it, making a difference between the man's interest and his act. The interest is set up as something ultimate and fixed, and the act is regarded as a mere subordinate means for subserving this presupposed interest. It is simply a tool. The same thing would apply to the utilitarian theories in their wider aspects as regards happiness, where the happiness is regarded as a fixed thing which is already known and the act is to be merely tributary to keeping up that totality of happiness.

On the basis of the other psychology of the self, the act is the man's interest. His interest is not something aside from it and beyond it so that the act comes in as an intervening state toward his interest, but you know his interest by seeing him act. He does what he does as his interest, not for his interest.

Now the defect on the side of the altruistic theory is precisely the same psychologically. They have exactly the same conception of the self that the egoistic or utilitarian schools have, but they see the practical moral objection to making that ultimate, and so they try to correct the deficiency by putting in another self. You must not act simply—or sometimes they put it as strongly as to say not at all—for your own interest, but always for the interest of some other self. Now the difficulty in that point of view has already been suggested. Why should anybody else's self be better than your own? If the self is a thing of a presupposed rigid kind, why should another self-end have any more claim than my self-end? Why should the self in anybody else have superiority over the self as found in you? Consistently you must either say that the self is a nonmoral principle or else that it is a moral principle. If it is a nonmoral end, then it is so wherever it is found. It is just as bad to further it in somebody else as in yourself. If it is everywhere a moral end, then the ego and the alter both stand exactly on the same plane, the same level. Whatever a man takes to be his interest, he does. A sane man could not possibly do anything excepting as his interest, but that does not mean that he sets up his own welfare, his own good as a thing to be attained at all hazards, and then makes everything else tributary means for getting this thing for himself. It means on the contrary that the moral problems arise because a man does not know what his interest is; and the whole moral process of deliberation and of effort and desire is a process of the discovery of interest, of finding out what one's value, what one's worth or meaning is.

We get two radically different conceptions of interest from the standpoint of the two psychological definitions of the self. It was said the other day that while the self is in a continual process of construction, it cannot be adequately made up excepting in terms of the content which it supplies for the situation in which the agent has to act. That would mean in terms of the egoism and altruism question, that the self cannot define itself excepting in terms of a larger whole, a larger situation in which others, as well as one's self as an agent of action, are involved. All action would be altruistic in the sense not that others are its end or aim but in the sense that in finding out what the self is, of valuing it in terms of the individual act that needs to be performed, one must have recourse to others who are involved as necessary conditions.

What is the criterion for an act of charity which is presented as a claim? Upon what basis does one decide whether he shall or shall not do something for a needy person who offers himself? There would be, on the basis of what has been said, two false and two right ways of getting at that. One of the false ways would be to take the past interest, the established interests and habits of the self as final and simply say: What would myself from the first up to the present time get out of it for me (meaning by me the acquired, presupposed self)? The other false way would be to say: Of course my moral duty is to do always what I can for somebody else and here is an opportunity for me to be benevolent, to be self-sacrificing, and if it is really such an opportunity it ought to be embraced. The fallacy is that although seemingly altruism and egoism are so opposed to each other, they both have the same fundamental psychology: that of supposing it possible to define the self either in the ego or the alter without reference to a comprehensive situation.

If we take the two right ways of getting at it, the question is either what am I myself with reference to this particular case, or what is the other man with reference to the particular case. What am I as identified in the act, or what is the other man, similarly identified? The real criterion is found in the ego or alter with reference to the whole situation. It is only as you get beyond the fixed self, the given self in either case, that you can get any criterion at all for dealing with the problem. Otherwise you must settle it on capricious, or arbitrary or sentimental grounds; arbitrarily, if you suppose there is some outside canon which fixes the question whether you are to give or not, or sentimental if you allow the feelings of the moment to determine what is to be done. The problem then between egoism and altruism is solved by recognizing that there is no such problem, the supposed distinction simply grows out of a false psychology of the self. All action is egoistic in the sense that the act is the self defined; it is all altruistic in the sense that one must, in defining one's self as end, take account of others, must define one's self in terms of relationship to others. . . .

The other aspect of the discussion is what we may term reflective egoism and reflective altruism. Both of these are equally virtuous or both are equally vicious. That reflective egoism is vicious we need not argue. That is what we mean by selfishness in the bad sense, when a man puts up his own welfare as a fixed given thing and then reduces other things to means for realizing it. The whole difficulty there is simply that one does not recognize the impossibility of what he is trying to do. There is no such self fixed there beforehand as an end. What the self is, what the end is, has to be found out experimentally through deliberation and through desire and effort. The self is always being discovered and valued, brought to consciousness. For that reason refl-ective selfishness in this sense is a comparatively rare thing. There are few people who have consciously and deliberatively set up their own welfare as a supreme end.

The form in which selfishness ordinarily presents itself is simply that of undue absorption in one's immediate interests. It is simply failure to mediate sufficiently the direction of attention and of interest. It is comparatively rarely that a man says: " I am going to have my own good at all hazards and I do not care how much I sacrifice other people." It comes in a much more subtle way than that. One is engaged on something which has a positive value; it is a good so far as it goes. Then the person becomes so absorbed in that immediate occupation which has defined himself in the past that he is not observant of new stimuli which would compel a broadening of the scope of activity, and which would involve that he subordinate this particular line of interest to something more comprehensive. The judgment that a man is selfish means that he ought to be defining himself on the basis of a wider situation, that he ought to be taking into account factors which as a matter of fact he is neglecting. It means inadequacy almost always. It generally means lack of adequate self-consciousness. It means a narrow vision of the situation which should be used to tell the self what it is.

On the other side, reflective altruism is vicious too. That is, to consciously make the welfare of others (whether their happiness or their moral good) the end, the supreme criterion, will always result in conduct which would be inadequate and defec-tive as much as if one consciously or thoughtlessly made one's self the supreme end. That point, probably, that altruism is defined in that sense as being as vicious as ego-ism, may not be quite so obvious. I will therefore suggest three or four reasons for considering it so. As an illustration: For what motive should business be carried on? How shall one define the end and the ultimate criterion? Is the only moral justifica-tion for a pursuit of a certain business or profession conscious desire as the supreme thing to do good to other people? If one says yes, aside from the fact that that would condemn about everybody that is doing business and following professions, there are two theoretical reasons why such a view is to be rejected. On one side you say the business is a simple means where the welfare of others, either as happiness or moral perfection, is the real end. That externality between the means and the end is a fatal objection to that point of view. That means that there is no adequate moral criterion within the business itself. It means that it does not carry its own moral standard and justification on with it. At every point you must get away from your business and think about the welfare of other people; and in that outside consideration, which is more or less remote and external to the thing you are doing, you must seek for justifi-cation and for guidance. That of course means that you cannot give your full interest to what you are doing. Nobody can do thoroughly well what does not command his full interest and attention. If a man cannot find his motive for action in what he is doing, he cannot do it with his whole being, and therefore he will do it imperfectly.

There is the contradiction. Any moral means, to be moral, must be one which is identified with end; it must be the end. In its immediate aspect it must be the end as it presents itself at this particular point in time and under these particular circumstances. If
you say that the justification for business is the contribution to the welfare of others,
then organic identification of means as end is lacking. You must get at it from the
other standpoint: a man must be made to believe that this particular line of action is
called for by the whole situation, and then believe that because it is called for it does
involve the welfare of others. There is an altruistic paradox as well as a hedonistic one.
The hedonistic paradox is that a man cannot secure happiness as the end unless he
forgets it. He must forget it and devote himself to the thing in hand in order to be
really happy. So here on the altruistic side, before he can really do good to others, he
must stop thinking about the welfare of others; he must see what the situation really
calls for and go ahead with that, and the reason is the same in both cases. Whenever
one makes his own good or the good of others the end, it becomes an extraneous end.

On the other side, what criterion have you by which to tell what the good of others really is? You are going to work for the good of others, making business a simple
means to the welfare of others. What is the content for the well-being of others or the
good of others? How are you going to tell what that really is? Because your means is
external to your end; you cannot give your whole attention to the means, and equally
when the end is external to the means. That means that it is inadequate, it is empty, it
has no definite content. Persons who persist on that theory are always thrown back on
a sort of emotional utilitarianism in order to define what the welfare of others is.
There is no rational way of telling what the welfare of others is. The man who looks
at the situation and goes on to see what he can do has a standard, a basis on which to
put content into welfare; it enables him to realize what the good of others is in the
abstract. But if you turn in the other direction and set up the good of others in the
abstract and reduce professional and industrial activity as mere means for that end,
you are at the mercy of any sentimentalist or any dogmatist to tell you what the real
good of people is.

The insufficiency of altruism in the sense of making the welfare of others the
supreme end of action may be further illustrated in two ways. Because of the lack of
any criterion as to what the good or welfare of others is on that basis, the natural,
practical tendency of altruism as a principle would be to induce selfishness in others.
It puts the other person, the alter, in the attitude of having something done for him.
It puts everybody in a passive or recipient attitude as regards others. It is true that
there is an active side (that is, everybody is to promote the welfare of everybody else),
but on the other side he is to be an object whose welfare is to be cultivated. I say the
practical tendency would be to cultivate in the individual a sense of his own happiness
or good as something which he has a right to demand to receive from others. The

thing not infrequently occurs in some families where the members of the family make self-sacrifice the supreme end. The result is that those upon whom the self-sacrifice is lavished tend to take it as a matter of course and to expect such treatment as their normal due. It has a tendency to exaggerate the sense of the ego and what is due to it: its rights, privileges, possessions. Moreover, if this principle were universalized— which it never has been (it has always been a class principle—that is, a principle of superiors in some form to inferiors, the conferring of benefits by one class upon another)—but if it were universalized, morality would be reduced to a competitive contest regarding self-sacrifice.

It comes out very neatly in Mr. Spencer's final ideal state where he states that the highest form of altruism consists in the waiving of the right to make other people happy.[229] The chief form which self-sacrifice can take is allowing somebody else to make you happy instead of your trying to make them happy. The greatest self-denial a man can exercise under those circumstances would be the denial of the pleasure he found in making other people happy and in waiving his rights and allowing others to do these things for him. The theoretical difficulty that underlies that absurd practical outcome is that there is no basis for the unification or organization of a system of complete altruism any more than of a system of complete egoism. You have so many distinct selves, you have no system, no organization which as a unity defines and measures each one of these egos. The result is that the moral claims of one individual would be apt to cut across, to a certain extent, those of others, and you must have some sort of compromise. That is where Spencer comes out with a sort of working compromise of the claims of these individuals in relation to each other.

With relation to the agent himself there are certain practical tendencies also likely to result which would not be at all desirable. It is very difficult practically to keep the desire to do good to others entirely without any flavor of the desire to regulate their conduct. The thoroughgoing and systematic altruist is quite likely, under the guise of doing good to others, unconsciously perhaps to set up a good and insist that others must have it whether or no, all the more so because the agent is really sacrificing himself in giving the other person that good. Virtually he says: What greater criterion of my sincerity can you demand than the fact that I am willing to sacrifice so much to give it to you? The fact that one is sacrificing for another is taken as evidence that that is the good. Of course puritanic morality is a very common thing on this side. What was a perfectly sincere desire for absolute freedom of thought became the standard to regulate the lives of others just at the point where one demands freedom for himself; that is, in the definition of what the good really is and in the selection of means for realizing it.

Moreover, another reaction upon the self which is not at all desirable is to build up what some author has called the "egoism of renunciation." It is quite possible to make this pleasure the end, in which case you have a refined form of hedonism. The feeling that one is sacrificing something, and the satisfaction that one gets out of that, is quite capable of becoming a person's working measure for the rightness of what he is doing, and the securing of that doing becomes the end, the ideal. One measures one's goodness by the amount that he does to promote the happiness of others, and from that point of view his goodness can be maintained only on the condition that he do as much of this as possible, and that works into the previous point of view. The conferring of pleasure upon others, since it is the measure of one's own moral attainments, lends itself really to subordinating other people as instruments to securing the proper plane of goodness on the part of one's self.

The previous criticisms may be summed up by saying that in this reflective altruism, or the promotion of the welfare of others as the supreme end and test of morality, there is no organizing principle and there is therefore no objective principle. We come back, in order to get a unified principle, to the conception of the self as the active synthesis of all the conditions, all the elements; and to the further fact that under different circumstances one arrives at and discovers that active synthetic self by throwing the emphasis upon either of the two poles involved in it. One can discover the act which will define and identify the self by going at it from either of two sides: either from the side of the capacities of the agent, or from the side of the needs of the situation. We get back to the conception of function as the working unity of organism and environment to the possibility and desirability under different circumstances of defining function in terms of organism at one time, or in terms of environment at another; but whichever we consciously emphasize, we select because we presuppose the relation to the other.

There is no way of telling what the capacities of the agent are, excepting as one takes for granted the environmental conditions with reference to which those powers are exercised. There is no telling, on the other hand, what the situation and its needs are, excepting as one takes for granted an agent free, with certain resources at his command.

Take the illustration given the other day of the relief of suffering. The self there, the right self, the psychological self has to be discovered in the act which will unify all the factors. One may arrive at a solution by saying: Here am I and I have certain powers and limitations. What I do here I cannot do somewhere else, it is a question of utilizing my power to the utmost—and decide the question by throwing the emphasis on that side. But it is obvious that he cannot tell what his powers are or how much he can do with them until he virtually assumes certain conditions with which they are to operate. He will take into account the claims of this particular person as compared with other claims which will be made upon him, and the fact that the time and energy that are spent here could be spent somewhere else. Or he can throw the burden of the problem on the other side and say: What are the real needs here? Just what are the claims of this man as compared with the claims of the other? If he puts it from that side, it is because he is assuming that he is there as the agent. The only reason that he asks about the needs of the situation is to get light upon the direction of himself as an agent, just as on the other side the only reason that he asks about himself as an agent, inquires into his own powers, is in order that he may determine what the active need of the whole situation is.

That might be summed up briefly by stating that the real self psychologically is always a synthesis of two distinct types and conditions, one of which we may call the agent or instrumental self, and the other of which we may call the conditions of the situation, or, briefly, the environment. Thus we arrive once more at the point I have spoken of two or three times, that the moment you give up the conception of the self as a fixed entity, the moment you give up the conception of the self as an ontological being already in existence and having certain powers already made with which it can produce certain acts or results, you get to the conception of the self as an active synthesis — that is, a unification — realized only in action of a variety of factors; and if you call part of those factors internal then you must call the others external, if you call part of them individual you must call the others social. An act as an act always transcends mere individuality — that is, mere absolute individuality. An act occurs in space and time and embodies these space and time factors which lie beyond the individual.

We have at least then, so to speak, as a presumption, this point of view for the consideration of the social ethics. The self, psychologically examined, turns out to be an active synthesis; therefore the self is a social self in the sense that it involves intrinsically within itself a content which lies beyond its own formed habits and its own achievements, and with reference to which all its attainments and accomplishments must be considered as purely instrumental, as so much capital with which to do business, as so much resources for laying hold of, appropriating, and working up into personal form the conditions and materials supplied by the environment. Thus, while the psychological examination throws itself into an investigation of the form, of the machinery of the self, this very examination finally compels us to go over to the social side. It is not simply that after we have completed the psychological investigation we can take up the social investigation, but that the process, the machinery revealed at the psychological examination, is seen to depend upon a content which is social; that that content is what constitutes the peculiar character which the form has and that the varieties in the content are what differentiate one form or mode from another.

Self-interest and morality [230]

The notion that real goodness, or virtue, consists essentially in abnegation of the self, in denying and, so far as may be, eliminating everything that is of the nature of the self, is one of the oldest and most frequently recurring notions of moral endeavor and religion, as well as of moral theory. . . . The notion arises from the tendency to identify the self with one of its own factors. It is one and the same self which conceives and is interested in some generous and ideal good that is also tempted by some near, narrow, and exclusive good. The force of the latter resides in the *habitual* self, in purposes which have got themselves inwrought into the texture of ordinary character. Hence there is a disposition to overlook the complexity of selfhood, and to identify it with those factors in the self which resist ideal aspiration, and which are recalcitrant to the thought of duty; to identify the self with impulses that are inclined to what is frivolous, sensuous, and sensual, pleasure-seeking. All vice being, then, egoism, selfishness, self-seeking, the remedy is to check it at its roots; to keep the self down in its proper place, denying it, chastening it, mortifying it, refusing to listen to its promptings. Ignoring the variety and subtlety of the factors that make up the self, all the different elements of right and of wrong are gathered together and set over against each other. All the good is placed once for all in some outside source, some higher law or ideal; and the source of all evil is placed within the corrupted and vile self. When one has become conscious of the serious nature of the moral struggle; has found that vice is easy, and to err "natural," needing only to give way to some habitual impulse or desire; that virtue is arduous, requiring resistance and strenuous effort, one is apt to overlook the habitual tendencies which are the ministers of the higher goods. One forgets that unless ideal ends were also rooted in some natural tendencies of the self, they could neither occur to the self nor appeal to the self. Hence everything is swept into the idea that the self is inherently so evil that it must be denied, snubbed, sacrificed, mortified.

Ayn Rand was born in St. Petersburg, Russia and emigrated to the United States in 1926. She wrote several philosophical novels, as well as a host of essays articulating her philosophy of "Objectivism." Her position on self-interest is unequivocal: the pursuit of rational self-interest forms, for each individual, the moral purpose of his life.

AYN RAND
(1905–1982)

Personal happiness as the moral purpose of human beings [231]

Yes, this is an age of moral crisis. Yes, you are bearing punishment for your evil. But it is not man who is now on trial and it is not human nature that will take the blame. It is your moral code that's through, this time. Your moral code has reached its climax, the blind alley at the end of its course. And if you wish to go on living, what you now need is not to *return* to morality—you who have never known any—but to *discover* it.

You have heard no concepts of morality but the mystical or the social. You have been taught that morality is a code of behavior imposed on you by whim, the whim of a supernatural power or the whim of society, to serve God's purpose or your neighbor's welfare, to please an authority beyond the grave or else next door—but not to serve *your* life or pleasure. Your pleasure, you have been taught, is to be found in immorality, your interests would best be served by evil, and any moral code must be designed not *for* you, but *against* you, not to further your life, but to drain it.

For centuries, the battle of morality was fought between those who claimed that your life belongs to God and those who claimed that it belongs to your neighbors—between those who preached that the good is self-sacrifice for the sake of ghosts in

heaven and those who preached that the good is self-sacrifice for the sake of incompe-
tents on earth. And no one came to say that your life belongs to you and that the
good is to live it.

Both sides agreed that morality demands the surrender of your self-interest and of
your mind, that the moral and the practical are opposites, that morality is not the
province of reason, but the province of faith and force. Both sides agreed that no
rational morality is possible, that there is no right or wrong in reason—that in reason
there's no reason to be moral.

Whatever else they fought about, it was against man's mind that all your moralists
have stood united. It was man's mind that all their schemes and systems were intended
to despoil and destroy. Now choose to perish or to learn that the anti-mind is the
anti-life.

Man's mind is his basic tool of survival. Life is given to him, survival is not. His
body is given to him, its sustenance is not. His mind is given to him, its content is not.
To remain alive, he must act, and before he can act he must know the nature and purpose of his action. He cannot obtain his food without a knowledge of food and of
the way to obtain it. He cannot dig a ditch—or build a cyclotron—without a knowledge of his aim and of the means to achieve it. To remain alive, he must think.

But to think is an act of choice. The key to what you so recklessly call "human
nature," the open secret you live with, yet dread to name, is the fact that *man is a being of
volitional consciousness*. Reason does not work automatically; thinking is not a mechanical
process; the connections of logic are not made by instinct. The function of your
stomach, lungs, or heart is automatic; the function of your mind is not. In any hour
and issue of your life, you are free to think or to evade that effort. But you are not free
to escape from your nature, from the fact that *reason* is your means of survival—so
that for *you*, who are a human being, the question "to be or not to be" is the question
"to think or not to think."

A being of volitional consciousness has no automatic course of behavior. He
needs a code of values to guide his actions. "Value" is that which one acts to gain and
keep, "virtue" is the action by which one gains and keeps it. "Value" presupposes an
answer to the question: of value to whom and for what? "Value" presupposes a standard, a purpose, and the necessity of action in the face of an alternative. Where there
are no alternatives, no values are possible.

There is only one fundamental alternative in the universe: existence or non-existence—and it pertains to a single class of entities: to living organisms. The existence
of inanimate matter is unconditional, the existence of life is not: it depends on a
specific course of action. Matter is indestructible, it changes its forms, but it cannot
cease to exist. It is only a living organism that faces a constant alternative: the issue of
life or death. Life is a process of self-sustaining and self-generating action. If an
organism fails in that action, it dies; its chemical elements remain, but its life goes out

of existence. It is only the concept of "Life" that makes the concept of "Value" possible. It is only to a living entity that things can be good or evil. . . .

Man has no automatic code of survival. His particular distinction from all other living species is the necessity to act in the face of alternatives by means of *volitional choice*. He has no automatic knowledge of what is good for him or evil, what values his life depends on, what course of action it requires. Are you prattling about an instinct of self-preservation? An *instinct* of self-preservation is precisely what man does not possess. An "instinct" is an unerring and automatic form of knowledge. A desire is not an instinct. A desire to live does not give you the knowledge required for living. And even man's desire to live is not automatic: your secret evil today is that *that* is the desire you do not hold. Your fear of death is not a love for life and will not give you the knowledge needed to keep it. Man must obtain his knowledge and choose his actions by a process of thinking, which nature will not force him to perform. Man has the power to act as his own destroyer—and that is the way he has acted through most of his history.

A living entity that regarded its means of survival as evil, would not survive. A plant that struggled to mangle its roots, a bird that fought to break its wings would not remain for long in the existence they affronted. But the history of man has been a struggle to deny and to destroy his mind.

Man has been called a rational being, but rationality is a matter of choice—and the alternative his nature offers him is: rational being or suicidal animal. Man has to be man—by choice; he has to hold his life as a value—by choice; he has to learn to sustain it—by choice; he has to discover the values it requires and practice his virtues—by choice.

A code of values accepted by choice is a code of morality.

Whoever you are, you who are hearing me now, I am speaking to whatever living remnant is left uncorrupted within you, to the remnant of the human, to your *mind*, and I say: There *is* a morality of reason, a morality proper to man, and *Man's Life* is its standard of value.

All that which is proper to the life of a rational being is the good; all that which destroys it is the evil.

Man's life, as required by his nature, is not the life of a mindless brute, of a looting thug or a mooching mystic, but the life of a thinking being—not life by means of force or fraud, but life by means of achievement—not survival at any price, since there's only one price that pays for man's survival: reason.

Man's life is the *standard* of morality, but your own life is its *purpose*. If existence on earth is your goal, you must choose your actions and values by the standard of that which is proper to man—for the purpose of preserving, fulfilling and enjoying the irreplaceable value which is your life.

Since life requires a specific course of action, any other course will destroy it. A being who does not hold his own life as the motive and goal of his actions, is acting on the motive and standard of *death*. Such a being is a metaphysical monstrosity, struggling to oppose, negate, and contradict the fact of his own existence, running blindly amuck on a trail of destruction, capable of nothing but pain.

Happiness is the successful state of life, pain is an agent of death. Happiness is that state of consciousness which proceeds from the achievement of one's values. A morality that dares to tell you to find happiness in the renunciation of your happiness—to value the failure of your values—is an insolent negation of morality. A doctrine that gives you, as an ideal, the role of a sacrificial animal seeking slaughter on the altars of others, is giving you *death* as your standard. By the grace of reality and the nature of life, man—every man—is an end in himself; he exists for his own sake, and the achievement of his own happiness is his highest moral purpose.

But neither life nor happiness can be achieved by the pursuit of irrational whims. Just as man is free to attempt to survive in any random manner, but will perish unless he lives as his nature requires, so he is free to seek his happiness in any mindless fraud, but the torture of frustration is all he will find, unless he seeks the happiness proper to man. The purpose of morality is to teach you, not to suffer and die, but to enjoy yourself and love. . . .

Sweep aside those hatred-eaten mystics, who pose as friends of humanity and preach that the highest virtue man can practice is to hold his own life as of no value. Do they tell you that the purpose of morality is to curb man's instinct of self-preservation? It is for the purpose of self-preservation that man needs a code of morality. The only man who desires to be moral is the man who desires to live. . . .

This much is true: the most *selfish* of all things is the independent mind that recognizes no authority higher than its own and no value higher than its judgment of truth. You are asked to sacrifice your intellectual integrity, your logic, your reason, your standard of truth—in favor of becoming a prostitute whose standard is the greatest good for the greatest number.

If you search your code for guidance, for an answer to the question: "What is the good?"—the only answer you will find is "*The good of others.*" The good is whatever others wish, whatever you feel they feel they wish, or whatever you feel they ought to feel. "The good of others" is a magic formula that transforms anything into gold, a formula to be recited as a guarantee of moral glory and as a fumigator for any action, even the slaughter of a continent. Your standard of virtue is not an object, not an act, nor a principle, but an intention. You need no proof, no reasons, no success, you need not achieve in *fact* the good of others—all you need to know is that your motive was the good of others, *not* your own. Your only definition of the good is a negation: the good is the "non-good for me."

Your code—which boasts that it upholds eternal, absolute, objective moral values and scorns the conditional, the relative and the subjective—your code hands out, as its version of the absolute, the following rule of moral conduct: If *you* wish it, it's evil;

if others wish it, it's good; if the motive of your action is *your* welfare, don't do it; if the motive is the welfare of others, then anything goes.

As this double-jointed, double-standard morality splits you in half, so it splits mankind into two enemy camps: one is *you*, the other is all the rest of humanity. *You* are the only outcast who has no right to wish or live. *You* are the only servant, the rest are the masters, *you* are the only giver, the rest are the takers, *you* are the eternal debtor, the rest are the creditors never to be paid off. You must not question their right to your sacrifice, or the nature of their wishes and their needs: their right is conferred upon them by a negative, by the fact that they are "non-you."

For those of you who might ask questions, your code provides a consolation prize and booby-trap: it is for your own happiness, it says, that you must serve the happiness of others, the only way to achieve your joy is to give it up to others, the only way to achieve your prosperity is to surrender your wealth to others, the only way to protect your life is to protect all men except yourself—and if you find no joy in this procedure, it is your own fault and the proof of your evil; if you were good, you would find your happiness in providing a banquet for others, and your dignity in existing on such crumbs as *they* might care to toss you.

You who have no standard of self-esteem, accept the guilt and dare not ask the questions. But you know the unadmitted answer, refusing to acknowledge what you see, what hidden premise moves your world. You know it, not in honest statement, but as a dark uneasiness within you while you flounder between guiltily cheating and grudgingly practicing a principle too vicious to name.

I, who do not accept the unearned, neither in values nor in *guilt*, am here to ask the questions you evaded. Why is it moral to serve the happiness of others, but not your own? If enjoyment is a value, why is it moral when experienced by others, but immoral when experienced by you? If the sensation of eating a cake is a value, why is it an immoral indulgence in your stomach, but a moral goal for you to achieve in the stomach of others? Why is it immoral for you to desire, but moral for others to do so? Why is it immoral to produce a value and keep it, but moral to give it away? And if it is not moral for you to keep a value, why is it moral for others to accept it? If you are selfless and virtuous when you give it, are they not selfish and vicious when they take it? Does virtue consist of serving vice? Is the moral purpose of those who are good, self-immolation for the sake of those who are evil?. . .

Under a morality of sacrifice, the first value you sacrifice is morality; the next is self-esteem. When need is the standard, every man is both victim and parasite. As a victim, he must labor to fill the needs of others, leaving himself in the position of a parasite whose needs must be filled by others. He cannot approach his fellow men except in one of two disgraceful roles: he is both a beggar and a sucker.

You fear the man who has a dollar less than you, that dollar is rightfully his, he makes you feel like a moral defrauder. You hate the man who has a dollar more than you, that dollar is rightfully yours, he makes you feel that you are morally defrauded. The man below is a source of your guilt, the man above is a source of your frustration. You do not know what to surrender or demand, when to give and when to grab, what pleasure in life is rightfully yours and what debt is still unpaid to others—you struggle to evade, as "theory" the knowledge that by the moral standard you've accepted you are guilty every moment of your life, there is no mouthful of food you swallow that is not *needed* by someone somewhere on earth—and you give up the problem in blind resentment, you conclude that moral perfection is not to be achieved *or desired*, that you will muddle through by snatching as snatch can and by avoiding the eyes of the young, of those who look at you as if self-esteem were possible and they expected you to have it. Guilt is all that you retain within your soul—and so does every other man, as he goes past, avoiding *your* eyes. Do you wonder why your morality has not achieved brotherhood on earth or the good will of man to man?

The justification of sacrifice, that your morality propounds, is more corrupt than the corruption it purports to justify. The motive of your sacrifice, it tells you, should be *love*—the love you ought to feel for every man. A morality that professes the belief that the values of the spirit are more precious than matter, a morality that teaches you to scorn a whore who gives her body indiscriminately to all men—this same morality demands that you surrender your soul to promiscuous love for all comers. . . .

Since childhood, you have been hiding the guilty secret that you feel no desire to be moral, no desire to seek self-immolation, that you dread and hate your code, but dare not say it even to yourself, that you're devoid of those moral "instincts" which others profess to feel. The less you felt, the louder you proclaimed your selfless love and servitude to others, in dread of ever letting them discover your own self, the self that you betrayed, the self that you kept in concealment, like a skeleton in the closet of your body. And they, who were at once your dupes and your deceivers, they listened and voiced their loud approval, in dread of ever letting you discover that they were harboring the same unspoken secret. Existence among you is a giant pretense, an act you all perform for one another, each feeling that he is the only guilty freak, each placing his moral authority in the unknowable known only to others, each faking the reality he feels they expect him to fake, none having the courage to break the vicious circle.

No matter what dishonorable compromise you've made with your impracticable creed, no matter what miserable balance, half-cynicism, half-superstition, you now manage to maintain, you still preserve the root, the lethal tenet: the belief that the moral and the practical are opposites. Since childhood, you have been running from the terror of a choice you have never dared fully to identify: If the *practical*, whatever you must practice to exist, whatever works, succeeds, achieves your purpose, whatever brings you food and joy, whatever profits you is evil—and if the good, the moral is the *impractical*, whatever fails destroys, frustrates, whatever injures you and brings you loss or pain—then your choice is to be moral or to live.

The sole result of that murderous doctrine was to remove morality from life. You grew up to believe that moral laws bear no relation to the job of living, except as an impediment and threat, that man's existence is an amoral jungle where anything goes and anything works. And in that fog of switching definitions which descends upon a frozen mind, you have forgotten that the evils damned by your creed were the virtues required for living, and you have come to believe that actual evils are the *practical* means of existence. Forgetting that the impractical "good" was self-sacrifice, you believe that self-esteem is impractical; forgetting that the practical "evil" was production, you believe that robbery is practical.

Accept the fact that the achievement of your happiness is the only *moral* purpose of your life, and that *happiness*—not pain or mindless self-indulgence—is the proof of your moral integrity, since it is the proof and the result of your loyalty to the achievement of your values. Happiness was the responsibility you dreaded, it required the kind of rational discipline you did not value yourself enough to assume—and the anxious staleness of your days is the monument to your evasion of the knowledge that there is no moral substitute for happiness, that there is no more despicable coward than the man who deserted the battle for his joy, fearing to assert his right to existence, lacking the courage and the loyalty to life of a bird or a flower reaching for the sun. Discard the protective rags of that vice which you called a virtue: humility—learn to value yourself, which means: to fight for your happiness—and when you learn that *pride* is the sum of all virtues, you will learn to live like a man.

As a basic step of self-esteem, learn to treat as the mark of a cannibal any man's *demand* for your help. To demand it is to claim that your life is *his* property—and loathsome as such claim might be, there's something still more loathsome: your agreement. Do you ask if it's ever proper to help another man? No—if he claims it as his right or as a moral duty that you owe him. Yes—if such is your own desire based on your own selfish pleasure in the value of his person and his struggle.

On helping others [232]

The psychological results of altruism may be observed in the fact that a great many people approach the subject of ethics by asking such questions as: "Should one risk one's life to help a man who is: a) drowning, b) trapped in a fire, c) stepping in front of a speeding truck, d) hanging by his fingernails over an abyss?"

Consider the implications of that approach. If a man accepts the ethics of altruism, he suffers the following consequences (in proportion to the degree of his acceptance):

1. Lack of self-esteem—since his first concern in the realm of values is not how to live his life, but how to sacrifice it.

2. Lack of respect for others—since he regards mankind as a herd of doomed beggars crying for someone's help.

3. A nightmare view of existence—since he believes that men are trapped in a "malevolent universe" where disasters are the constant and primary concern of their lives.

4. And, in fact, a lethargic indifference to ethics, a hopelessly cynical amorality— since his questions involve situations which he is not likely ever to encounter, which bear no relation to the actual problems of his own life, and thus leave him to live without any moral principles whatever.

By elevating the issue of helping others into the central and primary issue of ethics, altruism has destroyed the concept of any authentic benevolence or good will among men. It has indoctrinated men with the idea that to value another human being is an act of selflessness, thus implying that a man can have no personal interest in others—that *to value* another means to *sacrifice* oneself—that any love, respect, or admiration a man may feel for others is not and cannot be a source of his own enjoyment, but is a threat to his existence, a sacrificial blank check signed over to his loved ones.

The men who accept that dichotomy but choose its other side, the ultimate products of altruism's dehumanizing influence, are those psychopaths who do not challenge altruism's basic premise, but proclaim their rebellion against self-sacrifice by announcing that they are totally indifferent to anything living and would not lift a finger to help a man or a dog left mangled by a hit-and-run driver (who is usually one of their own kind).

Most men do not accept or practice either side of altruism's viciously false dichotomy, but its result is a total intellectual chaos on the issue of proper human relationships and on such questions as the nature, purpose, or extent of the help one may give to others. Today, a great many well-meaning, reasonable men do not know how to identify or conceptualize the moral principles that motivate their love, affection, or good will, and can find no guidance in the field of ethics, which is dominated by the stale platitudes of altruism.

On the question of why man is not a sacrificial animal and why help to others is not his moral duty, I refer you to, *Atlas Shrugged.* This present discussion is concerned with the principles by which one identifies and evaluates the instances involving a man's *nonsacrificial* help to others.

"Sacrifice" is the surrender of a greater value for the sake of a lesser one or of a nonvalue. Thus, altruism gauges a man's virtue by the degree to which he surrenders, renounces, or betrays his values (since help to a stranger or an enemy is regarded as more virtuous, less "selfish," than help to those one loves). The rational principle of conduct is the exact opposite: always act in accordance with the hierarchy of your values and never sacrifice a greater value to a lesser one.

This applies to all choices, including one's actions to other men. It requires that one possess a defined hierarchy of *rational* values (values chosen and validated by a rational standard). Without such a hierarchy, neither rational conduct nor considered value judgments nor moral choices are possible.

Love and friendship are profoundly personal, selfish values: love is an expression and assertion of self-esteem, a response to one's own values in the person of another. One gains a profoundly personal, selfish joy from the mere existence of the person one loves. It is one's own personal, selfish happiness that one seeks, earns, and derives from love.

A "selfless," "disinterested" love is a contradiction in terms: it means that one is indifferent to that which one values.

Concern for the welfare of those one loves is a rational part of one's selfish interests. If a man who is passionately in love with his wife spends a fortune to cure her of a dangerous illness, it would be absurd to claim that he does it as a "sacrifice" for *her* sake, not his own, and that it no difference to *him*, personally and selfishly, whether she lives or dies.

Any action that a man undertakes for the benefit of those he loves is *not a sacrifice* if, in the hierarchy of his values, in the total context of the choices open to him, it achieves, that which is of greatest *personal* (and rational) importance to *him*. In the above example, his wife's survival is of greater value to the husband than anything else that his money could buy, it is of greatest importance to his own happiness and, therefore, his action is *not* a sacrifice.

But suppose he let her die in order to spend his money on saving the lives of ten other women, none of whom meant anything to him—as the ethics of altruism would require. *That* would be a sacrifice. Here the difference between Objectivism and altruism can be seen most clearly: if sacrifice is the moral principle of action, then that husband *should* sacrifice his wife for the sake of ten other women. What distinguishes the wife from the ten others? Nothing but her value to the husband who has to make the choice—nothing but the fact that *his* happiness requires her survival.

The Objectivist ethics would tell him: your highest moral purpose is the achievement of your own happiness, your money is yours, use it to save your wife, *that* is your moral right and your rational, moral choice.

Consider the soul of the altruistic moralist who would be prepared to tell that husband the opposite. (And then ask yourself whether altruism is motivated by benevolence.)

The proper method of judging when or whether one should help another person is by reference to one's own rational self-interest and one's own hierarchy of values: the time, money, or effort one gives or the risk one takes should be proportionate to the value of the person in relation to one's own happiness. . . .

The virtue involved in helping those one loves is not "selflessness" or "sacrifice," but *integrity*. Integrity is loyalty to one's convictions and values; it is the policy of acting in accordance with one's values, of expressing, upholding, and translating them into practical reality. . . .

What, then, should one properly grant to strangers? The generalized respect and good will which one should grant to a human being in the name of the potential value he represents—until and unless he forfeits it.

On taking a rational view of one's self-interest [233]

There are four interrelated considerations which are involved in a rational man's view of his interests. . . . I shall designate these four as: (a) "Reality," (b) "Context," (c) "Responsibility," (d) "Effort."

(a) *Reality.* The term "interests" is a wide abstraction that covers the entire field of ethics. It includes the issues of: man's values, his desires, his goals and their actual achievement in reality. A man's "interests" depend on the kind of goals he chooses to pursue, his choice of goals depends on his desires, his desires depend on his values—and, for a rational man, his values depend on the judgment of his mind.

Desires (or feelings or emotions or wishes or whims) are not tools of cognition; they are not a valid standard of value, nor a valid criterion of man's interests. . . .

In choosing his goals (the specific values he seeks to gain and/or keep), a rational man is guided by his thinking (by a process of reason)—not by his feelings or desires. He does not regard desires as irreducible primaries, as the given, which he is destined irresistibly to pursue. He does not regard "because I *want* it" or "because I *feel* like it" as a sufficient cause and validation of his actions. . . .

Only an irrationalist (or mystic or subjectivist—in which category I place all those who regard faith, feelings, or desires as man's standard of value) exists in a perpetual conflict of "interests." Not only do his alleged interests clash with those of other men, but they clash also with one another. . . .

(b) *Context.* Just as a rational man does not hold any conviction out of context—that is: without relating it to the rest of his knowledge and resolving any possible contradictions—so he does not hold or pursue any desire out of context. And he does not judge what is or is not to his interest out of context, on the range of any given moment.

Context-dropping is one of the chief psychological tools of evasion. In regard to one's desires, there are two major ways of context-dropping: the issues of *range* and of *means.*

A rational man sees his interests in terms of a lifetime and selects his goals accordingly. . . . [H]e does not regard any moment as cut off from the context of the rest of his life, and . . . he allows no conflicts or contradictions between his short-range and long-range interests. . . .

A rational man does not indulge in wistful longings for ends divorced from means. He does not hold a desire without knowing (or learning) and considering the means by which it is to be achieved. Since he knows that nature does not provide man with the automatic satisfaction of his desires, that a man's goals or values have to be achieved by his own effort, that the lives and efforts of other men are not his property and are not there to serve his wishes—a rational man never holds a desire or pursues a goal which cannot be achieved directly or *indirectly* by his own effort.

It is with a proper understanding of this "*indirectly*" that the crucial social issue begins.

Living in a society, instead of on a desert island, does not relieve a man of the responsibility of supporting his own life. The only difference is that he supports his life by *trading* his products or services for the products or services of others. And, in this process of trade, a rational man does not seek or desire any more or any less than his own effort can earn. What determines his earnings? The free market, that is: the voluntary choice and judgment of the men who are willing to trade him their effort in return. . . .

It is in this sense that a rational man never holds a desire or pursues a goal which cannot be achieved by his own effort. He trades value for value. He never seeks or desires the *unearned*. If he undertakes to achieve a goal that requires the cooperation of many people, he never counts on anything but his own ability to persuade them and their voluntary agreement. . . .

Since he never drops the context of the issues he deals with, a rational man accepts that struggle as *to his interest*—because he knows that freedom is to his interest. He knows that the struggle to achieve his values includes the possibility of defeat. He knows also that there is no alternative and no automatic guarantee of success for man's effort, neither in dealing with nature nor with other men. So he does not judge his interests by any particular defeat nor by the range of any particular moment. He lives and judges long-range. And he assumes the full responsibility of knowing what conditions are *necessary* for the achievement of his goals.

(c) *Responsibility.* This last is the particular form of intellectual responsibility that most people evade. That evasion is the major cause of their frustrations and defeats.

Most people hold their desires without any context whatever, as ends hanging in a foggy vacuum, the fog hiding any concept of means. They rouse themselves mentally only long enough to utter an "*I wish*," and stop there, and wait, as if the rest were up to some unknown power.

What they evade is *the responsibility of judging the social world.* They take the world as the given. "A world I never made" is the deepest essence of their attitude—and they seek only to adjust themselves uncritically to the incomprehensible requirements of those unknowable others who did make the world, whoever those might be.

But humility and presumptuousness are two sides of the same psychological medal. In the willingness to throw oneself blindly on the mercy of others there is the implicit privilege of making blind demands on one's masters. . . .

In dropping the responsibility for one's own interests and life, one drops the responsibility of ever having to consider the interests and lives of others—of those others who are, somehow, to provide the satisfaction of one's desires.

Whoever allows a "somehow" into his view of the means by which his desires are to be achieved, is guilty of that "metaphysical humility" which, psychologically, is the premise of a parasite. As Nathaniel Branden pointed out in a lecture, "*somehow*" always means "*somebody.*"

(d) *Effort*. Since a rational man knows that man must achieve his goals by his own effort, he knows that neither wealth nor jobs nor any human values exist in a given, limited, static quantity, waiting to be divided. He knows that all benefits have to be produced, that the gain of one man does not represent the loss of another, that a man's achievement is not earned at the expense of those who have not achieved it.

Therefore, he never imagines that he has any sort of unearned, unilateral claim on any human being—and he never leaves his interests at the mercy of any one person or single, specific concrete. He may need clients, but not any one particular client—he may need customers, but not any one particular customer—he may need a job, but not any one particular job.

If he encounters competition, he either meets it or chooses another line of work. There is no job so low that a better, more skillful performance of it would pass unnoticed and unappreciated; not in a *free* society. Ask any office manager.

It is only the passive, parasitical representatives of the "humility metaphysics" school who regard any competitor as a threat, because the thought of earning one's position by personal merit is not part of their view of life. They regard themselves as interchangeable mediocrities who have nothing to offer and who fight, in a "static" universe, for someone's causeless favor.

A rational man knows that one does not live by means of "luck," "breaks," or favors, that there is no such thing as an "only chance" or a single opportunity, and that this is guaranteed precisely by the existence of competition. He does not regard any concrete, specific goal, or value as irreplaceable. He knows that only persons are irreplaceable—only those one loves. . . .

Such, in brief essence, are the four major considerations involved in a rational man's view of his interests.

David Gauthier was born in Toronto, received his doctorate from Oxford, and is currently Distinguished Service Professor at the University of Pittsburgh. In the following essay he takes a game-theoretic approach to ethics, attempting to demonstrate the advantages secured by those committed to morality.

DAVID GAUTHIER
(b. 1932)

Morality and self-interest [234]

I

Hume asks, rhetorically, "what theory of morals can ever serve any useful purpose, unless it can show, by a particular detail, that all the duties which it recommends, are also the true interest of each individual?" [235] But there are many to whom this question does not seem rhetorical. Why, they ask, do we speak the language of morality, impressing upon our fellows their duties and obligations, urging them with appeals to what is right and good, if we could speak to the same effect in the language of prudence, appealing to considerations of interest and advantage? When the poet, Ogden Nash, is moved by the muse to cry out:

O Duty,

Why hast thou not the visage of a sweetie or a cutie? [236]

we do not anticipate the reply:

O Poet,

I really am a cutie and I think you ought to know it.

The belief that duty cannot be reduced to interest, or that morality may require the agent to subordinate all considerations of advantage, is one which has withstood the assaults of contrary-minded philosophers from Plato to the present. Indeed, were it not for the conviction that only interest and advantage can motivate human actions, it would be difficult to understand philosophers contending so vigorously for the identity, or at least compatibility, of morality with prudence.

Yet if morality is not true prudence it would be wrong to suppose that those philosophers who have sought some connection between morality and advantage have been merely misguided. For it is a truism that we should all expect to be worse off if men were to substitute prudence, even of the most enlightened kind, for morality in all of their deliberations. And this truism demands not only some connection between morality and advantage, but a seemingly paradoxical connection. For if we should all expect to suffer, were men to be prudent instead of moral, then morality must contribute to advantage in a unique way, a way in which prudence—following reasons of advantage—cannot.

Thomas Hobbes is perhaps the first philosopher who tried to develop this seemingly paradoxical connection between morality and advantage. But since he could not admit that a man might ever reasonably subordinate considerations of advantage to the dictates of obligation, he was led to deny the possibility of real conflict between morality and prudence. So his argument fails to clarify the distinction between the view that claims of obligation reduce to considerations of interest and the view that claims of obligation promote advantage in a way in which considerations of interest cannot.

More recently, Kurt Baier has argued that "being moral is following rules designed to overrule self-interest whenever it is in the interest of everyone alike that everyone should set aside his interest."[237] Since prudence is following rules of (enlightened) self-interest, Baier is arguing that morality is designed to overrule prudence when it is to everyone's advantage that it do so—or, in other words, that morality contributes to advantage in a way in which prudence cannot.[238]

Baier does not actually demonstrate that morality contributes to advantage in this unique and seemingly paradoxical way. Indeed, he does not ask how it is possible that morality should do this. It is this possibility which I propose to demonstrate.

II

Let us examine the following proposition, which will be referred to as "the thesis": *Morality is a system of principles such that it is advantageous for everyone if everyone accepts and acts on it, yet acting on the system of principles requires that some person perform disadvantageous acts.*[239]

What I wish to show is that this thesis *could be true*, that morality could possess those characteristics attributed to it by the thesis. I shall not try to show that the thesis is true—indeed, I shall argue in Section V that it presents at best an inadequate conception of morality. But it is plausible to suppose that a modified form of the thesis states a necessary, although not a sufficient, condition for a moral system.

Two phrases in the thesis require elucidation. The first is "advantageous for everyone." I use this phrase to mean that *each* person will do better if the system is accepted and acted on than if *either* no system is accepted and acted on *or* a system is accepted and acted on which is similar, save that it never requires any person to perform disadvantageous acts.

Clearly, then, the claim that it is advantageous for everyone to accept and act on the system is a very strong one; it may be so strong that no system of principles which might be generally adopted could meet it. But I shall consider in Section V one among the possible ways of weakening the claim.

The second phrase requiring elucidation is "disadvantageous acts." I use this phrase to refer to acts which, in the context of their performance, would be less advantageous to the performer than some other act open to him in the same context. The phrase does not refer to acts which merely impose on the performer some short-term disadvantage that is recouped or outweighed in the long run. Rather it refers to acts which impose a disadvantage that is never recouped. It follows that the performer may say to himself, when confronted with the requirement to perform such an act, that it would be better *for him* not to perform it.

It is essential to note that the thesis, as elucidated, does not maintain that morality is advantageous for everyone in the sense that each person will do *best* if the system of principles is accepted and acted on. Each person will do better than if no system is adopted, or than if the one particular alternative mentioned above is adopted, but not than if any alternative is adopted.

Indeed, for each person required by the system to perform some disadvantageous act, it is easy to specify a better alternative—namely, the system modified so that it does not require him to perform any act disadvantageous to himself. Of course, there is no reason to expect such an alternative to be better than the moral system for everyone, or in fact for anyone other than the person granted the special exemption.

A second point to note is that each person must gain more from the disadvantageous acts performed by others than he loses from the disadvantageous acts performed by himself. If this were not the case, then some person would do better if a system were adopted exactly like the moral system save that it never requires *any* person to perform disadvantageous acts. This is ruled out by the force of "advantageous for everyone."

This point may be clarified by an example. Suppose that the system contains exactly one principle. Everyone is always to tell the truth. It follows from the thesis that each person gains more from those occasions on which others tell the truth, even though it is disadvantageous to them to do so, than he loses from those occasions on which he tells the truth even though it is disadvantageous to him to do so.

Now this is not to say that each person gains by telling others the truth in order to ensure that in return they tell him the truth. Such gains would merely be the result of accepting certain short-term disadvantages (those associated with truth-telling) in order to reap long-term benefits (those associated with being told the truth). Rather, what is required by the thesis is that those disadvantages which a person incurs in telling the truth, when he can expect neither short-term nor long-term benefits to accrue to him from truth-telling, are outweighed by those advantages he receives when others tell him the truth when they can expect no benefits to accrue to them from truth-telling.

The principle enjoins truth-telling in those cases in which whether one tells the truth or not will have no effect on whether others tell the truth. Such cases include those in which others have no way of knowing whether or not they are being told the truth. The thesis requires that the disadvantages one incurs in telling the truth in these cases are less than the advantages one receives in being told the truth by others in parallel cases; and the thesis requires that this holds for everyone.

Thus we see that although the disadvantages imposed by the system on any person are less than the advantages secured him through the imposition of disadvantages on others, yet the disadvantages are real in that incurring them is *unrelated* to receiving the advantages. The argument of long-term prudence, that I ought to incur some immediate disadvantage *so that* I shall receive compensating advantages later on, is entirely inapplicable here.

III

It will be useful to examine in some detail an example of a system which possesses those characteristics ascribed by the thesis to morality. This example, abstracted from the field of international relations, will enable us more clearly to distinguish, first, conduct based on immediate interest; second, conduct which is truly prudent, and third, conduct which promotes mutual advantage but is not prudent.

A and B are two nations with substantially opposed interests, who find themselves engaged in an arms race against each other. Both possess the latest in weaponry, so that each recognizes that the actual outbreak of full-scale war between them would be mutually disastrous. This recognition leads A and B to agree that each would be better off if they were mutually disarming instead of mutually arming. For mutual disarmament would preserve the balance of power between them while reducing the risk of war.

Hence A and B enter into a disarmament pact. The pact is advantageous for both if both accept and act on it, although clearly it is not advantageous for either to act on it if the other does not.

Let A be considering whether or not to adhere to the pact in some particular situation, whether or not actually to perform some act of disarmament. A will quite likely consider the act to have disadvantageous consequences. A expects to benefit, not by his own acts of disarmament, but by B's acts. Hence if A were to reason simply in terms of immediate interest, A might well decide to violate the pact.

But A's decision need be neither prudent nor reasonable. For suppose first that B is able to determine whether or not A adheres to the pact. If A violates, then B will detect the violation and will then consider what to do in the light of A's behavior. It is not to B's advantage to disarm alone; B expects to gain, not by his own acts of disarmament, but by A's acts. Hence A's violation, if known to B, leads naturally to B's counter-violation. If this continues, the effect of the pact is entirely undone, and A and B return to their mutually disadvantageous arms race. A, foreseeing this when considering whether or not to adhere to the pact in the given situation, must therefore conclude that the truly prudent course of action is to adhere.

Now suppose that B is unable to determine whether or not A adheres to the pact in the particular situation under consideration. If A judges adherence to be in itself disadvantageous, then it will decide, both on the basis of immediate interest and on the basis of prudence, to violate the pact. Since A's decision is unknown to B, it cannot affect whether or not B adheres to the pact, and so the advantage gained by A's violation is not outweighed by any consequent loss.

Therefore if A and B are prudent they will adhere to their disarmament pact whenever violation would be detectable by the other, and violate the pact whenever violation would not be detectable by the other. In other words, they will adhere openly and violate secretly. The disarmament pact between A and B thus possesses two of the characteristics ascribed by the thesis to morality. First, accepting the pact and acting on it is more advantageous for each than making no pact at all. Second, in so far as the pact stipulates that each must disarm even when disarming is undetectable by the other, it requires each to perform disadvantageous acts — acts which run counter to considerations of prudence.

One further condition must be met if the disarmament pact is to possess those characteristics ascribed by the thesis to a system of morality. It must be the case that the requirement that each party perform disadvantageous acts be essential to the advantage conferred by the pact; or, to put the matter in the way in which we expressed it earlier, both A and B must do better to adhere to this pact than to a pact which is similar save that it requires no disadvantageous acts. In terms of the example, A and B must do better to adhere to the pact than to a pact which stipulates that each must disarm only when disarming is detectable by the other.

We may plausibly suppose this condition to be met. Although A will gain by secretly retaining arms itself, it will lose by B's similar acts, and its losses may well outweigh its gains. B may equally lose more by A's secret violations than it gains by its own. So, despite the fact that prudence requires each to violate secretly, each may well do better if both adhere secretly than if both violate secretly. Supposing this to be the ease, the disarmament pact is formally analogous to a moral system, as characterized by the thesis. That is, acceptance of and adherence to the pact by A and B is more advantageous for each, either than making no pact at all or than acceptance of and adherence to a pact requiring only open disarmament, and the pact requires each to perform acts of secret disarmament which are disadvantageous.

Some elementary notation, adapted for our purposes from the mathematical theory of games, may make the example even more perspicuous. Given a disarmament pact between A and B, each may pursue two pure strategies—adherence and violation. There are then, four possible combinations of strategies, each determining a particular outcome. These outcomes can be ranked preferentially for each nation; we shall let the numerals 1 to 4 represent the ranking from first to fourth preference. Thus we construct a simple matrix,[240] in which A's preferences are stated first:

		B	
		adheres	violates
	adheres	2, 2	4, 1
A			
	violates	1, 4	3, 3

The matrix does not itself show that agreement is advantageous to both, for it gives only the rankings of outcomes given the agreement. But it is plausible to assume that A and B would rank mutual violation on a par with no agreement. If we assume this, we can then indicate the value to each of making and adhering to the pact by reference to the matrix.

The matrix shows immediately that adherence to the pact is not the most advantageous possibility for either, since each prefers the outcome, if it alone violates, to the outcome of mutual adherence. It shows also that each gains less from its own violations than it loses from the other's, since each ranks mutual adherence above mutual violation.

Let us now use the matrix to show that, as we argued previously, public adherence to the pact is prudent and mutually advantageous, whereas private adherence is not prudent although mutually advantageous. Consider first the case when adherence— and so violation—are open and public.

If adherence and violation are open, then each knows the strategy chosen by the other, and can adjust its own strategy in the light of this knowledge—or, in other words, the strategies are interdependent. Suppose that each initially chooses the strategy of adherence. A notices that if it switches to violation it gains—moving from 2 to 1 in terms of preference ranking. Hence immediate interest dictates such a switch. But it notices further that if it switches, then B can also be expected to switch—moving from 4 to 3 on its preference scale. The eventual outcome would be stable, in that neither could benefit from switching from violation back to adherence. But the eventual outcome would represent not a gain for A but a loss—moving from 2 to 3 on its preference scale. Hence prudence dictates no change from the strategy of adherence. This adherence is mutually advantageous; A and B are in precisely similar positions in terms of their pact.

Consider now the case when adherence and violation are secret and private. Neither nation knows the strategy chosen by the other, so the two strategies are independent. Suppose A is trying to decide which strategy to follow. It does not know B's choice. But it notices that if B adheres, then it pays A to violate, attaining 1 rather than 2 in terms of preference ranking. If B violates, then again it pays A to violate, attaining 3 rather than 4 on its preference scale. Hence, no matter which strategy B chooses, A will do better to violate, and so prudence dictates violation.

B of course reasons in just the same way. Hence each is moved by considerations of prudence to violate the pact, and the outcome assigns each rank 3 on its preference scale. This outcome is mutually disadvantageous to A and B, since mutual adherence would assign each rank 2 on its preference scale.

If A and B are both capable only of rational prudence, they find themselves at an impasse. The advantage of mutual adherence to the agreement when violations would be secret is not available to them, since neither can find it in his own over-all interest not to violate secretly. Hence, strictly prudent nations cannot reap the maximum advantage possible from a pact of the type under examination.

Of course, what A and B will no doubt endeavor to do is eliminate the possibility of secret violations of their pact. Indeed, barring additional complications, each must find it to his advantage to make it possible for the other to detect his own violations. In other words, each must find it advantageous to ensure that their choice of strategies is interdependent, so that the pact will always be prudent for each to keep. But it may not be possible for them to ensure this, and to the extent that they cannot, prudence will prevent them from maximizing mutual advantage.

IV

We may now return to the connection of morality with advantage. Morality, if it is a system of principles of the type characterized in the thesis, requires that some persons perform acts genuinely disadvantageous to themselves, as a means to greater mutual advantage. Our example shows sufficiently that such a system is possible, and indicates more precisely its character. In particular, by an argument strictly parallel to that which we have pursued, we may show that men who are merely prudent will not perform the required disadvantageous acts. But in so violating the principles of morality, they will disadvantage themselves. Each will lose more by the violations of others than he will gain by his own violations.

Now this conclusion would be unsurprising if it were only that no man can gain if he alone is moral rather than prudent. Obviously such a man loses, for he adheres to moral principles to his own disadvantage, while others violate them also to his disadvantage. The benefit of the moral system is not one which any individual can secure for himself, since each man gains from the sacrifices of others.

What is surprising in our conclusion is that no man can ever gain if he is moral. Not only does he not gain by being moral if others are prudent, but he also does not gain by being moral if others are moral. For although he now receives the advantage of others' adherence to moral principles, he reaps the disadvantage of his own adherence. As long as his own adherence to morality is independent of what others do (and this is required to distinguish morality from prudence), he must do better to be prudent.

If all men are moral, all will do better than if all are prudent. But any one man will always do better if he is prudent than if he is moral. There is no real paradox in supposing that morality is advantageous, even though it requires the performance of disadvantageous acts.

On the supposition that morality has the characteristics ascribed to it by the thesis, is it possible to answer the question "Why should we be moral?" where "we" is taken distributively, so that the question is a compendious way of asking, for each person, "Why should I be moral?" More simply, is it possible to answer the question "Why should I be moral?"

I take it that this question, if asked seriously, demands a reason for being moral other than moral reasons themselves. It demands that moral reasons be shown to be reasons for acting by a noncircular argument. Those who would answer it, like Baier, endeavor to do so by the introduction of considerations of advantage.

Two such considerations have emerged from our discussion. The first is that if all are moral, all will do better than if all are prudent. This will serve to answer the question "Why should we be moral?" if this question is interpreted rather as "Why should we all be moral—rather than all being something else?" If we must all be the same, then each person has a reason—a prudential reason—to prefer that we all be moral.

But, so interpreted, "Why should we be moral?" is not a compendious way of asking, for each person, "Why should I be moral?" Of course, if everyone is to be whatever I am, then I should be moral. But a general answer to the question "Why should I be moral?" cannot presuppose this.

The second consideration is that any individual always does better to be prudent rather than moral, provided his choice does not determine other choices. But in so far as this answers the question "Why should I be moral?" it leads to the conclusion "I should not be moral." One feels that this is not the answer which is wanted.

We may put the matter otherwise. The individual who needs a reason for being moral which is not itself a moral reason cannot have it. There is nothing surprising about this; it would be much more surprising if such reasons could be found. For it is more than apparently paradoxical to suppose that considerations of advantage could ever of themselves justify accepting a real disadvantage.

V

I suggested in Section II that the thesis, in modified form, might provide a necessary, although not a sufficient, condition for a moral system. I want now to consider how one might characterize the man who would qualify as moral according to the thesis—I shall call him the "moral" man—and then ask what would be lacking from this characterization, in terms of some of our commonplace moral views.

The rationally prudent man is incapable of moral behavior, in even the limited sense defined by the thesis. What difference must there be between the prudent man and the "moral" man? Most simply, the "moral" man is the prudent but trustworthy man. I treat trustworthiness as the capacity which enables its possessor to adhere, and to judge that he ought to adhere, to a commitment which he has made, without regard to considerations of advantage.

The prudent but trustworthy man does not possess this capacity completely. He is capable of trustworthy behavior only in so far as he regards his commitment as advantageous. Thus he differs from the prudent man just in the relevant respect; he accepts arguments of the form "If it is advantageous for me to agree[24] to do x, and I do agree to do x, then I ought to do x, whether or not it then proves advantageous for me to do x."

Suppose that A and B, the parties to the disarmament pact, are prudent but trustworthy. A, considering whether or not secretly to violate the agreement, reasons that its advantage in making and keeping the agreement, provided B does so as well, is greater than its advantage in not making it. If it can assume that B reasons in the same way, then it is in a position to conclude that it ought not to violate the pact. Although violation would be advantageous, consideration of this advantage is ruled out by A's trustworthiness, given the advantage in agreeing to the pact.

The prudent but trustworthy man meets the requirements implicitly imposed by the thesis for the "moral" man. But how far does this "moral" man display two characteristics commonly associated with morality—first, a willingness to make sacrifices, and second, a concern with fairness?

Whenever a man ignores his own advantage for reasons other than those of greater advantage, he may be said to make some sacrifice. The "moral" man, in being trustworthy, is thus required to make certain sacrifices. But these are extremely limited. And—not surprisingly, given the general direction of our argument—it is quite possible that they limit the advantages which the "moral" man can secure.

Once more let us turn to our example. A and B have entered into a disarmament agreement and, being prudent but trustworthy, are faithfully carrying it out. The government of A is now informed by its scientists, however, that they have developed an effective missile defense, which will render A invulnerable to attack by any of the weapons actually or potentially at B's disposal, barring unforeseen technological developments. Furthermore, this defense can be installed secretly. The government is now called upon to decide whether to violate its agreement with B, install the new defense, and, with the arms it has retained through its violation, establish its dominance over B.

A is in a type of situation quite different from that previously considered. For it is not just that A will do better by secretly violating its agreement. A reasons not only that it will do better to violate no matter what B does, but that it will do better if both violate than if both continue to adhere to the pact. A is now in a position to gain from abandoning the agreement; it no longer finds mutual adherence advantageous.

We may represent this new situation in another matrix:

		B	
		adheres	violates
	adheres	3, 2	4, 1
A			
	violates	1, 4	2, 3

We assume again that the ranking of mutual violation is the same as that of no agreement. Now had this situation obtained at the outset, no agreement would have been made, for A would have had no reason to enter into a disarmament pact. And of course had A expected this situation to come about, no agreement—or only a temporary agreement—would have been made; A would no doubt have risked the short-term dangers of the continuing arms race in the hope of securing the long-run benefit of predominance over B once its missile defense was completed. On the contrary, A expected to benefit from the agreement, but now finds that, because of its unexpected development of a missile defense, the agreement is not in fact advantageous to it.

The prudent but trustworthy man is willing to carry out his agreements, and judges that he ought to carry them out, in so far as he considers them advantageous. A is prudent but trustworthy. But is A willing to carry out its agreement to disarm, now that it no longer considers the agreement advantageous?

If A adheres to its agreement in this situation, it makes a sacrifice greater than any advantage it receives from the similar sacrifices of others. It makes a sacrifice greater in kind than any which can be required by a mutually advantageous agreement. It must, then, possess a capacity for trustworthy behavior greater than that ascribed to the merely prudent but trustworthy man (or nation). This capacity need not be unlimited; it need not extend to a willingness to adhere to any commitment no matter what sacrifice is involved. But it must involve a willingness to adhere to a commitment made in the expectation of advantage, should that expectation be disappointed.

I shall call the man (or nation) who is willing to adhere, and judges that he ought to adhere, to his prudentially undertaken agreements even if they prove disadvantageous to him, the trustworthy man. It is likely that there are advantages available to trustworthy men which are not available to merely prudent but trustworthy men. For there may be situations in which men can make agreements which each expects to be advantageous to him, provided he can count on the others' adhering to it whether or not their expectation of advantage is realized. But each can count on this only if all have the capacity to adhere to commitments regardless of whether the commitment actually proves advantageous. Hence, only trustworthy men who know each other to be such will be able rationally to enter into, and so to benefit from, such agreements.

Baier's view of morality departs from that stated in the thesis in that it requires trustworthy, and not merely prudent but trustworthy, men. Baier admits that "a person might do better for himself by following enlightened self-interest rather than morality."[242] This admission seems to require that morality be a system of principles which each person may expect, initially, to be advantageous to him, if adopted and adhered to by everyone, but not a system which actually is advantageous to everyone.

Our commonplace moral views do, I think, support the view that the moral man must be trustworthy. Hence, we have established one modification required in the thesis, if it is to provide a more adequate set of conditions for a moral system.

But there is a much more basic respect in which the "moral" man falls short of our expectations. He is willing to temper his single-minded pursuit of advantage only by accepting the obligation to adhere to prudentially undertaken commitments. He has no real concern for the advantage of others, which would lead him to modify his pursuit of advantage when it conflicted with the similar pursuits of others. Unless he expects to gain, he is unwilling to accept restrictions on the pursuit of advantage which are intended to equalize the opportunities open to all. In other words, he has no concern with fairness.

We tend to think of the moral man as one who does not seek his own well-being by means which would deny equal well-being to his fellows. This marks him off clearly from the "moral" man, who differs from the prudent man only in that he can overcome the apparent paradox of prudence and obtain those advantages which are available only to those who can display real restraint in their pursuit of advantage.

Thus a system of principles might meet the conditions laid down in the thesis without taking any account of considerations of fairness. Such a system would contain principles for ensuring increased advantage (or expectation of advantage) to everyone, but no further principle need be present to determine the distribution of this increase.

It is possible that there are systems of principles which, if adopted and adhered to, provide advantages which strictly prudent men, however rational, cannot attain.

These advantages are a function of the sacrifices which the principles impose on their adherents.

Morality may be such a system. If it is, this would explain our expectation that we should all be worse off were we to substitute prudence for morality in our deliberations. But to characterize morality as a system of principles advantageous to all is not to answer the question "Why should I be moral?" nor is it to provide for those considerations of fairness which are equally essential to our moral understanding.

SELECT
BIBLIOGRAPHY

Plato

Annas, Julia, *The Morality of Happiness* (Oxford: Oxford University Press, 1993). [Consult Annas on Aristotle and the Epicureans and Stoics as well.]

Irwin, Terence, *Plato's Ethics* (Oxford: Oxford University Press, 1995).

Kraut, Richard, "Egoism, Love, and Political Office in Plato," *Philosophical Review* 82 (1973), 330–44.

Mahoney, Timothy, "Do Plato's Philosopher-Rulers Sacrifice Self-Interest to Justice?" *Phronesis* 37 (1992), 265–282.

Aristotle

Annas, Julia, "Self-Love in Aristotle," *Southern Journal of Philosophy* 27, Supplement (1988), 1–18.

Homiak, Marcia, "Virtue and Self-Love in Aristotle's Ethics," *Canadian Journal Of Philosophy* 11 (Dec 1981), 633–51.

Kahn, Charles H., "Aristotle and Altruism," *Mind* 90 (1981), 20–40.

Madigan, Arthur, "*EN* IX 8: Beyond Egoism and Altruism?," *The Modern Schoolman* 62 (1985), 1–20.

Rogers, Kelly, "Aristotle on Loving Another for His Own Sake," *Phronesis* 39 (1994), 291–302.

Epicureanism

Mitsis, Philip, *Epicurus' Ethical Theory: The Pleasures of Invulnerability* (Ithaca, NY: Cornell University Press, 1988).

Preuss, Peter, *Epicurean Ethics: Katastematic Hedonism* (Lewiston, NY: E. Mellen Press, 1994).

Stoicism

Engberg-Pedersen, Troels, *The Stoic Theory of Oikeiosis* (Aarhus, 1990).

Inwood, Brad, *Ethics and Human Action in Early Stoicism* (Oxford: Oxford University Press, 1985).

Whitlock Blundell, Mary, "Parental Nature and Stoic *Oikeiosis*," *Ancient Philosophy* 10 (1990), 221–42.

Augustine

Deane, Herbert A., *The Political and Social Ideas of St. Augustine* (New York: Columbia University Press, 1963).

Nygren, Anders, *Agape and Eros, Part I—A Study of the Christian Idea of Love* (1930). *Part II—The History of the Christian Idea of Love* (1936). Rev. Ed. Translated by P. S. Watson (London, 1953). [Consult on Aquinas, too.]

O'Donovan, Oliver, *The Problem of Self-Love in St. Augustine* (New Haven, CT: Yale University Press, 1980).

Outka, Gene, *Agape: An Ethical Analysis* (New Haven, CT: Yale University Press, 1972). [Consult on Aquinas, too.]

Aquinas

Drum, Peter, "Religion and Self-Interest," *Sophia* 32 (1993), 50–53.

Hayden, R. Mary, "The Paradox of Aquinas's Altruism: From Self-Love to Love of Others," *Proceedings of the Catholic Philosophical Association* (1990), 72–83.

Langan, John, "Egoism and Morality in the Theological Teleology of Thomas Aquinas," *Journal of Philosophical Research* 16 (1991), 411–26.

——, "Morality, Egoism and Punishment In Thomas Aquinas," *Heythrop Journal* 22 (1981), 378–93.

Santurri, Edmund N., Response to Langan's "Egoism and Morality in the Theologi-
    cal Teleology of Thomas Aquinas," *Journal of Philosophical Research* 16 (1991), 427–30.

Hobbes

Gauthier, David, *The Logic Of Leviathan* (Oxford: Oxford University Press, 1969).
Hampton, Jean, *Hobbes and the Social Contract Tradition* (Cambridge: Cambridge Universi-
    ty Press), 1986.
Kavka, Gregory S., *Hobbesian Moral and Political Theory* (Princeton, NJ: Princeton Univer-
    sity Press, 1986).
Lloyd, S. A., *Ideals as Interests in Hobbes's "Leviathan": The Power of Mind Over Matter* (Cam-
    bridge: Cambridge University Press, 1992).
Lukac De Stier, Maria L., "Individual Egoism as Motivation for Human Praxis,"
    Hobbes Studies 6 (1993), 43–57.
McNeilly, F. S., "Egoism in Hobbes," *Philosophical Quarterly* 16 (1966), 193–206.

Spinoza

Bennett, Jonathan, *A Study of Spinoza's Ethics* (Indianapolis, IN: Hackett Publishing Co.,
    1984).
Curley, Edwin, *Behind the Geometrical Method: A Reading of Spinoza's Ethics* (Princeton, NJ:
    Princeton University Press, 1988).
Hampshire, Stuart, *Spinoza: An Introduction to his Philosophical Thought* (London: Penguin
    Books, 1951).
Wolfson, H. A., *The Philosophy of Spinoza* (Cambridge, MA: Harvard University Press,
    1934).

Mandeville

Dickey, Laurence, "Pride, Hypocrisy and Civility in Mandeville's Social and Histori-
    cal Theory," *Critical Review* 4 (1990), 387–431.
Kaye, F. B., Introduction to *The Fable of the Bees, or Private Vices, Publick Virtues*, Kaye, ed.
    (Oxford: Clarendon Press, 1924).
Rosenberg, Nathan, "Mandeville and *Laissez-Faire*," *Journal of the History of Ideas* 24
    (1963), 183–96.
Scott-Taggart, M. J., "Mandeville: Cynic or Fool?" *Philosophical Quarterly* 16 (1966), 221–32.

Butler

Duncan-Jones, Austin, *Butler's Moral Philosophy* (London: Penguin Books, 1952).

Henson, Richard G., "Butler on Selfishness and Self-Love," *Philosophy and Phenomenologi-cal Research* 49 (1988), 31–57.

Maxwell, J. C., "Disinterested Desires," *Mind* 52 (1943), 39–46.

Platt, Thomas W., "Self-Love and Benevolence: In Defense of Butler's Ethics," *South-western Journal of Philosophy* 3 (1972), 71–79.

Roberts, Tom Aerwyn, *The Concept of Benevolence: Aspects of Eighteenth-Century Moral Philoso-phy* (London: Macmillan and Co., Ltd., 1973). [Consult Roberts on other eigh-teenth-century figures as well.]

Rorty, Amelie Oksenberg, "Butler on Benevolence and Conscience," *Philosophy* 53 (1978), 171–84.

Sturgeon, Nicholas J., "Nature and Conscience in Butler's Ethics," *Philosophical Review* 85 (1976), 316–56.

Hutcheson

Jensen, Henning, *Motivation and the Moral Sense in Francis Hutcheson's Ethical Theory* (The Hague: Nijhoff, 1971).

Loughran, James N., "Francis Hutcheson: Benevolence as Moral Motivation," *History of Philosophy Quarterly* 3 (1986), 293–309.

Stewart, Robert M., "John Clarke and Francis Hutcheson on Self-Love and Moral Motivation," *Journal of the History of Philosophy* 20 (1982), 261–78.

Hume

Huff, Thomas, "Self-Interest and Benevolence in Hume's Account of Moral Obliga-tion," *Ethics* 83 (1972), 58–70.

Lipkin, Robert J., "Altruism and Sympathy in Hume's Ethics," *Australian Journal of Phi-losophy* 65 (1987), 18–32.

Mackie, J. L., *Hume's Moral Theory* (London: Routledge & Kegan Paul, 1980).

Mercer, Philip C., *Sympathy and Ethics: A Study of the Relationship between Sympathy and Morali-ty with Special Reference to Hume's Treatise* (Oxford: Clarendon Press, 1972).

Shaver, Robert, "Hume's Self-Interest Requirement," *Canadian Journal of Philosophy* 24 (1994), 1–17.

Smith, Norman Kemp, *The Philosophy of David Hume* (London: Macmillan and Co., 1941).

Smith

Campbell, T. D., *Adam Smith's Science of Morals* (London: Allen & Unwin, 1971).

Fleischacker, Samuel, "Talking to My Butcher: Self-Interest, Exchange, and Freedom in the *Wealth of Nations*," (forthcoming).

Hirschman, A. O., *The Passions and the Interests* (Princeton, NJ: Princeton University Press, 1977).

Lamb, Robert Boyden, "Adam Smith's System: Sympathy not Self-Interest," *Journal of the History of Ideas* 35 (1974), 671–82.

Macfie, A. L., *The Individual in Society* (Oxford: Oxford University Press, 1967).

Shack, George, "Self-Interest and Social Value," *Journal of Value Inquiry* 18 (1984), 123–37.

Werhane, Patricia, "The Role of Self-Interest in Adam Smith's *Wealth Of Nations*," *The Journal of Philosophy* 87 (1989), 669–80.

———, *Adam Smith and his Legacy for Modern Capitalism* (Oxford: Oxford University Press, 1991.)

Kant

Herman, Barbara, *The Practice of Moral Judgment* (Cambridge, MA: Harvard University Press, 1993).

Hill, Thomas E., Jr., "Beneficence and Self-Love: A Kantian Perspective," *Social Philosophy and Policy* 10 (1993), 1–23.

Paton, Herbert James, *The Categorical Imperative: A Study in Kant's Moral Philosophy*, 5th ed. (London: Hutchinson, 1965).

Sullivan, Roger J., *Immanuel Kant's Moral Theory* (Cambridge: Cambridge University Press, 1989).

Bentham

Goldworth, Amnon, "The Sympathetic Sanction and Sinister Interest in Bentham's Utilitarianism," *History of Philosophy Quarterly* 4 (1987), 67–78.

Halévy, Eli, *The Growth of Philosophical Radicalism* (New York: Augustus M. Kelley, 1949).

Lyons, David, *In the Interest of the Governed: A Study in Bentham's Philosophy of Utility and Law* (Oxford: Clarendon Press, 1973).

Stearns, J. Brenton, "Bentham On Public and Private Ethics," *Canadian Journal of Philosophy* 5 (1975), 583–94.

Mill

Berger, Fred R., *Happiness, Justice, and Freedom: The Moral and Political Philosophy of John Stuart Mill* (Berkeley, CA: University of California Press, 1984).

Green, Michele, "Sympathy and Self-Interest: The Crisis in Mill's Mental History," *Utilitas* 1 (1989), 259–77.

Lyons, David, *Rights, Welfare, and Mill's Moral Theory* (Oxford: Oxford University Press, 1994).

Norman, Richard, "Self and Others: The Inadequacy of Utilitarianism," *Canadian Journal of Philosophy* 5, Supp. (1979), 181–201.

Sidgwick

Brink, David O., "Sidgwick's Dualism of Practical Reason," *Australian Journal of Philosophy* 66 (1988), 291–307.

——, "Sidgwick and the Rationale for Rational Egoism," in Bart Schultz, ed., *Essays on Henry Sidgwick* (Cambridge: Cambridge University Press, 1992).

Crisp, Roger, "Sidgwick and Self-Interest," *Utilitas* 2 (1990), 267–80.

Frankena, William K., "Sidgwick and the Dualism of Practical Reason," *The Monist* 58 (1974), 449–467.

——, "Sidgwick's *Methods Of Ethics*, Edition 7, Note 1," in John Heil, ed., *Rationality, Morality and Self-Interest* (Maryland: Rowman & Littlefield, 1993).

Mackie, J. L., "Sidgwick's Pessimism," *Philosophical Quarterly* 26 (1976), 317–27.

Schneewind, J. B., *Sidgwick's Ethics and Victorian Moral Philosophy* (Oxford: Clarendon Press, 1977).

James

Smith, M. Brewster, "William James and the Psychology of Self," in Margaret E. Donnelly, ed., *Reinterpreting the Legacy of William James* (Washington D.C.: American Psychological Association, 1992).

Strube, Michael J., John H. Yost, and James R. Bailey, "William James and Contemporary Research of the Self: The Influence of Pragmatism, Reality, and Truth," in Donnelly, ed., *Reinterpreting the Legacy of William James*.

Nietzsche

Ansell-Pearson, Keith, *Nietzsche contra Rousseau: A Study of Nietzsche's Moral and Political Thought* (Cambridge: Cambridge University Press, 1991).

Hatab, Lawrence J., *A Nietzschean Defense of Democracy: An Experiment in Postmodern Politics* (Chicago: Open Court, 1995).

Houlgate, Stephen, "Power, Egoism and the 'Open' Self in Nietzsche and Hegel," *Journal of the British Society for Phenomenology* 22 (1991), 120–38.

Hunt, Lester, *Nietzsche and the Origin of Virtue* (New York: Routledge, 1991).

Kaufmann, Walter, *Nietzsche: Philosopher, Psychologist, Antichrist*, 3d ed. (New York: Vintage Books, 1968).

Schacht, Richard, *Nietzsche* (Boston: Routledge and Kegan Paul, 1983).

Thiele, Leslie Paul, *Friedrich Nietzsche and the Politics of Soul: A Study of Heroic Individualism* (Princeton, NJ: Princeton University Press, 1990).

Dewey

Cruz, Feodor F., *John Dewey's Theory of Community* (New York: Peter Lang, 1987).

Lemos, Noah M., "High-Minded Egoism and the Problem of Priggishness," *Mind* 93 (1984), 542–58.

Roth, Robert J., *John Dewey and Self-Realization* (Englewood Cliffs, NJ: Prentice-Hall, 1962).

Teehan, John, "Character, Integrity, and Dewey's Virtue Ethics," *Transactions of the Charles S. Peirce Society* 31 (1995), 841–63.

Rand

Den Uyl, Douglas, and Douglas B. Rasmussen, "Nozick on the Randian Argument," *The Personalist* 59 (April 1978), 184–205.

———, eds., *The Philosophic Thought of Ayn Rand* (Chicago: University of Illinois, 1984).

———, "Life, Teleology, and Eudaimonia in the Ethics of Ayn Rand," in *The Philosophic Thought of Ayn Rand* (Chicago: University of Illinois, 1984).

Flew, Antony, "Selfishness and the Unintended Consequences of Intended Action," in *The Philosophic Thought of Ayn Rand*.

Mack, Eric, "The Fundamental Moral Elements of Rand's Theory of Rights," in *The Philosophic Thought of Ayn Rand*.

Nozick, Robert, "On the Randian Argument," *The Personalist* 52 (Spring 1971), 282–304.

Gauthier

Morris, Christopher W., "The Relation between Self-Interest and Justice in Contractarian Ethics," *Social Philosophy and Policy* 5 (1988), 119–53.

Paul, Ellen Frankel, Fred D. Miller, Jr., and Jeffrey Paul, eds., *The New Social Contract: Essays on Gauthier* (New York: Basil Blackwell, 1988).

Superson, Anita M., "The Self-Interest Based Contractarian Response to the Why-Be-Moral Skeptic," *Southern Journal of Philosophy* 28 (1990), 427–47.

Vallentyne, Peter, ed., *Contractarianism and Rational Choice: Essays on David Gauthier's Morals by Agreement* (Cambridge: Cambridge University Press, 1991.)

Additional Twentieth-century Sources

Badhwar, Neera K., "Egoism and Altruism: Sometimes a False Dichotomy," *Social Philosophy and Policy* 10 (1993), 90–117.

———, "Virtue and Self-interest," *Social Philosophy and Policy* (forthcoming, 1997).

Baier, Kurt, *The Moral Point of View* (Ithaca, NY: Cornell University Press, 1958).

Broad, C. D., *Five Types of Ethical Theory* (London: Routledge and Kegan Paul, 1930).

Brunton, J. A., "Egoism and Morality," *Philosophical Quarterly* 6 (1956), 289–303.

Campbell, Richmond, *Self-Love and Self-Respect: A Philosophical Study of Egoism* (Ottawa: Published for the Canadian Association for Publishing in Philosophy by the Department of Philosophy of Carleton University, 1979).

Cottingham, John, "The Ethics of Self-Concern," *Ethics* 101 (1991), 798–817.

Falk, W. D., "Morality, Self, and Others," in Hector-Neri Castaneda and George Nakhikian, eds., *Morality and the Language of Conduct* (Detroit, MI: Wayne State University, 1963).

Foot, Philippa, "Morality as a System of Hypothetical Imperatives," *Philosophical Review* 81 (1972), 305–32.

Freud, Sigmund, *Civilization and Its Discontents*, James Strachey, trans. (New York: W. W. Norton, 1989).

Gauthier, David, *Moral Dealing: Contract, Ethics, and Reason* (Ithaca, NY: Cornell University Press, 1990).

Hampton, Jean, "Selflessness and the Loss of Self," *Social Philosophy and Policy* 10 (1993), 135–65.

Hare, R. M., "Universalizability," *Proceedings of the Aristotelian Society* 55 (1954–55), 295–312.

Heil, John, ed., *Rationality, Morality and Self-Interest* (Maryland: Rowman & Littlefield, 1993).

Kalin, Jesse, "In Defense of Egoism," in David Gauthier, ed., *Morality and Rational Self-Interest* (Englewood Cliffs, NJ: Prentice-Hall, 1970).

MacIntyre, Alisdair, "Egoism and Altruism," *The Encyclopedia of Philosophy*, vol. 2 (New York: Macmillan, 1967).

Mack, Eric, "How to Derive Ethical Egoism," *The Personalist* 52 (1971), 735–43.

Mansbridge, Jane J., ed., *Beyond Self-Interest* (Chicago: University of Chicago Press, 1990).

Medlin, Brian, "Ultimate Principles and Ethical Egoism," *Australasian Journal of Philosophy* 35 (1957), 111–18.

Nagel, Thomas, *The Possibility of Altruism* (Oxford: Oxford University Press, 1970).

Olson, R. G., *The Morality of Self-Interest* (New York: Harcourt, Brace & World, 1965).

Parfit, Derek, *Reasons and Persons* (Oxford: Oxford University Press, 1984).

Paul, Ellen Frankel, Fred D. Miller, Jr., and Jeffrey Paul, eds., *Altruism* (Cambridge: Cambridge University Press, 1993).

——, *Self-Interest* (Cambridge: Cambridge University Press, forthcoming in 1997).

Rawls, John, *A Theory of Justice* (Cambridge, MA: Harvard University Press, 1971).

Rogers, Kelly, "Beyond Self and Other," *Social Philosophy and Policy* (forthcoming, 1997).

Schmidtz, David, *Rational Choice and Moral Agency* (Princeton, NJ: Princeton University Press, 1995).

Smith, Tara, "Rights, Friends, and Egoism," *The Journal of Philosophy* 90 (1993), 144–48.

NOTES

1 See Neera K. Badhwar, "Virtue and Self-Interest" (forthcoming in *Social Philosophy and Policy*, 1997).

2 See, e.g., Thomas Nagel, *The Possibility of Altruism* (Oxford: Oxford University Press, 1970); David Schmidtz, "Reasons for Altruism," *Social Philosophy and Policy* 10 (1993), 52–68; Lawrence A. Blum, *Friendship, Altruism, and Morality* (Boston: Routledge and Kegan Paul, 1980).

3 Derek Parfit, *Reasons and Persons* (Oxford: Oxford University Press, 1984).

4 See, e.g., Jane J. Mansbridge, ed., *Beyond Self-Interest* (Chicago: University of Chicago Press, 1990).

5 See, e.g., Robert Axelrod, *The Evolution of Cooperation* (New York: Basic Books, 1984), David Gauthier, *Morals By Agreement* (Oxford: Oxford University Press, 1986), and Brian Skyrms, *The Dynamics of Rational Deliberation* (Cambridge, MA: Harvard University Press, 1990).

6 See, e.g., David Collard, *Altruism and Economy: A Study in Non-Selfish Economics* (Oxford: Oxford University Press, 1978), Milton L. Myers, *The Soul of Modern Economic Man: Ideas of Self-Interest, Thomas Hobbes to Adam Smith* (Chicago: University of Chicago Press, 1983), and Amartya Sen, *On Ethics and Economics* (Oxford: Oxford University Press, 1987).

7   See, e.g., Nancy Eisenberg, *Altruistic Emotion, Cognition, and Behavior* (Hillsdale, NJ: Lawrence Erlbaum Associates, 1986), Bruce A. Sevy, "On the Explanatory Power Of Self-Interest," *The American Psychologist* (1988), and Robert B. Cialdini, "Altruism or Egoism? That is (Still) the Question," *Psychological Inquiry* 2 (1991).

8   See, e.g., Richard Dawkins, *The Selfish Gene* (Oxford: Oxford University Press, 1976), and Helena Cronin, *The Ant and the Peacock: Altruism and Sexual Selection from Darwin to Today* (Cambridge: Cambridge University Press, 1991). See also Peter Singer, *The Expanding Circle: Ethics and Sociobiology* (New York: Farrar, Straus & Giroux, 1981).

9   James Buchanan and Gordon Tullock, *The Calculus of Consent* (Ann Arbor, MI: University of Michigan Press, 1962), and Howard Margolis, *Selfishness, Altruism, and Rationality: A Theory of Social Choice* (Cambridge: Cambridge University Press, 1982).

10   *Philosophical Dictionary*, "Egoism."

11   [*Gorgias* 483a–492c; *Republic* I.338c–344c.]

12   [Ibid., 506d–509c.]

13   [*Republic* IV.441e–445b.]

14   [Ibid., III.416d–IV.421c; *Laws* 903b–d.]

15   [*Laws* 731d–732b.]

16   [*Nicomachean Ethics* I.7 1097b23–1099b17.]

17   [Ibid., X.7–8 1177a11–1179a32.]

18   [Ibid., IX.4 1166a1–1168a27; *Rhetoric* I.11 1371b12–25.]

19   [Ibid., IX.8 1168a28–1169b2.]

20   [*Politics* II.5 1263a25–b26.]

21   [*Nicomachean Ethics* IX.6 1167a21–b15.]

22   [Epicurus, *Letter to Menoeceus* 127–32; Lucretius, *On the Nature of Things* II.1–61.]

23   [Lucretius, *On the Nature of Things* V.925–1157; Hermarchus, as reported by Porphyry in *On Abstinence* 1.7.1–9.4.]

24   [Torquatus, as reported by Cicero in *On Ends* 1.66–70; Plutarch, *Against Epicurean Happiness* 1097A; Epicurus, *Principal Doctrines*, #27.]

25   [Cicero, *De Finibus* III.16; Epictetus, *Discourses* II.xxii.]

26   [Cicero, *De Finibus* III.ix.]

27   [Epictetus, *Manual* #1, #8, #48; Marcus Aurelius, *The Meditations*, III.7, 9, 12.]

28   [Epictetus, *Discourses* I.xix, II.x; Cicero, *On Duties* III.v.21–vi.31.]

29   [*On Christian Doctrine*, Chapter 22].

30   *Jeremiah* xvii.5.

31   *Matthew* xxii.37–39. Compare *Leviticus* xix.18; *Deuteronomy* vi.5.

32   [*On Christian Doctrine*, Chapters 23–27.]

33   *Psalms* x.5.

34   *Matthew* xxii.37–40.

35   [*The City of God*, Book XIV, Chapter 13; *Sermons on Selected Lessons of the New Testament*, Sermon XLVI.]

36 2 *Timothy* iii.2.

37 *Luke* xv.17.

38 *Luke* xv.18.

39 *Jeremiah* xvii.5.

40 *Ecclus.* x.13.

41 *Matthew* vii.18.

42 *Defecit.*

43 *Psalms* lxxiii.18.

44 [*Tractates on the Gospel of St. John*, Tractate LI.]

45 *Matthew* iv.7.

46 *Chapter* xxi.18, 19.

47 [*Letters of St. Augustine*, CXXX.VII.14; *The City of God*, Book X, Chapter 3.]

48 *Matthew* xxii.37–40.

49 *Psalms* lxxiii.28.

50 *Exodus* xxii.20.

51 [*The City of God*, Book XIV, Chapter 28.]

52 *Psalms* iii.3.

53 *Psalms* xviii.1.

54 *Romans* i.21–25.

55 I *Corinthians* xv.28.

56 [*Summa Theologiae* 1a2ae. 77, 4. Section headings in this chapter are Aquinas' own.]

57 Cf. *Summa Theologiae* 1a2ae. 84, 2 ad 3; 2a2ae. 25, 7 ad 1; 153, 5 ad 3. II *Sent.* 42, 2, 1. *De Malo* VIII, 1 ad 19.

58 *Leviticus* 19,18.

59 *Romans* 7,8.

60 *Glossa Ordinaria.* PL 114, 491. *Glossa Lombardi.* PL 191, 1416.

61 *Summa Theologiae* 1a2ae. 23,4; 30,2.

62 *Psalms* 79,17.

63 *Enarr. in Psalm.* 79,17. PL 36, 1027.

64 *De Civitate Dei* XIV, 28. PL 41, 436.

65 1a2ae. 75,1.

66 *Summa Theologiae* Cf. *sed contra* above.

67 In the body of the article.

68 Aristotle, *Ethics* IX, 4. 1166a31–2; & 9, 1170b 6–7.

69 [*Summa Theologiae* 1a2ae. 73, 1.]

70 *Summa Theologiae* 1a2ae. 65, 1 and 2.

71 *De Civitate Dei* XIV, 28. PL 41, 436. *Enarrationes in Psalmos*, 64 PL 36,775.

72 *Ethics* II, 8. 1108b27–30.

73 [*Summa Theologiae* 1a2ae. 84, 2.]

74 *De Civitate Dei* XIV, 28. PL 41,436.

75   *Ecclesiasticus* 10,15.

76   Cf. art. 1, note 4.

77   The Wise Man (*Sapientis*), or the author of a sapiential book, is Jesus son of Sira, cf. *Ecclesiasticus* 50,29.

78   *Ecclesiasticus* 10,17.

79   [*Summa Theologiae* 2a2ae. 25, 7.]

80   Cf. *Summa Theologiae* 1a2ae. 29,4. II *Sent.* 42, 11, 2, ii ad 2; III *Sent.* 27, Expos. litt. *De Caritate* 12 ad 6, *In Psalmos* 10.

81   *De Civitate Dei* XIV, 28. PL 41, 436.

82   *De Divinis Nominibus* 4. PG 3,708. St. Thomas, *lect.* 9.

83   *Psalm* 10,6.

84   II *Corinthians* 4,16.

85   *Ethics* IX, 4. 1166a3. St Thomas, *lect.* 4.

86   *Psalms* 49, 21.

87   See note 2.

88   Body of the art.

89   [*Summa Theologiae* 1a2ae. 29, 4.]

90   Cf. *Summa Theologiae* 2a2ae. 25,7, III *Sent.* 27, Exposit. text. In *Psalm.* 10. In *Ephes.* 5, *lect.* 9.

91   *Psalms* 10, 6.

92   *De consolatione philosophiae* II, pros. 5. PL 63,690.

93   *Ephesians* 5, 29.

94   *De divinis nominibus* 4. PG 3, 732

95   *Summa Theologiae* 1a2ae. 26, 4.

96   [*Summa Theologiae* 1a1ae. 60, 3.]

97   Cf. Ibid., 1a2ae. 26, 4; 29, 4. *In De div. nom.* 4, *lect.* 9 & 10.

98   Art. 2.

99   *De divinis nominibus* 4. PG 3, 713.

100 Aristotle, *Ethics* IX, 4. 1166a1.

101 Aristotle, *Ethics* I, 6. 1096a19.

102 In the body of the article.

103 [*Summa Theologiae* 1a1ae. 60, 5.]

104 Cf. *Summa Theologiae* 1a2ae; 109, 3. 2a2ae. 26, 3. II *Sent.* 3(2), 3. III, 29, 3. *In De div. nom.* 4, *lect.* 9 & 10. *Quodl.* 1, 8.

105 Art. 4.

106 *De civitate Dei* XII, 9. PL 41, 357.

107 Ibid. XIV, 28. PL 41, 436.

108 *Deuteronomy* 6, 5; cf. *Matthew* 22, 36–40.

109 Aristotle, *Physics* II, 8. 199a9.

110 In the body of the article.

111 To this extent, then, "friendship-love" of an angel for God is *natural* to him; cf. art 3 above, note b.

112 [*Summa Theologiae* 2a2ae. 25, 12.]

113 III *Sent.* 28, 7. *De Caritate* 7.

114 *In. Joannis Evang.* LXXXIII. On *John* 15, 12. PL 35, 1846.

115 *De Doctr. Christ.* 1, 23. PL 34, 27.

116 Arts 3, 6 & 10 above. 2a2ae. 23, 1 & 5 above.

117 [*Summa Theologiae* 2a2ae. 26, 3.]

118 Cf. III *Sent.* 29, 3. *De Caritate* 4 ad 2; 9.

119 *Ethics* IX, 4 & 10. 1161a1 & 1168b5.

120 *De Doctr. Christ.* 1, 22. PL 34, 27.

121 [*Summa Theologiae* 2a2ae. 26, 4.]

122 Cf. *Summa Theologiae* 2a2ae. 44, 8 ad 2. III *Sent.* 29, 5. *De Caritate* 9, In II *Tim.* 3, *lect.* 1.

123 Art. 2 above.

124 *Proverbs* 12, 26.

125 I *Corinthians* 13, 5.

126 *Leviticus* 19, 18; *Matthew* 22, 39.

127 *Summa Theologiae* 2a2ae. 25, 7.

128 Art. 2 above; *Summa Theologiae* 2a2ae. 25, 12.

129 In the body of the article.

130 *Epist.* CCXXI. PL 33, 963.

131 Art. 3.

132 [*Summa Theologiae* 2a2ae. 25, 4.]

133 Cf. III *Sent.* 28,6. *De Caritate.* 7.

134 *In Evang.* 1,17. PL 76, 1139.

135 *Ethics* VIII, 2. 1158b28.

136 *Summa Theologiae* 2a2ae. 23,1.

137 I *Corinthians* 13,4.

138 II *Timothy*, 3,1,2.

139 *Leviticus* 19,18.

140 *Summa Theologiae* 2a2ae. 23,1.

141 *De Divinis Nominibus* 4. PG3, 709. [Cf. also *Summa Theologiae* 1a2ae. 28,1 where St. Thomas explains that the affective union caused by love is the very love itself: also *Summa Theologiae* 1a, 20, 1 ad 3. 1a2ae, 25, 2 ad 2.]

142 *Ethics* IX, 4. 1166a1 cf.8. 1168b5.

143 [*Leviathan*, Part I, Ch. vi, xi.]

144 [Ibid., Part I, Ch. xiii.]

145 [Ibid., Part I, Ch. xiv.]

146 [Ibid., Part I, Ch. xv.]

147 [*Ethics*, Part III, with omissions.]

148 [Given the "geometric" method employed in Spinoza's *Ethics*, he will frequently make reference to other parts of his argument that play a supporting role in the point under discussion. He usually summarizes those parts when they are mentioned, but the reader may wish to look up the original passages himself. Using the current reference as an example, the reference system works as follows: "Cor.Pr.25,I" refers to *Ethics*, Part I, Proposition 25, Corollary.]

149 [The term "conatus" plays an important role in Spinoza's psychology. It expresses Spinoza's view that each thing exemplifies an inherent tendency towards self-preservation and activity. This term has a long history, going back to Cicero, who used it to express Aristotle's and the Stoics' notion of impulse (*horme*). It was later used by medieval and early modern philosophers, such as Hobbes, to connote the natural tendency of an organism to preserve itself. For a history of this term consult H. Wolfson, *The Philosophy of Spinoza* (New York, 1969), volume 2, pp. 195–199—Feldman.]

150 ["By an adequate idea I mean an idea which, in so far as it is considered in itself without relation to its object, has all the properties—that is, intrinsic characteristics—of a true idea (*ideatum*)" (Def.4,II). Again: "Falsity consists in the privation of knowledge which inadequate ideas, that is, fragmentary and confused ideas, involve" (Pr.35,II).]

151 [*Ethics*, Part IV, with omissions.]

152 [*The Fable of the Bees, or Private Vices, Public Benefits.*]

153 Ibid.

154 [Sermon #11.]

155 [Sermon #11.]

156 [Sermon #2.]

157 [*An Inquiry Concerning Moral Good and Evil*, Section II, "Concerning the immediate motive to virtuous action," §§I–II.]

158 [See Sect. I. Not reprinted here.]

159 ["Concerning the immediate motive to virtuous action," §III.]

160 Ibid., section II, §IV.]

161 These several motives of interest, which, some allege, do excite us to benevolence, operate upon us in a very different manner. Prospect of external advantage of any kind in this life from our fellows, is only a motive to the volition of external actions immediately, and not to raise desire of the happiness of others. Now being willing to do external actions which we know do in fact promote the happiness of others, without any desire of their happiness, is not approved as virtuous; otherwise it were virtue to do a beneficent action for a bribe of money.

The prospect of rewards from the deity of future pleasures, from the self-approbation of our moral sense, or of any pleasure attending an affection itself, are only motives to us to desire or wish to have the affection of benevolence in our hearts, and consequently, if our volition could raise affections in us, these motives would make us will or choose to raise benevolent affections. But these prospects cannot be motives to us from self-love, to desire the happiness of others, for from self-love we only desire what we apprehend to be the means of private good. Now having those affections is the means of obtaining these private goods, and not the actual happiness of others, for the pleasure of self-approbation, and divine rewards, are not obtained or lost according as others are happy or miserable, but according to the goodness of our affections. If therefore affections are not directly raised by volition or choice, prospects of future rewards or of self-approbation cannot directly raise them.

162 ["Concerning the immediate motive to virtuous action," section II, §V.]
163 [Ibid., §X.]
164 See the *Fable of the Bees*, p. 68, 3rd edition.
165 [*A Treatise of Human Nature*, Book III, Part II, Section II.]
166 [Ibid.]
167 [*An Inquiry Concerning the Principles of Morals*, Section IV, Part II.]
168 [Ibid., Appendix II.]
169 [*An Inquiry Concerning the Principles of Morals*, Conclusion, Part II.]
170 [*The Theory of Moral Sentiments*, Part I, Section i, Ch. I; Part VII, Sect. iii, Ch. I.]
171 [Ibid., Part III, Section ii, Ch. III.]
172 [Ibid., Part II, Section ii, Ch. II.]
173 [Ibid., Part I, Section i, Ch. V; Part III, Ch. iii; Part III, Ch. iii.]
174 [*An Inquiry into the Nature and Causes of the Wealth of Nations*, Book I, Ch. ii.]
175 [Ibid., Book IV, Ch. ii.]
176 [*Foundations of the Metaphysics of Morals*, Section II, §§415–419.]
177 [Ibid., Section I, §§395–396.]
178 [Ibid., Section I, §§400–401; §§397–399.]
179 [Ibid., Section II, §§406–407.]
180 [*Lectures on Ethics*, "Duties to Oneself."]
181 [Ibid., "Self-love."]
182 "A Table of the Springs of Action," in John Bowring, ed., *The Works of Jeremy Bentham*, Vol. 1 (New York: Russell and Russell, Inc., 1962), Section I (f).
183 *The Constitutional Code*, Introduction, Sect. II, pp.5–6.
184 *Deontology*, I.1.
185 See *The Methods of Ethics*, Book III, Chapter xiii, §3.
186 *Psychologische Analysen auf Physiologischer Grundlage*. This work does not exist in English translation.
187 [*An Introduction to the Principles of Morals and Legislation*, Ch. I, §§1–6.]
188 [*The Constitutional Code*, Book I, Ch. 9.]
189 [*Deontology*, I.15.]

190 [Editorial correction by Goldworth.]

191 [Editorial correction by Goldworth.]

192 [Bentham also wrote at the top of this sheet: "Quote the Poet—'Self and social interests are the same'." (The reference is to Pope, *Essay on Man*, iv.396: "That true Self-love and Social are the same.")—Goldworth.]

193 [Bentham wrote the following note at the top of the sheet: "Conflict between self- and extra-regarding—but not more than between one branch and another of self-regarding. Say or do what one will, every case will in every instance be determined by the predominant interest. As intercourse and intellectuality encrease, the force of social interest encreases."—Goldworth.]

194 [*An Introduction to the Principles of Morals and Legislation*, Ch. XVII, §§7–20, with omissions.]

195 On occasions like this the legislator should never lose sight of the well known story of the oculist and the sot. A countryman who had hurt his eyes by drinking, went to a celebrated oculist for advice. He found him at table with a glass of wine before him. "You must leave off drinking," said the oculist. "How so?" says the countryman; "you don't, and yet methinks your own eyes are none of the best."—"That's very true friend," replied the oculist: "but you are to know, I love my bottle better than my eyes."

196 Ch. XVI (Division) 52.

197 A woman's headdress catches fire: water is at hand: a man, instead of assisting to quench the fire, looks on, and laughs at it. A drunken man, falling with his face downwards into a puddle, is in danger of suffocation: lifting his head little on one side would save him: another man sees this, and lets him lie. A quantity of gunpowder lies scattered about a room: a man is going into it with a lighted candle: another, knowing this, lets him go in without warning. Who is there that in any of these cases would think punishment misapplied?

198 [*On Liberty*, Ch. I; Ch. IV.]

199 [*Considerations on Representative Government*, Ch. VI.]

200 [Samuel Taylor Coleridge, "The Statesman's Manual," in *On the Constitution of Church and State, and Lay Sermons* (London: Pickering, 1839), 220.—Robson.]

201 [*On the Subjection of Women*, Ch. II; Ch. IV.]

202 [*The Methods of Ethics*, Book I, Chapter ix, §3.]

203 It would seem that, according to the common view of "good," there are occasions in which an individual's sacrifice of his own good on the whole, according to the most rational conception of it that he can form, would apparently realize greater good for others. Whether, indeed, such a sacrifice is ever really required, and whether, if so, it is truly reasonable for the individual to sacrifice his own good on the whole, are among the profoundest questions of ethics: and I shall carefully consider them in subsequent chapters (especially Book iii. chap. xiv.). I here

only desire to avoid any prejudgment of these questions in my definition of "my own good."

204 As before said (chap. iii. §4), so far as my "good on the whole" is adopted as an end of action, the notion of "ought"—implying a dictate or imperative of Reason—becomes applicable to the necessary or fittest means to the attainment of the adopted end.

205 [*The Methods of Ethics*, concluding chapter.]

206 See J. S. Mill's treatise on Utilitarianism (chap. iii. *passim*): where, however the argument is not easy to follow, from a confusion between three different objects of inquiry: (1) the actual effect of sympathy in inducing conformity to the rules of Utilitarian ethics, (2) the effect in this direction which it is likely to have in the future, (3) the value of sympathetic pleasures and pains as estimated by an enlightened Egoist. The first and third of these questions Mill did not clearly separate, owing to his psychological doctrine that each one's own pleasure is the sole object of his desires. But if my refutation of this doctrine (Book i. chap. iv. §3) is valid, we have to distinguish two ways in which sympathy operates: it generates sympathetic pleasures and pains, which have to be taken into account in the calculations of Egoistic Hedonism; but it also may cause impulses to altruistic action, of which the force is quite out of proportion to the sympathetic pleasure (or relief from pain) which such action seems likely to secure to the agent. So that even if the average man ever should reach such a pitch of sympathetic development, as never to feel prompted to sacrifice the general good to his own, still this will not prove that it is egoistically reasonable for him to behave in this way.

207 I do not, however, think that we are justified in stating as *universally* true what has been admitted in the preceding paragraph. Some few thoroughly selfish persons appear at least to be happier than most of the unselfish; and there are other exceptional natures whose chief happiness seems to be derived from activity, disinterested indeed, but directed towards other ends than human happiness.

208 See chap. iii. §3 of this Book, pp. 432–33.

209 See Book iii. chap. i. §2; also Book iii. chap. ii . §1.

210 It is not necessary, if we are simply considering Ethics as a possible independent science, to throw the fundamental premiss of which we are now examining the validity into a Theistic form. Nor does it seem always to have taken that form in the support which Positive Religion has given to Morality. In the Buddhist creed this notion of the rewards inseparably attaching to right conduct seems to have been developed in a far more elaborate and systematic manner than it has in any phase of Christianity. But, as conceived by enlightened Buddhists, these rewards are not distributed by the volition of a Supreme Person, but by the natural operation of an impersonal Law.

211 It may be well to remind the reader that by "adequate" is here meant "sufficient to make it the agent's interest to promote universal good"; not necessarily "proportional to Desert."

212 I cannot fall back on the resource of thinking myself under a moral necessity to regard all my duties *as if they were* commandments of God, although not entitled to hold speculatively that any such Supreme Being really exists. I am so far from feeling bound to believe for purposes of practice what I see no ground for holding as a speculative truth, that I cannot even conceive the state of mind which these words seem to describe, except as a momentary half-willful irrationality, committed in a violent access of philosophic despair.

213 ["The Consciousness of Self," from *The Principles of Psychology*, Volume I, pp. 317–329.]

214 The *kind* of selfishness varies with the self that is sought. If it be the mere bodily self; if a man grabs the best food, the warm corner, the vacant seat; if he makes room for no one, spits about, and belches in our faces—we call it hoggishness. If it be the social self, in the form of popularity or influence, for which he is greedy, he may in material ways subordinate himself to others as the best means to his end; and in this case he is very apt to pass for a disinterested man. If it be the "other-worldly" self which he seeks, and if he seeks it ascetically—even though he would rather see all mankind damned eternally than lose his individual soul— "saintliness" will probably be the name by which his selfishness will be called.

215 Lotze, *Med. Psych.* 498–50l; *Microcosmos* bk. II. chap. v. §§3, 4.

216 *Psychologische Analysen auf Physiologischer Grundlage. Theil* II. *ute Hälfte*, §11. The whole section ought to be read.

217 [*The Will to Power*, §246; *Twilight of the Idols*, §§33, 35.]

218 [*Geneaology of Morals*, Essay 1, §2.]

219 Cf. *Beyond Good and Evil*, section 257.

220 [*The Will to Power*, §362; *The Gay Science*, §21; *The Will to Power*, §269.]

221 *Obhut ober sich selbst.*

222 [*The Gay Science*, §162; *Daybreak*, §281; *The Will to Power*, §§369, 372, 785, 873; *Beyond Good and Evil*, §220.]

223 Notably Kant.

224 [*Daybreak*, §516; *The Will to Power*, §§918, 919; *Beyond Good and Evil*, §287.]

225 [Cf. Aristotle's *Nicomachean Ethics* (1169a): "The good man ought to be a lover of self, sinse he will then act nobly, and so both benefit himself and his fellows; but the bad man ought not to be a lover of self, since he will follow his base passions, and so injure both himself and his neighbors" (Rackham translation). Cf. also the long note for section 212. . . . —Kaufmann.]

226 [*Lectures on Psychological and Political Ethics: 1898*, Chapter 6, Section 2.]

227 See Auguste Comte, *System of Positive Polity* (London: Longmans, Green, 1875), I, 73–75, and *The Positive Philosophy of Auguste Comte* (London: Jay Chapman, 1853), II, 554–55.

228 For an analysis of this aspect of Eliot, see Josiah Royce, "George Eliot as a Religious Teacher," in *Fugitive Essays* (Cambridge, Mass.: Harvard University Press, 1920), 260–89.

229 Spencer, *The Data of Ethics*, Sec. 98.

230 [*Ethics*, Chapter XVIII, §1.]

231 [*Atlas Shrugged*, Part III, Ch. 7]

232 [*The Virtue of Selfishness*, Chapter 3, "The Ethics of Emergencies."]

233 [Ibid., Chapter 4, "The 'Conflict' of Men's Interests."]

234 ["Morality and Advantage", *Philosophical Review*, Vol. 76 (1961), 460–475.]

235 David Hume, *An Enquiry Concerning the Principles of Morals*, sec. ix. pt. ii.

236 Ogden Nash, "Kind of an Ode to Duty."

237 Kurt Baier, *The Moral Point of View: A Rational Basis of Ethics* (Ithaca, 1958), p. 314.

238 That this, and only this, is what he is entitled to claim may not be clear to Baier, for he supposes his account of morality to answer the question "Why should we be moral?," interpreting "we" distributively. This, as I shall argue in Sec. IV, is quite mistaken.

239 This thesis is not intended to state Baier's view of morality. I shall suggest in Sec. V that Baier's view would require substituting "everyone can expect to benefit" for "it is advantageous to everyone." The thesis is stronger and easier to discuss.

240 Those familiar with the theory of games will recognize the matrix as a variant of the Prisoner's Dilemma. In a more formal treatment, it would be appropriate to develop the relation between morality and advantage by reference to the Prisoner's Dilemma. This would require reconstructing the disarmament pact and the moral system as proper games. Here I wish only to suggest the bearing of game theory on our enterprise.

241 The word "agree" requires elucidation. It is essential not to confuse an advantage in agreeing to do x with an advantage in saying that one will do x. If it is advantageous for me to agree to do x, then there is some set of actions open to me which includes both saying that I will do x and doing x, and which is more advantageous to me than any set of actions open to me which does not include saying that I will do x. On the other hand, if it is advantageous for me to say that I will do x, then there is some set of actions open to me which includes saying that I will do x, and which is more advantageous to me than any set which does not include saying that I will do x. But this set need not include doing x.

242 Baier, *op. cit.*, 314.

ACKNOWLEDGMENTS AND SOURCING

$\mathcal{A}$ brief word about texts and sourcing. Spelling has been made consistent across texts and modernized where appropriate. Most original footnotes have been retained. The square-bracketed [ ] footnotes accompanying each section-heading provide sourcing; when a note refers to more than one source, the order of sources it lists will reflect the order in which the texts appear in that section. Selections from different sections of a single text are separated by a double space, and from different texts by triple dots (• • •). Some bracketed footnotes are my own and others belong to the original editors of the texts here reprinted, and their names appear at the end of such notes. The angle brackets < > in the chapters on the Epicureans and Stoics are inserted by the translators, and surround bits of text suspected to have fallen out of the original texts.

Anthologies tend to be collaborative efforts, and I have received support, comments, and suggestions on text-selection from: Julia Annas, John Biro, David O. Brink, Neera K. Badhwar, Allan Gotthelf, Lester Hunt, Bonnie Kent, R. G. Frey, R. M. Hare, Fred D. Miller, Jr., Mark Riebling, and David Schmidtz. Michael Pakaluk and James Hullett gave me helpful publishing advice. I thank Robert W. Riebling for his assistance with translations, and Blake Landor for his help with historical sources. I was able to complete a good deal of work on the anthology in the spring of 1995 while holding a visiting fellowship at the Social Philosophy and Policy Center at Bowling Green State University. Thanks to all the members of the Center for their help, and especially to Waldemar Hanacz, my research assistant while in Bowling Green, and Fred Miller, from whom I have learned so much about both ancient and moral philosophy. I am grateful to the Division of Sponsored Research at the University of Florida for equipment and research assistance grants, and to the staff and faculty at the department of philosophy. A special thanks goes to Virginia Dampier, who provided extra clerical assistance. I thank my editor at Routledge, Maureen McGrogan, and her assistant, Laska Jimsen, for backing the project and helping me see it through the final stages. Ronald, Frances, Jason, Dalia, Ahuva, Tova, Hanna, and Herschel Rogers, and Hyman and Sonia Blumenstein, provided love and moral support. Finally, my greatest debt is to Joseph N. Windham, my research assistant in Gainesville, who spent countless hours tracking down sources, making library runs, writing permissions requests, and scanning and proofing texts. Joe's tireless effort and unflagging enthusiasm made it possible for me to complete this project on time and with great enjoyment. Any errors that remain in the final manuscript are, of course, my sole responsibility.

• • •

Excerpts from St. Thomas Aquinas: *Summa Theologica*, translated by The Fathers of the English Dominican Province, copyright © 1964 by McGraw Hill Book Company, reprinted by permission of McGraw Hill Book Company.

Excerpts from Aristotle: Selections from *Nicomachean Ethics* (trans. W.D. Ross), *Rhetoric* (trans. W. Rhys Roberts), and *Politics* (trans. B. Jowett) from *The Complete Works of Aristotle*, edited by J. Barnes, copyright © 1984 by Princeton University Press, reprinted by permission of Princeton University Press.

Excerpts from St. Augustine of Hippo: *A Selected Library of the Nicene and Post-Nicene Fathers of the Christian Church*, edited by Philip Schaff, copyright © 1956 by W. R. Eerdmans Publishing Co., reprinted by permission of W. R. Eerdmans Publishing Co.

Excerpts from Marcus Aurelius: *The Meditations*, translated by G. M A. Grube, copyright © 1983 by Hackett Publishing Company, Inc., reprinted by permission of Hackett Publishing Company, Inc.

Excerpts from Jeremy Bentham: *Deontology Together with A Table of the Springs of Action and The Article on Utilitarianism*, edited by Amnon Goldworth, copyright © 1983 by Clarendon Press (Oxford University Press), reprinted by permission of Clarendon Press.

Excerpts from Jeremy Bentham: *The Works of Jeremy Bentham*, edited by John Bowring, copyright © 1962 by Russell & Russell Inc., reprinted by permission of Russell & Russell Inc.

INDEX